The Invisible
Faculty

Judith M. Gappa
David W. Leslie

The Invisible Faculty

*Improving the Status
of Part-Timers
in Higher Education*

Jossey-Bass Publishers · San Francisco

Substantial discounts on bulk quantities of Jossey-Bass books are available to corporations, professional associations, and other organizations. For details and discount information, contact the special sales department at Jossey-Bass Inc., Publishers. (415) 433-1740; Fax (415) 433-0499.

For sales outside the United States, contact Maxwell Macmillan International Publishing Group, 866 Third Avenue, New York, New York 10022.

Manufactured in the United States of America

The paper used in this book is acid-free and meets the State of California requirements for recycled paper (50 percent recycled waste, including 10 percent postconsumer waste), which are the strictest guidelines for recycled paper currently in use in the United States.

10% POST CONSUMER WASTE

The ink in this book is either soy- or vegetable-based and during the printing process emits fewer than half the volatile organic compounds (VOCs) emitted by petroleum-based ink.

Library of Congress Cataloging-in-Publication Data

Gappa, Judith M.
    The invisible faculty : improving the status of part-timers in higher education / Judith M. Gappa, David W. Leslie.
        p.   cm.—(The Jossey-Bass higher and adult education series)
    Includes bibliographical references and index.
    ISBN 1-55542-517-8
    1. College teachers, Part-Time—United States.   2. College teachers, Part-time—Employment—United States.   I. Leslie, David W.   II. Title.   III. Series.
    LB2331.72.G37   1993
    378.1'2—dc20   92-36906
                                                                                CIP

FIRST EDITION
HB Printing   10 9 8 7 6 5 4 3 2 1   *Code 9314*

The Jossey-Bass
Higher and Adult Education Series

Contents

Preface

Just as we completed the manuscript for *The Invisible Faculty,* we received a newspaper clipping that essentially explains why we spent so many months and did so much work to put the book together. The newspaper story goes as follows: "A . . . poet nominated for [the National Book Award] says she was dropped from the . . . University faculty because she publicly criticized the school's treatment of its adjunct faculty. In a recent article in [the local newspaper] she said: '. . . . Because I am . . . an adjunct faculty [member], I am denied access to the support and encouragement that full-time faculty are entitled to. . . . [We] receive no benefits, no health insurance, no pension, no paid vacation, no office space, no telephone, and no sabbatical' " ("National Book Award Nominee," 1991).

This brief news item is a fitting introduction to our book because it highlights one of the fundamental questions our study has raised: How can institutions expect people of talent to contribute to quality educational programs when those same people are victims of medieval employment conditions?

The National Education Association (NEA) invited us to appear at a forum during its 1988 annual meeting to react to its draft policy statement on part-time faculty. Our inspection of the draft, and of the policy statements of other educational organizations, raised a second fundamental issue, which we address in this study.

There seemed to be a commonly held theory that solving the part-time faculty "problem" required eliminating part-time teaching or reducing it to the extent possible. This struck us as utterly unrealistic and potentially dangerous to the long-term vitality of the total faculty work force. In our view, nothing in the national statistics or in our experience with individual colleges and universities even remotely suggested that radical cutbacks in part-time faculty were feasible. Tight budgets, scarce talent, shifting enrollment patterns, and other factors seem to point to increasing rather than decreasing part-time, temporary, and other nontraditional appointments.

We decided that it was important to try to find out whether our concerns about policy and practice regarding part-time faculty were valid by undertaking a national study to examine in an open and nonjudgmental way the current employment conditions of part-time faculty. Few studies of any real scope had been undertaken on this topic since the late 1970s, and those had left many questions unanswered.

Our previous work on the subject had perhaps predisposed us to be sympathetic toward part-time faculty, whom we knew to be capable, dedicated, and productive people. We also knew that institutions gained a great deal when they employed practicing professionals, retired teachers, artists and musicians, and aspiring academics with advanced degrees as part-time faculty members. What we did not know was how all sides now viewed part-time academic work and its consequences for individuals and the institutions where they were employed. What we thought was needed was a view from ground level that could serve as a basis for more thoughtful policy development.

Description of Our Study

We conducted site visits at eighteen colleges and universities, chosen in part to represent all types of institutions of higher education and in part because some had experimented with policies and practices regarding part-time faculty employment. At each site institution, we conducted individual and group interviews with chief academic officers, deans, department chairs, tenured faculty members involved in faculty governance and development, and part-timers. We gathered information from the part-timers themselves about their educational and employment backgrounds and their perceptions of their part-time faculty jobs. We also gathered information from administrators and senior faculty members about institutional policies and practices governing the employment of part-timers, and their views of the benefits and weaknesses of using part-time faculty. Over a seven-month period in 1990–91, we interviewed a total of 467 people, including part-time faculty members, deans, department chairs, central administrators, and senior faculty leaders. Interview data were buttressed by analyses of written policies, procedures, handbooks, and other materials collected at each site institution.

We found more than we had expected, both positive and negative. We found extraordinary people teaching part-time for the widest imaginable variety of reasons under the broadest imaginable sets of conditions. We also found institutions employing part-time faculty for a great variety of reasons. We found, in short, not a "system" for using part-timers but a wildly random collection of institutional and departmental practices. We likewise found a discomforting universality in the feelings of part-time faculty that somehow they were being exploited, and blatantly so.

Overview of the Contents

The complexity of our data presented an enormous challenge as we began to write the book. On the one hand, we decided that the present system, as we had observed it, had to be laid out for honest scrutiny. We also decided that the dependence of the tenure system on the employment of low-paid temporary faculty needed to be confronted. On the other hand, we are both seasoned academics, having served in a variety of faculty and administrative posts ourselves. As insiders in the system that we were prepared to criticize, we understand how difficult it is to effect change.

To accomplish our two objectives of describing the present situation and making recommendations for change, we divided the book into two parts. In Part One, Chapters Two through Eight, we analyze the current environment for part-time faculty. In Part Two, Chapters Nine through Thirteen, we identify key trends in the employment of part-time faculty and delineate forty-three recommended practices for institutions to follow. These recommendations are based primarily on the real experiences of the institutions we visited as well as on what the people we interviewed told us was needed to improve current conditions.

To meet the needs and interests of a diverse audience, our coverage of the current environment for part-time faculty in Part One purposely encompasses all aspects of part-time faculty employment. We recognize that some readers may not be interested in every topic covered. We remind them that our purpose has been to provide a comprehensive profile of the current situation as a foundation for recommendations for change, and we encourage readers to skim topics not germane to their immediate concerns or interests.

In Chapter One, we describe the factors that led us to conduct our study, the methods we employed, and the themes that kept recurring as our site visits progressed. These themes are expanded on throughout the book.

Chapter Two provides a broad overview of the part-time faculty. We describe part-timers' demographic characteristics, academic backgrounds, motivations for teaching part-time, and satisfactions and dissatisfactions with their roles. The extraordinary diversity of this group cannot be overdrawn, and in our portrait, we cover as many aspects of the population as necessary to represent it fairly.

Chapter Three begins with a description of the varied work history of part-time faculty. The categorization of part-timers that we suggest essentially focuses on the kinds of work and career paths that individual part-timers are following. The lines we have drawn between the categories are somewhat arbitrary. Not every part-time faculty member will find a clear "home" in one category or another, and many part-timers have moved between categories at different stages in their lives and careers outside academia. However, we believe that the categories are useful for policy makers' understanding of the need for flexible and varied approaches to part-time employment practices and give us convenient labels to differentiate between part-timers in the book.

Next, in Chapter Four, we cover the external policy environment as it affects both policy and practice within colleges and universities. Part-time employment at public institutions is affected by a patchwork of state- and system-level policies and regulations. Some general principles can be identified, but it is clear that little policy coherence can be found among the states. Institutions may often have to define their own policies and practices with the help of legal counsel familiar with established law in a particular jurisdiction.

Many institutions in our study reported that fiscal conditions played a substantial part in shaping the extent to which part-time faculty are employed. In Chapter Five, we examine fiscal conditions separately from other external factors because they are so influential and because we believe attention must be called to the consequences of basing on fiscal circumstances fundamental educational decisions about who shall teach. In this chapter, we begin our in-depth discussion of the underlying conditions that have led to the bifurcation of the faculty, a theme on which we build in subsequent chapters.

Institutions of higher learning use part-time faculty for a wide array of reasons. Chapter Six explores the reasons, as well as ways in which use differs from institution to institution. Our major concern about the use of part-timers is that some institutions engage in what we call unplanned or out-of-control use. We contrast out-of-control use with the situations we found at institutions that planned and managed their use of part-time faculty, at least to some extent.

Institutions have widely varying policies and practices of their own about the terms and conditions of part-time faculty employment. Standards for hiring, length and terms of appointments, pay and benefits, supervision and evaluation, and job security are described in Chapter Seven. Frequently, great discretion and responsibility in the realm of part-time faculty hiring and supervision are given to department chairs. We explore the effect of this discretion, both within departments and institutions and on part-time faculty.

Institutions, and departments within institutions, also vary greatly in the degree to which part-timers participate as members of the academic community, a phenomenon we refer to as *integration*. We are concerned that such integration is not sufficiently advanced at many institutions; we assess the conditions that favor or discourage it in Chapter Eight. Examples of what we call comprehensive professional development programs are included. Some institutions have made active efforts to include part-time faculty in their overall human resource plan, thus helping part-timers to be more effective teachers and creating high morale at the same time.

In Part Two, our focus shifts from the present to the future. In Chapter Nine, we synthesize key trends about which we heard over and over again in different contexts. These trends highlight the need for changes in the academic profession, including more thoughtful use of part-timers, fairer employment policies for part-timers, and better integration of part-time faculty. In Chapters Ten, Eleven, and Twelve, we offer a total of forty-three recommended practices for making the needed changes. We developed our recommendations by looking at what our site institutions were doing and by listening to their suggestions for change. We believe that these practices represent a comprehensive approach that can correct some of the most difficult problems.

In Chapter Ten, we suggest that institutions learn to plan and manage their use of part-time faculty to help meet their educational goals, instead of allowing fiscal conditions to dictate staffing decisions. In Chapter Eleven, we advocate fairness toward part-timers. Colleges and universities need to be clear about their policies, provide information to part-timers and department administrators, and eliminate exploitation and arbitrary treatment. Finally, in Chapter Twelve, we recommend practices that can help part-timers grow and develop professionally and participate actively as valued members of the department. Drawing on the best practices we found at the institutions we visited, we offer suggestions about orientation, mentoring, in-service programs, assessment, and incentives.

We briefly revisit the themes of the preceding four chapters (including our recommended practices) in Chapter Thirteen, which focuses on how institutions can be strengthened through constructive and purposeful use of part-timers. We believe that the incremental improvements we recommend in the second part of the book are well within reach of every college and university that employs part-time faculty. We urge that the forty-three recommended practices be implemented to change and improve a system that seems to us morally and educationally unsustainable.

Resource A at the end of the book lists the eighteen site institutions. Resource B contains the questionnaire we used in our interviews.

Audience

We have written this book for college and university presidents, chief academic officers, deans, department chairs, and full- and part-time faculty. While our primary focus is the institutional environment, *The Invisible Faculty* may also be helpful to system and state administrators and national policy makers concerned with program quality, planning, and faculty development.

We have written about the rapidly shifting context for the academic career, the desirability of bringing part-time faculty into the mainstream of academic life, and the pressing need to change employment practices and policies that affect part-timers. Institutional leaders will find that we question the fiscal and managerial soundness of indiscriminate use of part-time faculty, in substantial part because such use is unfair to part-timers and impairs their ability to do their jobs. Deans, department chairs, and tenured faculty members will find that we place the task of integrating part-time faculty into the mainstream primarily on them. We urge them to adopt the point of view that *all* faculty, regardless of status, should be involved directly in ensuring high-quality educational programs. Part-time faculty may discover that we think they, too, can take some responsibility for improving the system. Although they are right to expect a greater financial return for their investment of time and effort, they need to work more closely with full-time faculty members and students and make a professional commitment to their institutions. Each of these audiences will learn that our major conclusion is that educational considerations, *not money*, should drive the system.

We hope that *The Invisible Faculty* will provoke debate. We think the system is overdue for change. If our conclusions help frame the issue and promote a willingness to discuss new ideas, we will have done what we hoped to do. There remains much to accomplish, however, and the pace of change in the world outside may outstrip the more contemplative, deliberate pace of academe. We believe that a much more forward-looking and urgent strategy is needed, and we congratulate those with the courage to get started—among them the people whose ideas are expressed in this book.

Acknowledgments

We owe many debts to people who have encouraged, supported, helped, and counseled us throughout this effort. They are, of course, not responsible for our errors, our misjudgments, or our conclusions. Without their continued interest, however, we might not have persisted.

Foremost, we wish to thank Peggy Heim for urging us to collaborate on this project and for committing the Teachers Insurance and Annuity Association/College Retirement Equities Fund (TIAA/CREF) support to it. Ralph Lundgren at the Lilly Endowment has been similarly supportive, and we acknowledge the endowment's funding with gratitude. With grants from both TIAA/CREF and Lilly, we were able to interview more than 460 people at eighteen institutions, a time- and labor-intensive task we could not have completed otherwise.

At the outset, we convened an advisory panel that helped us sharpen and focus our approach. Joan Stark and Wilbert McKeachie of the University of Michigan and the National Center for Research to Improve Postsecondary Teaching and Learning, Malcolm Lowther of the University of Michigan, Sean Fanelli of Nassau Community College, Robert Berry of Loyola University of Chicago, and Thomas Maher of Saint Francis College (Pennsylvania) offered us a variety of perspectives, criticized our proposed design, and helped us refine our direction. At the completion of the site visits, William Farr of York University, Donald Hoyt of Cuyahoga Community College, and Sonia Patten, a part-timer at Macalester College, took the time to read and critique parts of the manuscript.

Gale Erlandson, senior editor for the Higher and Adult Education Series at Jossey-Bass, offered us superb guidance in the preparation of this book. We benefited greatly, too, from the helpful suggestions offered by Robert Boice, Ellen Chaffee, and Malcolm Lowther, each of whom patiently read the entire manuscript with careful attention and great insight.

We are also indebted to James Fairweather of the Center for the Study of Higher Education at the Pennsylvania State University for producing special tables based on data gathered from the National Center for Education Statistics' 1988 National Survey of Postsecondary Faculty.

Closer to home, we could not have completed our site visits and manuscript without the support of Diane Lenartz at Purdue University, Mary Ann Brown at San Francisco State University, and Jan Basile at Florida State University, who were indispensable on the administrative end of the project; we also learned an enormous amount about how to get our computers to talk to each other as a result of their patient instructions.

Florida State graduate students Joy Myers, Elaine Fygetakis, and Yu-Jen Tsai assisted at various stages of the project: Joy Myers proved to be an incisive reader as the final manuscript took shape; Elaine Fygetakis and Yu-Jen Tsai were helpful in our initial literature search.

Our spouses, Joe Gappa and Jan Leslie, deserve more thanks than we can offer here. They accommodated our frenetic travel schedules, accepted our preoccupation with transcribing and recording the interviews and endured our hibernation with the manuscript throughout months of pure obsession.

The eighteen site institutions we visited deserve a special note of gratitude. Although there are too many people to thank individually, we were invariably treated courteously and welcomed by administrators and faculty alike at each site institution. Coordinators at the institutions set up elaborate schedules, gathered pertinent materials before our arrival, and responded to numerous requests for additional information. Department chairs and other administrators were very generous with their time during our visits, as were part-time faculty members, who often made a special trip to the campus to participate in the interviews.

Everywhere, we appreciated the candor and objectivity with which people responded to our questions. We were unknown to almost everyone with whom we talked, and we were exploring a sensitive and provocative subject. We think the importance of the issue was itself the stimulus for people to share information and points of view; almost every interview session took on a momentum of its own and provided us with richer data than we had expected.

We are especially grateful to the 240 part-time faculty members who took the time to be interviewed. Taken together, they constitute a group whose energy, spirit, dedication to teaching, broad experience, and professionalism obviously strengthen the institutions and the students they serve. They freely shared their stories and their hopes with us, and it is to them that this book is dedicated.

January 1993

Judith M. Gappa
West Lafayette, Indiana

David W. Leslie
Tallahassee, Florida

The Authors

Judith M. Gappa is vice president for human relations and professor of educational administration at Purdue University. She received both her B.A. (1968) and M.A. (1970) degrees in musicology from George Washington University and her Ed.D. degree (1973) in educational administration (higher education) from Utah State University. From 1980 to 1991, she was associate vice president for faculty affairs at San Francisco State University, where she was responsible for the annual appointment of approximately one thousand part-time faculty members. Previously, Gappa had held positions at Utah State University and the National Center for Higher Education Management Systems in Boulder, Colorado. She has been a member of the faculty at San Francisco State University and Utah State University.

David W. Leslie is professor of education at Florida State University. He received his B.A. degree (1964) in psychology from Drew University, his M.Ed. degree (1965) in school psychology from Boston University, and his Ed.D. degree (1971) in higher education from the Pennsylvania State University. He has served on the faculties of the University of Virginia, the University of Illinois (where he also served as executive assistant to the president), and Illinois State University and has been department head at both Illinois State

xxi

University and Florida State University. From 1987 to 1989, Leslie served as resident scholar with the Florida Department of Education. He is former president of the Association for the Study of Higher Education. Leslie currently serves as review essay editor for the *Review of Higher Education.*

The Invisible
Faculty

One

Confronting Myths and Realities About Part-Time Faculty Members

The academic profession, currently buffeted by economic hard times and facing major demographic changes, has entered the 1990s with a sense of foreboding. It has faced critical times before. The Great Depression of the 1930s was traumatic. World War II threatened the survival of many institutions and changed others irreversibly. The 1950s brought McCarthyism to the campus. In the 1960s, student protests rocked campuses with violence and rebellion. Growth, retrenchment, government intrusion, assorted fiscal hard times, and the emergence of faculty unionism made the decades of the 1970s and 1980s a period of continuous adaptation to "crises" of one kind or another. These crises appear to be accelerating.

Campuses in the 1990s are faced with a national economic recession, the prospect of dramatically increasing enrollments, prospective retirements of large cohorts of senior faculty in a short period of time, the wearing out of infrastructures, and a host of other problems. Institutions of higher education are approaching the twenty-first century with skepticism and caution.

The tenure system has served the present generation of faculty (and its predecessors) well for fifty years. However, many institutions are no longer willing or able to make the fiscal, moral, and intellectual commitments that tenure requires to all, or even most, faculty members for decades ahead. Tenure, originally promulgated to protect faculty from abuses of academic freedom, has

1

become a job security system without parallel in other professions. Accordingly, institutions have sought additional flexibility in staffing by gradually using more part-time and temporary faculty to whom they need not make commitments for more than an academic term or a year at a time.

At many institutions, the use of part-time and temporary faculty has become a way of life. Budgets are balanced and classes assigned on the assumption that 20, 30, or 50 percent of all undergraduate sections will be taught by faculty members who are hired for a temporary assignment. Although perhaps 270,000 people— somewhere between 35 and 38 percent of all faculty members—are now teaching part-time in colleges and universities, they remain a largely unrecognized, underrewarded, and invisible part of the academic profession (National Center for Education Statistics [NCES], 1989). And part-time faculty are not only increasing in numbers; they are growing angry, which leads them on occasion to seek remedies for their exploitive working conditions through unionization or other sources of redress.

Thus, the academic profession has slowly but inexorably become bifurcated into two faculties: the tenured "haves" and the temporary, part-time "have-nots" (Bowen & Schuster, 1986; National Education Association [NEA], 1988). The reason for the two faculties is that the one sustains the other: the low costs and heavy undergraduate teaching loads of the have-nots help make possible the continuation of a tenure system that protects the jobs and perquisites of the haves. Because tenured faculty benefit directly and personally from this bifurcation of the academic profession, they have a vested interest in maintaining it.

We are not alone in recognizing the emergence of two faculties. Our colleagues in Canada conducted a parallel study at approximately the same time we did and recently concluded: "The absence of data on higher education's part-time work force has hidden not only the extent to which universities have become dependent upon part-timers economically, but also the degree to which two large, but essentially separate faculties have emerged in our institutions. On the one side is the full-time faculty, who have . . . substantial . . . control over [their work]. . . . On the other side are the part-timers, whose work is marked by curricular routinization of courses, standardized pedagogy, course replication, piecework payment, and managerial coordination" (Rajagopal & Farr, n.d. (a), p. 22).

In some ways, particularly in the degree to which fiscal stress seems to have played a role in the emergence of part-time employment, Canadian colleges and universities present a harbinger of a more stringent and conflict-prone future for U.S. institutions. The two situations are not qualitatively different, and the findings of the Canadian study are so strikingly similar to our own that we feel compelled to call attention to them.

The central thesis of this book is that it is time for institutions of higher education that hire and use part-time faculty to end the current bifurcated system. The major advocates of the status quo are many of the tenured faculty members who are its beneficiaries. But we believe that they, too, are becoming attuned to the creaks and cracks in an obsolete system. Administrators, pressed with fiscal problems and uneasy about future resources, are increasingly reluctant to make tenure commitments and are choosing more and more frequently to employ part-time faculty as a viable alternative. This alternative, which started out to be a "temporary solution," has become a "permanent fix."

Background

This book reports the results of a study conducted during the 1990–1991 academic year that was originally intended to examine some of the myths, issues, and problems associated with employing part-time faculty. We define part-time faculty as those individuals who are temporary, nontenure-track faculty employed less than full-time. Infrequently, we include doctoral degree candidates teaching part-time within the scope of this definition. However, when they are included, they are employed as part-time faculty members, not as graduate teaching assistants.

In the process of conducting the study, our concerns and interests broadened because no study of part-time faculty is complete without an examination of their relationships to the tenured faculty. During the study we gradually reached the perspective that part-time faculty are or should be an integral part of the whole faculty. We hope our recommendations for change, based upon the results of our study, will serve to improve not only the lives of the part-timers themselves but the health of the academic profession as a whole.

There is little basic scholarship on part-time faculty. Two major studies on the use of part-time faculty were conducted in the late 1970s by Tuckman and associates and by Leslie, Kellams, and Gunne. The main sources of research and policy development include Leslie (1978); Parsons (1980); Leslie, Kellams, & Gunne (1982); Gappa (1984); and Biles & Tuckman (1986). Howard Tuckman has also published a series of economic analyses of part-time faculty compensation. While numerous articles and reports have appeared in the journals and the ERIC system, most are based on experiences of individuals or single institutions. Some present highly subjective polemical arguments.

More recently, new hard data on part-time faculty have become available. The National Center for Education Statistics' 1988 National Survey of Postsecondary Faculty (see NCES, 1990) included responses from more than 2,000 regular and temporary part-timers in its sample. Results from that survey provide the most comprehensive current picture of who the part-time faculty are and of their attitudes on a variety of issues. (Published reports of similar recent faculty surveys conducted by the Carnegie Foundation for the Advancement of Teaching [CFAT, 1989] and the Higher Education Research Institute [Astin, Korn, & Dey, 1991] do not provide analyses of responses from part-time faculty.)

Rationale for Our Study

Notwithstanding the lack of research and the absence of hard data about part-timers between the mid 1970s and 1988, several key policy statements during the 1980s did address the use of part-time faculty. These statements often made bluntly negative assumptions about the impact part-timers have had (or will have) on quality. *Involvement in Learning* (Study Group on the Conditions of Excellence in American Higher Education, 1984), for example, cites the inability of part-time faculty to make a primary commitment to the college or university and asserts that such a commitment underlies the ability of faculty to create conditions for effective learning. The report concludes that "one full-time faculty member is a better investment than three part-timers" (p. 36). A similarly negative assessment was made in *Transforming the State Role in Undergraduate Education* (Working Party on Effective Action to Improve Undergraduate Education, 1986), a report of the Education Commission of the States: "[Use of part-time faculty] can . . . inhibit faculty collegiality, instructional continuity, and curricular coherence" (p. 19). The National Education Association (NEA) issued a policy statement on use of part-time faculty, *Report and Recommendations on Part-Time, Temporary, and Nontenure Track Faculty Appointments,* in 1988. This statement advocates reducing the number of part-time and temporary faculty and cites the "negative impact" of practices that represent abuses of such appointments. It expresses concern that fiscal and administrative imperatives may drive institutions to use more part-time faculty than is educationally sound (p. 12).

From our earlier work on part-time faculty, we had reached conclusions at some variance with the prevailing assumptions and the conventional mythology these policy statements exemplify. For example, it has never been clear to us that "part-time faculty" represent anything like a homogeneous population or that all institutions use part-time faculty in the same ways. If the use of part-timers varies and if part-time faculty themselves have such widely differing backgrounds, it does not make sense to us to issue sweeping policy statements based on assumptions about part-time faculty as a homogeneous group of itinerant workers who are potentially damaging to academic quality.

Second, is it realistic to expect that institutions will reduce the use of part-time or temporary faculty—that the "problem" will be brought under control and eliminated? We could envision no scenario that would permit drastic changes in staffing practices. In fact, most trends pointed to tighter fiscal constraints, more enrollment pressures, increased volatility in the "market" for academic programs, shifting supply-demand factors in the faculty labor market (Bowen & Schuster, 1986; Bowen & Sosa, 1989), and a general need for more flexibility. Policy statements calling for fewer part-time or temporary faculty and more tenure-track positions appear to fly in the face of all the evidence. It seemed clear to us that the pressure in the coming years would be on the side of using more rather than fewer part-time and temporary faculty.

Third, we know of many aspiring academics who lead complex lives and cannot expect to pursue an academic career that requires a full-time commitment to scholarly activity over an entire career. Emerging shifts in the professional life cycles of faculty—care-giving and spousal roles; recognition of the need to learn, grow, and change in adulthood; and the extension of productive years beyond the traditional age of sixty-five—have led us to think about where the next generation of faculty will come from, what kinds of conditions they will work under, and what alternative career opportunities might be available within the academic profession.

Fourth, part-time faculty have been widely alleged to have a negative impact on "quality." Very little hard evidence of this has been developed, however, and most of the allegations do not correspond well with our previous findings. We found that part-time faculty vary widely in their teaching performance, but we found little to suggest that they are at the root of any systematic decline in the quality of higher education. To the contrary, we also found that part-time faculty are, for the most part, superbly qualified for their teaching assignments, highly committed, and conscientious about doing their jobs. Although they are, as alleged, often unavailable for advising, committee work, and other noninstructional duties, this is also not part of their assignment. We wondered whether part-time faculty were perhaps taking some of the blame for shortcomings in a system where they are the victims of shortsighted and exploitive practices.

Finally, it seemed to us that very little was being said or done nationally about how to improve the quality of education in institutions that rely heavily on part-time faculty. So much has been said about how and why using part-time faculty is undesirable and about the resulting erosion of quality that an almost self-fulfilling prophecy has infected the whole climate in which academic staffing decisions are made.

Very simply, no one had looked closely at the realities within institutions, and no one had assessed the validity of the assumptions being made. Little constructive advice was available to institutions struggling to meet their obligations by relying on part-time faculty.

Periodically in recent years, we had been asked by various groups, organizations, and institutions to reflect on or react to issues presented by the employment of part-time faculty. We grew increasingly uncomfortable doing so because most of what we had to say was based on research done a decade or more ago. Furthermore, we became more concerned because of the growing gap between the reality of the inexorably increasing use of part-time faculty and the rhetoric of those who deplored the impact of such use.

We concluded that the time for "further study" had finally arrived and undertook the effort whose results are reported in this book. It should be clear that we had a point of view when we started, that we had a mission in mind. As we began our study, we felt strongly that an objective analysis of the current situation was needed and that nothing would be gained by situating ourselves with advocates of any particular position. We wanted instead to focus on what the data told us about current use of part-time faculty and the policies (or lack thereof) guiding practices at varying types of institutions. What we thought the academic community needed to hear was that part-time faculty are among us in substantial numbers. They do important work for our institutions, and they are likely to continue to do so in the future. We can neither ignore their presence nor engage in the wishful fantasy that some day all faculty will be full-time and on the tenure track.

This point of view led us to take on a mission. Very little has been said about how to improve the quality of education when part-timers carry a significant amount of an institution's teaching load. We wanted to know what had been done and what could be done to help part-time faculty do a better job of teaching. We wanted to know what could be done to improve their morale and commitment to the institutions where they work. We wanted to know how their aspirations for career development could be addressed. In short, we wanted to look for practices that we could recommend to help part-time faculty contribute to stronger programs and institutions while finding personal and professional satisfaction in work that has often been ignored and devalued.

This study has become essentially two studies in one. On the one hand, we looked as deeply as we could at the current realities and have reported "what is." On the other hand, we looked for good practices and for ideas about "what ought to be." Inevitably, as our study progressed, we were confronted with the division of the academic profession into two separate faculties as the core issue underlying both current realities and good or bad practices.

Methods

We used several sources of data for this book. We visited seventeen colleges and universities in the United States and one university in Canada. We conducted ERIC searches and screened the literature on part-timers. We also searched state and federal government court cases decided in the last five years. We researched state laws affecting part-time academic employment through direct correspondence with state attorneys general and analysis of statutes. We commissioned a special analysis of the data on part-time faculty from the National Center for Education Statistics' 1988 National Survey of Postsecondary Faculty to supplement the survey data published by NCES. When the data about part-timers from the special analysis of the survey results are used, they are cited as NSOPF '88. When the survey results published by NCES (in the publication *Faculty in Higher Education Institutions*) are used, they are cited as NCES, 1990.

The eighteen site institutions were chosen because they represented all types of institutions, all regions of the country, both public and private control, and both unionized and nonunionized environments. Seven of the eighteen institutions were selected in part because they have experimented with policies or practices pertaining to part-time faculty that seem to hold some promise. (See Table 1.1 for more information about the characteristics of the site institutions; these institutions are also listed in Resource A.)

At each of our site institutions, we conducted individual and group interviews with the chief academic officer, deans, department chairs, and part-time faculty. At many of these institutions, we also interviewed senior faculty involved in governance and union leaders. The individuals selected for interviews varied from institution to institution, depending on organizational structures and the peo-

Table 1.1. Characteristics of Site Institutions.

Type	Location	Control
Universities (6)	U.S. West (4)	Private (7)
Comprehensive colleges (4)	U.S. Midwest (5)	Public (10)
Liberal arts colleges (3)	U.S. South (3)	Mixed (1)[a]
Community colleges (5)	U.S. East (5)	
	Canada (1)	

[a]The Canadian institution has a self-perpetuating board and private charter; it is funded by the provincial government.

ple's availability during the site visits. At all institutions, the chief academic officer or the person centrally responsible for part-time faculty employment was interviewed. In addition, a substantial number of deans and department chairs were interviewed. Senior faculty leaders were chosen by campus liaisons because of their current active participation in academic senates, unions, or faculty development programs. Part-time faculty were selected on the basis of our criteria. We were seeking a balance of disciplines, length of employment, and other variables among the part-timers interviewed.

All of the interviews were conducted by the authors according to a structured format, which was developed with the assistance of a panel of project advisers. The questionnaires were then pretested. At one pretest site, we kept separate records of interviews and compared transcriptions to check inter-rater concordance. We also reorganized our interview questions to eliminate duplication and increase the efficiency of the site-visit process. The structured questionnaires (see Resource B) and other explanatory materials were sent to campus liaisons early to assist them with their arrangements for the site visits.

Our site visits typically covered two days of interviews. We usually began by interviewing the chief faculty personnel officer and going over supplementary information with the campus liaison. Interview sessions were conducted separately for deans, department heads, and part-timers. The interviews were usually conducted with small groups of two to five individuals, though some were with one person, depending upon the size of the campus and the availability of key people. Site institutions agreed to participate in the study under the condition that only exemplary practices would be attributed to them. Individuals agreed to be interviewed under the condition that their remarks would not be attributed to them by name. We have made every effort to ensure the anonymity of institutions and individuals in this book.

Transcriptions of our site interviews began contemporaneously with each visit and were completed within a few days of the visit's end. Over a seven-month period, we interviewed 240 part-time faculty members, 146 department chairs, 58 central administrators (including deans), and 23 faculty leaders—a total of 467 individuals.

In reporting our findings, we use both statistical data from our analysis of the NCES National Survey of Postsecondary Faculty and more anecdotal data from our site interviews. Although reporting anecdotal data can lead to impressions or conclusions that do not fairly represent the central tendencies in the population, we have tried to present anecdotes as powerful representations of commonly perceived realities. In most cases, the anecdotes are reflections of a point of view we heard a sufficient number of times to make us aware of an issue. In all cases, anecdotes are from one individual; they are not composites of several people's comments. Interview data are also buttressed by written policies, procedures, and other materials that we collected at each site institution.

Several cautions to the reader are necessary. Readers should keep in mind that variability is the rule in almost all aspects of this field. Part-timers are an extraordinarily diverse population, and institutions have widely varying attitudes and policies that affect part-time faculty employment. In fact, some readers may see their own institutions as exceptions to many of our generalized findings. What we have tried to accomplish is to draw a composite picture of common issues, problems, themes, and trends that run through most of our data and that have a bearing on the direction of policy and practice.

Readers should also be aware that we have reported what we found during our visits at our site institutions during the 1990–91 academic year. Programs and ideas attributed to institutions were those that were in place at the time of our visits. Since that time, people and programs may have come and gone, and we do not wish to suggest that the same programs are necessarily still in place. The examples we have chosen are just that—examples that readers may find helpful in formulating strategies for their own institutions. Moreover, during our interviews, we guaranteed individual anonymity. We have made every effort to preserve that confidentiality and discourage any attempts on the part of readers to attribute comments or situations to any particular site institution or individual.

A final and more personal word is needed on method. Most of our interview sessions prompted far more complex and emotional responses to our questions than we had anticipated. Part-time faculty, for example, often stayed beyond the appointed time to share their personal experiences and views. Many were simply intrigued that someone wanted to hear about their experiences. Some obviously wanted to vent frustration. Others had constructive recommendations for policy or practice. We have tried to capture the depth of feeling and the informal comments of individuals in these off-the-cuff sessions in our quotations. On a number of occasions, we also found ourselves in small group interview sessions that turned into fascinating roundtable discussions where participants would share perspectives and argue about solutions to problems. The issues we were raising were so seldom aired on their campuses and were so salient to the participants that this opportunity to talk was simply too tempting to resist. As a result, our interview transcripts are full of sidebar conversations, digressions, and impromptu discussions. This provided far richer data than we had thought we would gather and presented us with a more complex analytical task than we had anticipated. However, the obvious spontaneity of the participants and the insights we gained from listening to them share information and opinions provided us with perspectives we could not have obtained by sticking to a scripted interview. Although we almost always asked the questions we planned in advance to ask, on occasion it seemed far wiser to take what was offered serendipitously and fit it into the larger tapestry of results as best we could.

Recurrent Themes

At the conclusion of our site visits, we prepared a technical report based on our independent reviews of the complete set of transcribed interview data from each site institution. In this technical report we summarized the principal themes that had emerged in our site visits. We shared the technical report with key administrators at each of our site institutions prior to the actual writing of this book.

These themes have persisted through many rewritings of the manuscript and recur throughout the book. We introduce them here as a composite snapshot of our findings from the site visits, and so that our readers can attend to them in subsequent chapters.

A central theme is that faculties are bifurcated into high- and low-status "castes." We think such bifurcation is damaging to the general ethic of community that academics have long honored and also damaging to the quality of education. It is especially dangerous at a time when institutions are confronting an impending shortage of full-time faculty, an expanded educational agenda, and fiscal difficulties that demand focused, efficient programs. Institutions can and must do more to overcome the bifurcation of their faculties and to foster a unity of purpose that is reinforced by a new sense of community.

There is no longer any point to arguing over the place of part-time faculty in American colleges and universities. Part-timers now carry a significant part of the responsibility for teaching, especially at the lower-division level of undergraduate education. While one might wish that the situation were different, and while in a perfect world it might be so, it is not so now. What we hope to accomplish with this book is to focus attention on the need to integrate part-time faculty into the academic community as full partners enjoying the professional respect and regard of their colleagues. In the process, they need to be supported in their efforts to offer good instruction and they need no less fair or humane treatment than their full-time colleagues.

Another important theme has to do with the role of department chairs. They are the principal point of contact with part-timers, and how department heads perform their supervisory responsibilities makes an enormous difference. Part-timers are quick to sense whether they are valued and respected by the treatment they receive from the department chair. We think that department chairs in departments using substantial numbers of part-timers are underprepared and administratively overwhelmed in trying to deal responsibly with part-time faculty issues. Institutions can and should provide department chairs with more orientation and support.

We have also found an unfortunate tendency to "blame the victims" in much of what is written and assumed about part-time faculty. For the most part, we believe such blame is drastically misplaced. Part-time faculty are not responsible for whatever declines may be occurring in the quality of postsecondary education. Rather, colleges and universities should look carefully within themselves to question whether they have done all they can to support good instruction, committed faculty, and effective programs. Where part-time faculty do not have the proper tools to do their jobs, and we found that they often do not have any support at all, it is usually because the institution has failed in some significant way to provide what is needed.

We refer at several points to the "false economies" of part-time faculty employment. One of those false economies is failing to account for the burdens that accrue to full-time faculty as more part-timers take on teaching assignments. Another is the assumption that part-timers can teach as well as full-time faculty without the same level of support that full-time faculty enjoy. We would be quicker to accuse institutions of ignoring part-timers' needs and interests and exploiting them than we would be to denigrate the contributions part-time faculty make to quality educational programs.

Part One

The Current
Environment for
Part-Time Faculty

The chapters in this part describe what we learned in our study about part-time faculty and the campus employment policies and practices under which they work. We concentrate here on the complex realities affecting part-time employment in higher education now, the "what is" part of our study.

We look first at part-timers—their backgrounds and work experiences, their varied motivations for teaching on a part-time basis, and the extent of their satisfaction or dissatisfaction with their academic working environment. We then consider external influences on colleges and universities as they affect institutional policies and practices regarding part-time faculty. Since fiscal conditions play a substantial part in shaping the extent to which colleges and universities use part-timers, we examine these conditions separately from other external factors. We then move to the institutional setting in which part-timers work. First, we report the wide variety of reasons colleges and universities have for using part-time faculty. Here we look at planned and unplanned or out-of-control use of part-time faculty. Next, we examine the terms and conditions underlying part-time faculty employment and the degree to which employment policies and practices are centrally controlled or left to the discretion of the department chairs to "do what they think best." Finally, we conclude Part One with an assessment of the conditions

15

within departments and institutions that encourage or discourage the integration of part-timers as full participants in the academic community. Proactive efforts to orient, support, and assist part-timers are described here.

Two

Who Are
the Part-Time Faculty?

Part-time faculty members bring variety, energy, enthusiasm, and a wide array of backgrounds and experiences to colleges and universities. Too often we have heard and read stereotypical descriptions of "part-timers" as an anonymous mass of laboring drones who supposedly detract from the quality of education. Although they are often treated as second-class citizens, perhaps because these myths are widely believed, the 240 part-time faculty members we interviewed emerged as professional, committed, and fascinating human beings whom we came to respect, appreciate, and enjoy. The extraordinary range of their accomplishments and experiences enhances the richness of instruction and contributes to the diversity of all types of institutions we visited.

In this chapter we draw on statistical data from the National Survey of Postsecondary Faculty (NSOPF '88) and on the interviews we conducted at eighteen site institutions. We report on part-timers' demographic characteristics, academic preparation, and length of service, and we examine their motivations to teach as well as their satisfactions and dissatisfactions.

We call the reader's attention especially to the wide diversity represented among part-time faculty. It is important to appreciate this diversity and to understand what it adds to classroom and campus life. When part-time faculty are seen in the full complexity of their humanity and their professional aspirations, one can better appreciate what is to be gained from positive actions to support and more fully involve part-timers in the academic community.

The Life Story of a Part-Timer

We begin with the story of one part-timer's career because it covers so well the range of circumstances, motivations, and choices we heard in our interviews. At different points in her life she has progressed through most of the employment categories we describe in the next chapter. She is currently employed in two nontenure-track positions at two different academic institutions, a common phenomenon among part-timers. Her story also exemplifies two central themes of these chapters: part-timers are exceptionally well qualified for their assignments, and part-timers are a rich resource to higher education, with much to offer their students and their institutions. They also have to confront complex circumstances in their lives, and they often cope heroically.

> I have an M.S. in sociology from a midwestern land-grant university and a Ph.D. in anthropology from another midwestern university. I started my Ph.D. in 1977 and finished in 1990.
>
> I was a faculty wife for a long time. I followed my faculty husband around, had children. In 1965, we went to the University of _____ . I had two young children by this time. I got depressed really fast. A professional institute in the city where we were living needed someone to teach anthropology through extension. I really loved it. I taught two or three courses. Then we went to a university town in the Midwest. I got my master's there. Then I taught at the university as a part-timer. Then we moved to _____ for a year. I worked full-time at a publishing firm. I taught one course for a small liberal arts college in the evening. . . .
>
> After my husband accepted a faculty position in another state, . . . I was admitted to the Ph.D. program at the University of _____ , and I paid for it by

teaching at _____ , where we were living. I taught two-thirds time there and drove to the city, 220 miles one way, once a week for the Ph.D. program. I had two children, the Ph.D. program, and my teaching; and I did this for two years.

When I finished my dissertation research, I was employed full-time by a department in the medical school in the city where we now live. I am now an assistant professor there, and it is my primary appointment. It is a nontenure-track appointment. I am on the professional academic track because I do not have an M.D. I got the Ph.D. in 1990. I have been in this job for eight years, the salary is commensurate with the tenure-track's, the benefits package is good, and I do a lot of interesting research.

I started teaching part-time [at a nearby college] three years ago. I usually teach one course a semester, I advise seniors on final honors papers on a volunteer basis, and I work with the department faculty from time to time as a member of students' committees. I teach here to keep up my teaching skills in mainline anthropology. I also teach medical students from time to time. . . .

I'm fine with where I am. There were such profound difficulties for me in the 1950s and early 1960s because of my gender. I came from a relatively poor family. I had no money; could not raise the money to go to medical school—medicine was my first choice of profession. I had done all my undergraduate work in three years and graduated Phi Beta Kappa. I was accepted into medical school but still could not get monetary support, probably because I was a woman. I have had heavy family responsibilities along the way. My mother-in-law, mother, and father all had significant medical problems and needed care at one point or another. Also, I was part of a dual-career couple. Life is crazy. Life is especially complex for women. So right now I am just fine with where I am. . . . I am having a marvelous time of it.

Demographic Characteristics

According to recent estimates, there are about 270,000 part-time faculty teaching in American institutions of higher education. They make up 34.6 percent of the total faculty (NCES, 1989). On average they devote 13.4 hours a week or 42 percent of their total working time to part-time employment in a college or university, and their assignment is predominantly teaching.

Age

Part-time faculty tend to be younger than full-time faculty. (See Table 2.1.)

The part-timers we interviewed, as might be expected, expressed very different life concerns, career interests, and plans, depending on their age and where they were in their careers. We talked with many individuals who were in transition from full-time careers to part-time teaching, often as part of their plans for retirement, and to others who had already retired from a primary job. One assessed his current situation in this way:

> After I retired, I wanted to get back to my first love, which is teaching. I come from a family of educators and always felt I was teaching, even when I was in administration. My students are the same generation as my kids, and I like working with them. I can use

Table 2.1. Age Comparison of Part- and Full-Time Faculty.

	Under 30 years	30–44 years	45–59 years	60–65 years	65+ years
Part-time	6.2%	51.9%	31.9%	5.2%	4.8%
Full-time	2.6%	38.9%	45.9%	8.8%	3.8%

Source: NSOPF '88 (data abstracted).

my experiences as case material to foster critical thinking and challenge able students. I don't have to do
this. I am well off financially, with retirement pay,
investments, and an inheritance. So I'm doing exactly
what I want to be doing for the first time in my life.
There is no financial pressure; I can leave when I want
to. I take great pride in being part of the education
process in the United States. We are responsible for
producing the scientists, doctors, and lawyers, the people who have made this country so great.

The younger people we interviewed typically were trying to
complete their academic or professional training, were starting families, and were looking for entry to academic (or other) careers while
trying to decide how mobile (upwardly, downwardly, and geographically) they wanted to be. In most cases, they had significantly
more pressing economic concerns than did those in the middle or
older age brackets. One young woman described her current situation and plans this way:

I want to be an academic, but I don't want to go
through the hoops of the doctorate or do research. I've
found out that there is no upward mobility for part-
time faculty and that it is tough to find opportunities.
I am getting good experience here. I'm allowed to develop and teach my own critical writing course, which
I enjoy. I'd like to teach more literature courses than
writing. What I do in the future depends on my husband's career, and whether we stay in the area.

Some of the younger people are no longer at the truly beginning stages of their academic careers. They teach part-time because
no full-time positions are open to them in their particular field or
because they want to establish a track record at a particular institution while hoping that this will help them as candidates for the
next opening in their field. We have labeled these individuals *aspiring academics* and will discuss their plight in more detail in
Chapter Three.

Ethnicity

Racial and ethnic minorities make up only 9.2 percent of all part-time faculty, a slightly lower percentage than that of full-time faculty, 10.7 percent of whom are members of racial and ethnic minorities (NSOPF '88). This lack of diversity also characterized our interviewees. While we had speculated that part-time faculty employment would offer institutions an excellent opportunity to hire teachers from racial and ethnic minorities, considerations of affirmative action or diversity did not appear to play an important role in the recruitment and employment of minority candidates at most of the institutions we visited. National data imply, in fact, that just the opposite appears to be occurring. One of our site institutions was troubled by the lack of diversity. In its *Data Book*, a manual that describes its curricula, students, and faculty, it states: "The [part-time] faculty is 76% male; it is also 96% white, compared to 82% for the student body. There are only five minority members: four black and one Asian. Considering both the current reality and the apparent trends for the future, some recruitment effort to further diversify the faculty seems in order" (Saint Mary's College, 1989, p. 46).

The reflections of one African American part-timer may be instructive. He holds a Ph.D. and has postdoctoral experience in his discipline, prior teaching experience at other institutions, and a full-time clinical practice. He had been employed at a major research university on a part-time basis for more than five years when we interviewed him. He described his situation and his views of the institution's posture on affirmative action as follows:

> I enjoy teaching. I can satisfy that interest . . . [and] it gives me variety. Seeing clients all day every day, this gives me variety. [I also do it] for the money. I teach here part-time because that is all they will hire me for. Whether you want more is beside the point. They decide. I told the chair I'm going to leave if I can't get up to .50 FTE and teach every quarter. He replied, "Well, that's too bad. I won't discuss it." . . . Overall, I am about 90 percent satisfied with the teaching. It is rewarding. But all part-time faculty feel isolated. Like

the ghost that goes between people, they see you, they are cordial, but you don't really count. [I represent] a way to achieve diversity. I feel the students should see me—not the students of color but the white students. Students need it. Yet the department chair says, "Well, OK, go [find work elsewhere]." There are not that many people [of color] coming through the pipeline. You [should] take advantage of where you can get them.

The largest concentration of racial and ethnic minority members participating in our interviews was at a large urban community college, where seven of the twenty-five part-time faculty members were from underrepresented groups. Their reasons for teaching part-time exemplify those expressed by others at all our institutions. One African American has taught psychology since 1979. On the outside, he works full-time as an associate director of a drug dependency program and has been a mental health professional for twelve years. He comes from a welfare family and could not read when he got to college. Now he wants to help others from a similar background.

I have experiences I can share with students. I can relate to them and they can understand. I do it for the love of teaching and working with people from the same kind of background I had, not for the money.

Another African American we interviewed has taught courses in social problems and race relations part-time since 1969. He likes to teach these specific courses at his campus, which is almost exclusively white and serves the middle-class suburbs of a large city.

I can talk to my students about all blood being red in a racist system. [This] campus has few Afro-American students. I can talk with these kids about things they don't usually talk about: the contributions of African Americans to the nation. I can see the impact on the students' lives. I challenge the ones from the "good"

suburban schools who may think they are better prepared than the kids from the [city] schools. I go one-
on-one with the minority students who need help and
a personal touch. I get lots of satisfaction out of the
feedback I get from the kids.

The most important conclusion we can offer, however, is
that reflected in the national data: with only 9.2 percent of the part-
time faculty coming from underrepresented groups, institutions are
missing out on an opportunity to enrich their programs with diverse perspectives. Most institutions need to recruit—more actively
than they have in the past—minority professionals employed in a
primary job elsewhere who might also be interested in part-time
teaching.

Gender

According to the NSOPF '88 survey, 58 percent of the part-time
faculty are men and 42 percent are women. By contrast, 73 percent
of full-time faculty are male and 27 percent are female. Although
the common supposition that women constitute a majority of the
part-timers is clearly not true, it is just as clear that women are
disproportionately represented as part-timers. Lundy and Warme
(1990, p. 219) confirm that "gender influences who chooses, or is
assigned to, part-time teaching." The fact that the part-time academic work force is far more female than the full-time academic
work force may be an indicator of the inflexibility of a tenure system
that often conflicts with women's prime childbearing years. Women
who wish to balance their commitments to family and career are
forced by this system to accept less rewarding and secure forms of
work. While this is true for men too, women are disproportionately
affected.

The participation of men and women varies widely by type
of institution, with women ranging from 23 percent of the part-
timers at private doctorate-granting universities to 60 percent at
liberal arts colleges. (See Table 2.2).

Similar variation among men and women as part-timers is
found among the disciplines. Within four-year institutions, women

Table 2.2. Gender Distribution by Type of Institution.

Institution type	Part-time faculty	
	Men	Women
All institutions	57.9%	42.1%
Public research	66.1	33.9
Private research	55.3	44.7
Public doctoral	40.7	59.3
Private doctoral	76.9	23.1
Public comprehensive	50.3	49.7
Private comprehensive	60.1	39.9
Liberal arts	40.2	59.9
Public two-year	60.7	39.3

Source: NSOPF '88 (data abstracted).

represent 25 percent of the *part-time* faculty in business, 39 percent in the natural sciences, 41 percent in the social sciences, 50 percent in the health sciences, 54 percent in education, 59 percent in the fine arts, and 67 percent in the humanities. However, women represent only 24 percent of the *full-time* faculty in the fine arts and 33 percent in the humanities. This pattern of proportionally low representation of women in the full-time faculty and high representation in the part-time faculty did not occur for men in any discipline (NSOPF '88).

In our interviews the numbers of men and women were about equal. The problems and issues they raised, however, reflected substantially different concerns, leading us to conclude that there are important gender-related issues in the use of part-time faculty. For example, we tended to find more men than women who were teaching part-time while they held full-time professional positions elsewhere and, conversely, more women than men teaching part-time who were at least partially dependent upon their part-time faculty income.

I am now ABD [all but dissertation] from [the state university]. I also have an M.A. in English from there. I am teaching three technical writing sections here and two at [the local community college]. I have taught as many as three courses while a full-time doc-

toral student taking three courses. I am a single parent
[age forty] with a $40,000 debt from going to school.
I used to want to teach part-time and write on the side,
but I've now taken on so much debt that I have to find
a full-time job.

These conflicted motives and the perpetual double bind that
hinders many women from realizing their career ambitions were
explicitly recognized by some part-timers as a source of vulnerability and as stemming from stereotyping of female roles:

We are concerned about the gender aspects of part-
time work. Women are relegated to the "conceptual"
ghetto; their roles are stereotyped, and they do the
lower-level teaching. . . . Women and younger people
are easily exploited and very vulnerable in this system.

Marital Status

In contrast to full-time faculty, among whom more males (83 percent) are married than females (63 percent), among part-timers more
nearly equal numbers of male and female faculty members are married—78 percent of the men and 71 percent of the women (NSOPF
'88). This does not vary substantially by type of institution and was
often reported by those we interviewed to be an important factor
underlying the choice of part-time employment.

Marriage and family commitments are closely related to geographical immobility, which was frequently cited as a reason for
choosing part-time over full-time work. (Other than marriage, full-
time professional commitment was the principal factor in unwillingness to move.) Very few of the part-timers we interviewed who
were not full-time graduate students indicated that they were willing to relocate.

Marital status tended to have a disproportionate impact on
many of the women we interviewed, who, torn by conflicts requiring choices between a challenging academic career and marriage
and child rearing, found themselves in part-time positions with

limited future potential and opportunities for professional growth. Typical of many institutions, it was reported at one that

> Many of our daytime adjuncts are women with master's degrees and families who want daytime part-time work.

A young woman at another institution described her own motives to teach part-time in words that confirm this pattern:

> The schedule is important to me. And the department meets my scheduling needs. I can only teach between 8 A.M. and 2 P.M. because of my children's schedule. I do not have any other employment, and I don't want it now.

Another faced a somewhat more trying situation:

> I'm not a 100 percent gung-ho career woman. I have family responsibilities but no other full-time employment. I have one severely handicapped child. My kids are out [of school] at 3 P.M. They are more important [than career ambitions]. I am not geographically mobile. I don't have other employment, but I would like an opportunity to get on the tenure track.

The emergence of interest in academic careers on the part of larger numbers of women has resulted in change at some institutions, but residual exploitation is visible at others. On balance, the women and men who participated in our interviews expressed the need for more options than the traditional full-time, seven-year up-or-out ritual in their pursuit of academic careers. As one woman stated:

> I am teaching part-time because my husband has a tenured position in geography. Our youngest child is one and the oldest is four and a half. For me, the ideal would be a half-time tenured job. This would be per-

fect. I've kept up my research and publishing, and I coedit an academic journal. But I don't have part-time tenure because of institutional rigidity.

Care-giving responsibilities—more often shared by men and women now than in previous generations—and spousal commitments have led individuals to accept part-time positions that do not afford any more promise or security than semester-by-semester appointments. With the exception of some extraordinarily purposeful and committed individuals who have overcome very long odds, the lack of options has led to widespread alienation and despair among a talented generation of hopeful academics.

Dual-Career Academic Couples

Within the group of people trying to balance career and family or other responsibilities, we encountered dual-career academic couples. On occasion, and particularly at liberal arts colleges, part-timers fully qualified for full-time academic positions taught part-time because they had accompanied a spouse who had a tenure-track offer. These tended to be couples just starting academic careers.

Some institutions have made efforts to accommodate dual-career couples when both spouses are attempting to pursue their respective academic careers while raising a family at the same time.

> I am here because my husband is here. He has a tenure-track position. . . . We share India as a common interest in our academic careers. Now that I've finished my Ph.D., I want to begin working again but I don't want a full-time position because I have three small children. We applied jointly [for a single position] and were finalists at [one institution]. But [this one] offered him the job and me a one-third time position. We were happy with this offer. . . . I am not absolutely sure about the security of my job. I understand that it is ongoing, but I don't know. If my job disappears, I'll look for a full-time position. Now, I don't want more than one-third.

Campuses in rural locations often employ "trailing spouses" in part-time positions. A faculty member in classical studies at a small rural liberal arts college described his own experience:

> I came here with my wife, who is in the English Department, in 1975. I was working on a Ph.D. in classical archeology [and] spent fourteen years excavating in Israel. [After] I received the Ph.D., [I] taught in a private boys' school while my wife was at Berkeley. When I came [here], no courses were being taught in my field. I got the Classics Department to let me teach a course in Greek archeology. Roman archeology followed the next year. Then I taught Roman one semester, Greek the next. Then the man who taught Greek retired. I started teaching ancient Greek. I [eventually] got to two courses a semester. . . . Then I got the department to put in a 300-level topics course in Latin. For a long time I have been teaching three courses a semester [full-time load] for part-time pay. I was glad to get the money, and positions were frozen. Now I teach Greek and Roman archeology and art, Latin, medieval art, and architecture.

Another partner in a dual-career academic couple had fared much better. She had just finished her Ph.D. in sociology and had come to a liberal arts college

> Because my husband got a full-time job at _____ and they offered me a part-time position. I've been here for two and one-half years. I found out I was being cut four months ago. I started looking immediately. I was *lucky*. I got a full-time tenure-track position at another liberal arts college in the area. It was offered two weeks ago!

Not many dual-career couple stories end this happily. A woman with a Ph.D. in political science had been on federal research funding for a project on racism and ethnicity and had taught at several urban institutions. When her husband had relocated to a small rural campus, she had followed him. Her current assignment was split: she taught one course in each of three departments.

> We did not negotiate spousal employment, but they knew about my qualifications. My husband liked the job and the institution, and he got the job. I like the education environment and the campus but not the town. I am only here because of the family. I have little children. One is eighteen months old. Commuting is not feasible. Later I may consider splitting the family and commuting. This is an option. I am getting frustrated with my underemployment and the underutilization of my skills and training. I have a good record of scholarly accomplishment.

In summary, although women are far more likely to be affected by the constraints of marital and family roles, we also encountered men who had assumed care-giving roles and had chosen part-time work to accommodate these other responsibilities. Regardless of gender, we were struck by the degree to which people of talent, energy, commitment, and obvious qualification had been relegated to marginal positions in academic life by their marital and familial situations.

Although it is still rare, we did find institutions willing to make part-time tenure-track appointments. At one time, it was popular to advocate "shared" academic positions. One institution we visited had experimented with such positions and recounted almost total failure. One couple sharing a position had divorced. Another had experienced a divergence of professional interests. And in a third, the performance of one spouse was far inferior to that of the other, resulting in an offer of tenure to the superior one—who in this case was the woman—with predictable consequences. The institution no longer considers shared positions an option. Admittedly, this is a sample of one, but it serves to highlight all that can go wrong, and it emphasizes the serious need for career options.

More often, institutions are accommodating spouses via part-time "temporary" positions. For many of these new-generation academic couples, the usual temporary part-time assignment is unsatisfying and unpromising and therefore both demeaning and unacceptable. Increasingly, this is true for both husbands and wives who agree to accompany the spouse who accepts a full-time academic job. It may be the best and only option available, however, and many will accept it in order to maintain a family unit. Nevertheless, substantial pressure is likely to arise to broaden the range of options available, including the establishment of part-time, tenure-track positions. Part-time positions with entrée to full career status are at the top of the list of changes many of those now teaching part-time want and need.

Academic Background

Part-time faculty are far better qualified for their assignments than might be commonly assumed. We found in our interviews an astounding range in the academic and experiential qualifications of individual part-timers. In many instances, the part-timers were more than qualified to perform their duties.

We heard very few expressions of concern about part-timers' qualifications in our interviews with department chairs and deans, even though some of our interviewees did candidly share with us episodic and incidental information that illustrates some of the dangers inherent in hiring part-timers. We consider these incidents more a matter of how institutions screen and select their teaching faculty than a critique of the part-timers' qualifications.

The NSOPF '88 data show that 28.5 percent of all part-time faculty have doctoral or professional degrees, 42.7 percent have master's degrees, and 28.8 percent have bachelor's or other degrees. There are important variations by institutional type. At public and private research institutions, the proportion of part-time faculty with doctoral degrees is 68 percent and 50 percent, respectively, while the public two-year institutions most often hire people with master's or bachelor's degrees.

The important issue is not what the national data on the academic qualifications of part-timers show but whether individual part-time faculty members are academically and experientially qualified for the assignments they have. The aggregate data tend to obscure the variations in individuals' overall qualifications. We will highlight these variations in three examples, sorted by type of institution, which illustrate the unique qualifications of part-timers for their particular assignments.

Part-timers at research universities and comprehensive regional universities generally have a high level of academic qualifications. For example, at one of our research universities, fourteen of the sixteen part-timers interviewed have doctoral or professional degrees. The two remaining individuals are practitioners in health care specialties and hold master's degrees. Those with doctoral degrees received them from prestigious institutions across the country and are fully qualified (in our view and in theirs) by training, experience, and current assignment to be in tenure-track positions. In many cases, these women and men were seeking simultaneously to pursue mainstream academic careers and to meet family responsibilities. Some of them have been teaching part-time for years and are actively involved in governance and union activity to improve the part-time faculty "career." Most of them are strong advocates of tenure for part-time people.

At another university, all the part-timers we interviewed have doctoral degrees in their fields from that institution or from nearby universities. At the time of our interviews, these part-timers were geographically bound and for the most part were seeking academic careers within a reasonable commuting distance.

A different pattern was observed at an urban university. This university hired doctoral students from its own programs and those of other universities in the same city to staff its undergraduate courses. These doctoral students were hired as part-timers, not as graduate teaching assistants. The university saw this practice as mutually beneficial. The doctoral students needed income on which to live while completing their programs and would benefit from the teaching experience when they finished their degrees and sought tenure-track positions. In the interim, the university benefited from their "cutting edge" knowledge of their discipline in the classroom.

Saint Mary's College in Moraga, California, just east of San Francisco, exemplifies the richness and variety in the backgrounds of part-time faculty we found at most of our site institutions, irrespective of type. Its *Data Book* (1989) for the School of Extended Education describes the academic backgrounds of its part-timers:

> For 127 faculty there are 61 different patterns of degrees. Forty-six people (36%) hold doctorates; many hold multiple master's degrees; nine have JDs. Only one holds no graduate degree. . . . Some faculty are also actively working on further degrees. Some faculty have gone the traditional route of doing all their academic work before embarking on their professional career[s]; others have spaced their degrees throughout. One, for example, received his M.A. in 1950 and his Ph.D. in 1987, at the age of 69. Another attained his B.S. in 1942, his M.B.A. in 1963, and his Ph.D. in 1989, at age 68. These are indeed lifelong learners [p. 46].

Of the twenty-five part-timers we interviewed at Saint Mary's School of Extended Education, ten have Ph.D.'s, four more were ABD, one person has three master's degrees, and the rest have either one or two master's degrees. The mix of academic backgrounds was extraordinary. For example, one individual has a Ph.D. in pharmacy combined with an M.B.A. in corporate finance. Another has a master's degree in health care administration and a second master's in business administration and is also a registered nurse. These individuals' academic qualifications were uniquely suited to their teaching assignments in a health sciences administration program for an adult population.

The large majority of part-time faculty we interviewed at community colleges hold a master's degree, and several hold two or more. Most part-timers at the community colleges in our study did not typically express interest in pursuit of doctoral (or other advanced professional) degrees. However, there were exceptions. Perhaps the most extraordinarily multitalented of all is a woman who holds master's degrees in music, mathematics, and business and was, at the time of our visit, a Ph.D. candidate in music.

At one typical community college, of twenty-six part-timers interviewed, two hold the baccalaureate only, fifteen hold one master's degree, two have more than one master's, four have a Ph.D., and one has an M.D. It should be emphasized strongly, however, that the degrees these part-timers hold do not represent the extraordinary diversity of backgrounds and experience they bring to the classroom.

For example, the M.D. runs a large soft-drink distributorship and has consulting medical practices with a number of Caribbean nations. He trained with a prominent heart-transplant team and received his degree from historically black institutions. Two of the individuals with master's degrees retired from careers as executives with Fortune 500 companies. One began teaching after realizing that he knew more about the subject than the instructor when he himself took the course after retirement. Two others have experience as elected or appointed local government officials. Two of the Ph.D.'s have international backgrounds: one is an immigrant from Eastern Europe and the other has benefited from two Fulbright fellowships. In general, at the time of our visit all of the part-timers at this institution had broad professional and community involvements that provided them with extremely rich backgrounds in their teaching fields.

As these examples show, the wide variety of academic backgrounds makes sense when individual situations are known. Many of the part-timers we interviewed were at mid career. In some cases they had extensive work experience and were teaching part-time as specialists in their field. In other cases they were changing career direction and/or field and making the transition to teaching from other employment. Some of them were highly ambivalent about the "worth" of a doctoral degree. They were uncertain as to whether they wanted to make the investment of time to earn a degree that they saw as having little relationship to teaching performance. They were clear that they did not want a Ph.D. in order to do research, and they were not sure they wanted a "regular" academic position badly enough to make the sacrifices necessary to complete a Ph.D. degree. They simply wanted to teach!

Length of Employment at Current Institution

Part-time faculty are not purely migrant labor. Many have taught at their institutions for extended periods of time, and some have long and even distinguished records of teaching. (See Table 2.3.)

Table 2.3. Percentage of Part-Time Faculty by Number of Years
at Current Institution.

Institution type	Fewer than 4 years	4–6 years	7–9 years	10–19 years	20+ years
All institutions	51.5%	15.5%	11.1%	15.5%	6.5%
Public research	42.7	14.9	13.4	17.2	11.8
Private research	47.9	14.1	10.4	12.7	14.9
Public doctoral	49.1	14.9	16.8	15.1	4.1
Private doctoral	35.7	21.4	15.4	19.2	8.4
Public comprehensive	52.8	14.9	11.7	15.6	5.0
Private comprehensive	57.0	15.3	8.6	11.5	7.6
Liberal arts	59.8	8.6	9.1	17.0	5.5
Public two-year	52.5	15.6	11.6	14.9	5.4

Source: NSOPF '88 (data abstracted).

NSOPF '88 data show that relatively greater numbers of part-timers at doctoral institutions have extremely long service (twenty years or more) and that relatively greater numbers of part-timers at comprehensive and liberal arts colleges typically have shorter service (under four years).

Among our part-timers we also found extensive employment experiences interwoven within academic backgrounds that make them ideally suited for teaching. These profiles of qualifications are in and of themselves the most powerful reason we found for the continuing use of part-time faculty in higher education. The range of employment experiences, when combining employment outside and inside academe, is so great that we have made it the focus of the next chapter. In this chapter we will look at employment experience only from the perspective of the length of time spent teaching at the current institution.

In our interviews, we found that most of the variance in length of service is more directly associated with individuals' circumstances, choices, and career histories than it is with any kind of institutional policy or practice. Graduate students teaching part-time for money, and people in periods of career transition tend to have been at their institutions less time than others. Those in rural institutions, fully prepared academics, and many of the specialists employed full-time elsewhere tend to have had longer-term affiliations with their institutions.

There also appears to be some systematic variation among academic disciplines in the typical length of service of part-time faculty. For example, NSOPF '88 data show that more than 50 percent of the part-timers in business and 49 percent in health sciences have been at their institutions seven or more years. However, only 27 percent of those in the humanities and 22 percent of those in the social sciences have been at their institutions for seven or more years. Certainly, the marketplace has something to do with these differences; we were repeatedly informed that surpluses of trained people in the social sciences and humanities had led to fairly extensive use of part-time appointments. We also learned that it is difficult to compete with the salaries available in the private sector in fields such as business and the health sciences. Academic departments in these fields, as one alternative to competing with "outside" salaries for full-time faculty, offer part-time positions instead to selected individuals with needed expertise. Those brought to the campus to teach a course or two in their field of expertise tend to have longer-term relationships with their institutions.

There was considerable variation in length-of-time-at-institution among our sites. Most were characterized by a combination of relatively new and long-term part-timers. Almost perfectly representative of the national experience was the distribution at one community college: of the forty-four part-timers interviewed, ten were in their first year, five were in their second year, fourteen were in their third through fifth years, nine had taught between five and ten years, and five had taught more than ten years. We are aware of several cases in which individuals have taught part-time for as long as thirty (and more) years at the same institution.

Motivation

Part-time faculty choose to teach for a wide variety of reasons. Morton and Rittenburg (1986) factor-analyzed a set of possible motivations and were able to identify six principal groupings. The main identifiable reason was to pursue professional growth. The second most important, but a distant second, was the economic motive

(p. 11). Other motivations (such as personal development, social interaction, and community or professional service) were primarily intrinsic in character. Our own data also suggest that intrinsic motivations are particularly strong and that economic motives—while critically important for some part-timers—are not the principal reason for entering part-time teaching.

Intrinsic Motivation

Part-time faculty have both intrinsic and extrinsic motivations to teach. Those with intrinsic motivations are almost always also employed elsewhere and are motivated to teach part-time because of the satisfaction the work itself brings them. The part-timers with whom we talked are dedicated to their teaching and the constituencies they serve and committed to the good of society. A substantial number, particularly those in a life transition or working in careers that do not fully satisfy their needs and interests, expressed their attraction to and enthusiasm for teaching.

Part-timers across all categories, but particularly those who are employed in a primary occupation elsewhere, often indicate that they feel obligated to return debts they owe to institutions, to society, or even to parents. One man approaching retirement grew up with parents who taught. He told us:

> I can trace my interest in teaching to my father, who taught in New York City in the Depression years. I have carried on that interest and have been involved in some kind of education for a long time. . . . The money isn't as important to me as the intrinsic satisfaction. I am in [teaching] because I love it. I always learn more than the students. I'd like to teach full-time at the end of my career. I feel everyone should give something back, and I am a "rabbi" at heart.

Another, a young woman in her first teaching job, indicated that her engineering work did not satisfy her need to work with people. She also cited a sense of social obligation:

> I think that education is very important and that the
> United States is falling behind. I feel I have a respon-
> sibility to help turn it around before it is too late.

A part-timer at a Catholic institution cited the moral priority in
these terms:

> The students are good and work hard. The curriculum
> is good. [My co-religionists and I] value education as
> part of our personal value system. We are also giving
> back a bit to the profession.

At the same institution, one of the part-timers felt obligated as an
alumna:

> I am the product of [this program]. I believe in it and
> in the institution, and I want to give something back.

An altruistic sense about helping others who come from similar backgrounds to one's own and who face risks one has already
confronted and beaten motivates part-timers from diverse backgrounds. They feel they have a special ability to capture the imag-
ination of young people from their particular ethnic or cultural
background. This is a particular concern of several who hope to
improve the educational status and life chances of young African
American men. These part-timers feel they can serve as role models
and mentors and are in positions to open career pathways. As one
African American part-timer in social work put it:

> I believe . . . African American students need role
> models, and I want to play this role.

Extrinsic Motivation

Money, status, and entrée to a full-time academic position are important motivations for many part-timers. Although we found these
the most thwarted of part-timers' desires in practice, they nevertheless form a substantial core of reasons why many people elect this

kind of employment. Those in metropolitan areas, especially, echoed a familiar theme:

> It is expensive to live in Toronto [or Washington, or New York, or San Francisco], particularly for people who want to own their own homes.

More poignant was the point made by a woman whose retirement plan had not been adequate:

> I need the money to live on in retirement.

On the other hand, the large majority of those we interviewed indicated that they are not making enough money as part-time faculty to continue teaching for that reason alone:

> I could make more money as an agricultural economist in government or the private sector—or even teaching in public school. I have been offered twice my present salary by my former students! But I like it here.

Although we encountered few cases of economic desperation, part-time work is clearly at least a temporary last resort for some:

> This year my husband lost his job. I need money.

Aspirations to secure a tenure-track position and full professional status clearly motivate some part-timers:

> The college should recognize good performance. Some of us would like to have rewards in the form of full-time positions; we would like to feel there is a way to get those jobs if we have done our work well.

Another, contemplating a career change, said,

> My engineering practice is very solitary. I would like to teach full-time. Doing it part-time is getting my

foot in the door and gaining the skills and experience
I'll need.

Satisfactions and Dissatisfactions

According to the NSOPF '88 survey, 87 percent of all the part-time
faculty surveyed stated that they were somewhat (46 percent) or very
(41 percent) satisfied with their jobs. This level of satisfaction is
almost identical to that of full-time faculty who responded to the
same survey. The percentage declined slightly to 78 percent for
those who identified themselves as aspiring to a full-time faculty
position. On the other hand, part-timers expressed markedly less
satisfaction with specific aspects of their jobs.

Most of the part-timers we interviewed derive their principal
satisfaction from the intrinsic rewards of teaching. Part-time faculty
love to teach! They are excited and challenged by their students and
the engagement in teaching and learning:

> It's like having three hundred kids you don't have to
> share the bathroom with!

Depending upon the type of assignment the part-timers had,
their comments about why they enjoy teaching so much varied.
Some enjoy the diversity in preparation and background of their
students.

> I am thrilled to be teaching the *lowest level of math*
> that is available. Kids that just can't make it are a
> challenge and a satisfaction. I prefer them to the hon-
> ors kids. The kid that hates school is the kid I love.

Another reported that she enjoys giving students individual attention and seeing their progress:

> Our students don't have very good preparation in
> high school. . . . I stopped writing [professionally]
> and started teaching because I liked doing tutoring
> and working with [students]. I don't want to be

immersed in some arcane subject like seventeenth-century literature. I have a lot of intrinsic interest and skill in teaching writing, and I like doing just what I'm doing here. I know there is a tremendous demand for good writing instructors—something full-time faculty don't much like to do. I really like seeing the tough cases make it. [Part-time faculty] are uncluttered with the responsibilities of full-time faculty. All we do is teach, and we have the time to do it well. Kids at the big universities don't get the individual attention they get here.

Teaching adult students is a particular source of enthusiasm:

The nature of the program keeps me here. The students are adults, experienced, and know what they want. . . . The students are good and work hard, the curriculum is good . . . lots of personal satisfaction in it for me.

Emphasizing the purely intrinsic satisfactions, one woman, the chief executive officer of an oil company that she owns, noted:

My students appreciate what I am doing. I don't need the money. I make several million dollars a year.

Despite their frustrations and unhappiness with their career choices or life-styles or with the employment policies or practices at their institutions, part-timers remain very committed to teaching at the college level. As one said,

I didn't intend to go full-time, but I loved part-time and decided to make a career out of it. Some part-time faculty don't want to be full-time faculty but just love to teach. In the private sector, management is too constraining. The corporate environment is too stultifying. I have a lot of control in teaching, and the challenges are endless.

This former part-time faculty member at a community college is now a department chair!

However much pleasure part-timers may receive while teaching, they are dissatisfied with many aspects of their employment. Part-timers who work at other jobs in addition to their part-time faculty employment are among the most critical of the way they are treated. They have broad experience in the real world of corporate, government, and artistic life, and they can compare the way they are treated in academe with what they are accustomed to elsewhere. Many offer a cynical assessment of the petty and thoughtless treatment they receive and are often highly aware of the inequities in their employment despite their academic backgrounds and their stature in other arenas.

Some general dissatisfactions with status and working conditions surfaced throughout our interviews. The foremost is vulnerability. One part-timer characterized the conflicts inherent in part-time faculty status perfectly:

> If you fall in love, you want a commitment. The institution won't make a commitment [to me]. Thus, as a part-timer I am vulnerable.

Others were more forceful:

> We are basically in the same position as migrant workers. There is a lot of wasted energy and unnecessary expense in trying to stay alive with part-time teaching.

Potential conflicts are never far beneath the surface:

> There is confusion—power, guilt relationships, and powerful feelings. The tenured faculty [have power] over the part-time. They are expendable. The part-time [have power] over the tenured. We have the numbers and we control the enrollment. The tenured faculty have their schedules and [other perks] at our

expense, and they feel guilty. They know there are inequities.

Dissatisfaction with second-class status was almost universal among the part-timers we interviewed. Over and over again, whether they were aspiring to an academic career or teaching one night a week as specialists, part-timers constantly alluded to their status in a bifurcated academic career system. They expressed anger and frustration about their treatment, work loads, salaries and benefits, and lack of appreciation for their efforts. They often felt deep anxiety about the temporary and indefinite nature of their employment. Many expressed clear annoyance over their lack of consultation and involvement in decisions affecting them, an annoyance that was only exacerbated by their feeling that protesting or demanding a more substantive role would jeopardize their continued employment.

While the sense of a lack of power and ability to influence their employment is pervasive, some part-timers are aggressively and creatively pursuing a better situation for themselves and, at some campuses, collectively for the good of the group. We encountered individuals in leadership roles at many campuses, particularly at institutions with collective bargaining. As one part-timer remarked about empowerment:

> There are lots of things part-time faculty don't know they can do. You can just call the provost and ask for a meeting. A lot of it is the way we feel rather than the way others act. I chose to be a part-time faculty member. I don't want committees and so on. I consider myself as basically freelance. I just call the provost and say, "I want to talk to you about my salary." It's just knowing what to do. I was here for seven years before I knew to do this. I met with the provost for fifteen minutes and got a $2,000 raise.

Conclusion

This chapter has provided a look at the talented, dynamic, and dedicated people who teach part-time. They express far more enthusiasm for teaching—especially for the intrinsic satisfactions they experience—than is commonly assumed. At the same time, they are very vocal about being second-class citizens in a bifurcated academic profession.

We conclude that they do not get the kind of respect and attention they deserve. This is a truly talented work force, but its potential remains largely ignored and therefore untapped. By failing to see the invisible faculty in its midst, the academic community is missing an opportunity to develop some of the best potential teaching talent it will have available in the foreseeable future.

Three

Employment Profiles
of Part-Timers

Part-time faculty come from extraordinarily varied and interesting work lives. We interviewed corporate executives and "starving poets," medical doctors and massage therapists, chemists and coaches, musicians and politicians, entrepreneurs and entertainers. Typically, part-time faculty have other work and sources of income. The large majority spend less than half their time teaching and derive an average of 18 percent of their total income from this source (NSOPF '88).

To explore how teaching fits in with their other work and activities, we asked about professional experiences, other jobs, and other teaching assignments. We also asked whether part-time faculty experienced conflicts among their roles and what their career aspirations were. Our goal was to understand the whole person so that we could better understand why people chose to teach part-time and what this decision meant to their lives and careers.

We were able to recognize four major clusters of academic background, employment history, and motivations. These clusters are only partly consistent with the popular and widely referenced typology generated a number of years ago by Howard Tuckman's (1978) research, which we summarize for the purpose of comparison.

We can see clearly that part-timers are not a monolithic group of marginal employees. We have identified four distinct sub-populations that we describe in this chapter. We show how individuals within each of these groups need varying career options and patterns of work and compensation in order to better meet their needs and those of the institutions they serve.

Categorizing Part-Timers' Employment Experiences

The diversity of employment experience we encountered in our site visits was first recognized and documented in a path-breaking study by Howard Tuckman in 1978. From the results of a survey of 3,763 part-time faculty members, Tuckman and his associates developed a taxonomy of part-timers based on their reasons for choosing part-time employment. This taxonomy contains seven categories:

1. *Semiretireds* (2.8 percent of Tuckman's total sample) were former full-time academics or professionals who were teaching fewer hours and were less concerned about future job prospects than the part-timers in other categories.
2. *Graduate students* (21.2 percent of the total sample) were usually employed as part-timers in institutions other than the one in which they were pursuing a graduate degree. They were teaching to gain experience and to augment income.
3. *Hopeful full-timers* (16.6 percent of the sample) were those who could not find full-time academic positions but wanted them. Tuckman also included those who were working enough part-time hours at one or more institutions to constitute full-time employment but under several contracts, each of which only provided part-time status.
4. *Full-mooners* (27.6 percent of the sample) were individuals who held another primary job of at least thirty-five hours a week. Tuckman characterized these individuals as spending relatively little time preparing lectures and other teaching activities and limiting the number of hours they taught. He also included here tenured faculty teaching overload courses.
5. *Homeworkers* (6.4 percent of the sample) worked part-time be-cause they cared for children or other relatives. Part-time employment might be the sole source of support for the home-worker's household or it might supplement the income of a spouse.
6. *Part-mooners* (13.6 percent) consisted of people working part-

time in one academic institution while holding a second job of fewer than thirty-five hours a week elsewhere. Reasons given for holding two jobs simultaneously were economic necessity, psychic rewards not obtainable from one job only, concern about future employment prospects, and highly specialized skills that could be used by one employer only to a limited extent.

7. *Part-unknowners* (11.8 percent) were part-time faculty whose reasons for working part-time were either unknown, transitory, or highly subjective. (See Tuckman, 1978.)

Tuckman's typology continues to provide a foundation for viewing part-time faculty employment experiences and motivations. While Tuckman and Pickerill (1988) note that no recent data permit a new test of this typology, we encountered part-timers who fit neatly into the typology among the 240 part-timers we interviewed. Our interviews indicate, however, that there are some important changes to be taken into account. For example, we found that the "full-mooners" were very dedicated to their teaching and spent a great deal of time in preparation, and we found that the label "homeworkers" now encompasses a much broader array of people with a wide variety of care-giving roles and life-style concerns. Because the interview data gave us much more information about other components of people's lives, we found the patterns of work experience and motivation too complex to fit into the narrow categories Tuckman's typology suggests.

On the basis of our interviews, we have broadened Tuckman's typology into four loose categories: career enders; specialists, experts, and professionals; aspiring academics; and freelancers. We will briefly define these four categories from the perspective of Tuckman's typology and then look at each one in turn, using our site visit interviews to draw a more comprehensive picture.

We have retained Tuckman's category of semiretireds but renamed it *career enders*. We have broadened it to include those who are already fully retired and those who are in transition from well-established careers (mostly outside of higher education) to a preretired or retired status in which part-time teaching plays a significant role. From our interviews, we would estimate that the percentage of part-timers who are retired or semiretired is now much higher than Tuckman's figure of 3 percent would suggest.

We have changed Tuckman's category of full-mooner to a designation of *specialist, expert, or professional* with a primary, usually full-time, career elsewhere. This group of people comes to higher education from a wide range of fields and careers and teaches for the love of it rather than because of a need for income. Some are hired as specialists to teach in their discipline; others are specialists in their primary occupation but teach as generalists. These specialists, experts, or professionals formed a significant portion of our total sample.

We have relabeled Tuckman's hopeful full-timers *aspiring academics* because the focus of their career aspiration is not necessarily to teach full-time but to be fully participating, recognized, and rewarded members of the faculty with a status at least similar to that currently associated with the tenure-track or tenured faculty. We include as aspiring academics only those part-timers who possess the terminal degree and want full-time academic careers and ABD doctoral students. Among the aspiring academics, we distinguish between truly part-time faculty and those who have managed to become "full-time" part-timers because they have a combination of part-time appointments at the same institution or at several institutions. (This latter group is frequently referred to as "freeway fliers.") In some cases, these full-time part-timers carry teaching loads that are greater than full-time. We also include in this group those who are fully qualified but who are "stuck," the geographically immobile who have chosen a part-time teaching career because of family or other obligations.

We have been unable to estimate how common the freeway flier phenomenon may be. We found individual part-timers at virtually every institution in our sample who held more than one part-time teaching job. Yet nowhere did it appear to be the principal mode of employment for part-timers, contrary to the standard myth we have heard repeated many times. A study conducted by the Office of the Chancellor of the California Community Colleges (1987, p. 8) estimated the number of aspiring academics in this subgroup at about one-quarter of all part-timers, a proportion that was found to be increasing. An earlier study conducted by Dykstra (1983), on the other hand, found little evidence of "crosstown teaching" in the Columbus, Ohio, metropolitan area. Anecdotal evidence from our study suggests that this form of employment, undertaken out of economic necessity, is probably more common in large metropolitan areas, and it may be more consequential for individuals and institutions in those areas. Further direct study of this phenomenon is needed, with particular attention to geography.

Our final category is a composite of Tuckman's part-unknowners, part-mooners, and homeworkers that we have broadened and relabeled *freelancers*. It is a composite of all part-timers whose current career is the *sum* of all the part-time jobs or roles they have, only one of which is part-time teaching in higher education. Freelancers are part-time faculty in higher education by choice; they are not aspiring academics.

We found a good example of the mixture of part-timers among the different groups in our interviews at one large community college. Of the forty-four part-time faculty members we interviewed, eight were otherwise unemployed (four of these by choice), six were self-employed in their own businesses, six had other full-time jobs at the same institution, five were teaching elsewhere, five were retired, three were artists, three had corporate jobs, three were graduate students, two were musicians, two were state government administrators, and one reported that he was a starving poet and massage therapist. Seventeen of the forty-four part-timers considered their part-time employment at the community college to be their primary employment.

Career Enders

Among the career enders we interviewed, one had just begun teaching international economics at a university. He had done his graduate work in the 1950s and had been a full-time faculty member for four years. He then went into the foreign service as an economic adviser in Vietnam and other Asian locations. Subsequently, he was employed by the Department of Commerce, U.S. Agency for International Development (USAID), and several major corporations. Upon his retirement from the government, he established a real estate partnership to buy inner-city property in Washington, D.C.

Continuously seeking a challenge, he had just taken up part-time teaching.

Another career ender we interviewed had been retired for a longer period of time but continued to work part-time where he had spent his career, in education:

> I taught in the public schools for twenty years and then was a principal. I spent thirty-three years in public education. I've been teaching at the local community college and at _____ for three years. I'm retired, but I currently serve on a part-time basis as the truant officer for the _____ schools and sell as much fish as I can catch in my spare time.

Others we interviewed had more prosaic reasons for teaching in retirement, such as those offered by a woman recently retired from teaching:

> I'm glad to be out of the junior high school setting. Now that I'm retired, I need a routine and a structure. This provides me with that.

Another, a man retired from a career in public administration, said,

> I've always taught, and now that I'm retired the routine is useful to keep me on track. I enjoy this because it keeps me in touch with young people and intellectually alive. I do four courses a term and love teaching.

As current faculty members reach retirement age in progressively larger numbers in the coming years, we expect that many will choose to teach part-time while phasing into full retirement. If this trend develops, it will mean that substantial numbers of experienced faculty may become available, altering the present marketplace for faculty in ways we do not yet foresee.

Specialists, Experts, and Professionals

According to NSOPF '88 data, over half of the part-time faculty in all institutions (52.5 percent) have other full-time employment.

This ranges from a low of 37 percent at liberal arts colleges and public doctorate-granting institutions to a high of 67 percent at private doctorate-granting universities. There is also variation among disciplines. Only 19 percent of those in the humanities have full-time positions elsewhere, while 59 percent of those in education, 67 percent in business, and 73 percent in engineering work full-time at other jobs.

Those who do have full-time positions elsewhere tend to have been employed at their colleges or universities as part-time faculty members for a longer period of time. About 60 percent of the part-timers who have full-time positions elsewhere have been employed more than four years as compared with an average of 48.6 percent for all part-time faculty. Similarly, the higher the terminal degree, the more likely the part-time faculty member is to have full-time employment elsewhere. Across all types of institutions, 61 percent of the part-time faculty who have doctoral or professional degrees also have full-time employment elsewhere, but only 47 percent of those with master's degrees and 52 percent of those with bachelor's degrees work full-time elsewhere (NSOPF '88).

At virtually every institution in our study, we interviewed part-timers who have full-time jobs as professionals or managers. They have advanced training in fields such as medicine, allied health, biochemistry, mathematics and statistics, public administration, business, education, social work, law, and criminal justice. Some of them teach courses closely related to their primary occupation; some of them were hired as generalists for courses such as basic mathematics. For almost all, their teaching represents a professional commitment, a community service, and a source of personal satisfaction.

Since most of the part-time faculty we interviewed who also have full-time positions elsewhere already enjoy comparatively high salaries and relative employment security, they have little economic need or motive to teach part time. They are teaching because they want to. Usually, they do not experience conflict with their full-time jobs:

> My superiors and subordinates on my full-time job are
> supportive. They don't see my teaching as competi-

tive. This job keeps me fresh and enthused. I recruit
volunteers from classes to help out at the facilities. I
can use real life examples in class.

At San Jose State University, we interviewed the dean of the
School of Engineering who talked about his proximity to Silicon
Valley and the need to graduate quality engineers:

To make sure we graduate quality engineers, we must
have part-timers. Industry understands this. People
from the companies come in at all times of day. [We
have] a partnership concept. . . . Teaching at San Jose
State is part of the part-timers' outside work assignment with their companies.

Some fast-track professionals enjoy the intrinsic rewards of
teaching but do not always appreciate or understand the folkways
of academic life. One Ph.D. in economics had worked for a Big
Eight accounting firm and subsequently formed his own company.
He currently teaches microeconomics and would be well qualified
for a tenure-track position, but he has reservations:

I just enjoy teaching. The rest of what [the faculty] are
involved in is a pain in the butt. Committee work is
redundant and a waste of time. Also, academic work
is not as financially rewarding as work in the private
sector. I decided to leave academe because of finances.
But I like being in the classroom. Teaching is much
more fulfilling than work in the private sector. Right
now I have the best of both possible worlds.

One individual with a Ph.D. in mathematics and statistics
had originally considered an academic career. Instead he had become a statistical systems analyst for a research institute. Then he
worked at the Department of Health, Education and Welfare setting
up medical data bases and data analysis systems. He is currently
employed in a management position as a senior statistician with
another major federal agency. Despite his decision to forego an

academic career, he has been teaching evening courses since receiving his Ph.D.

> It is *fun*. I enjoy teaching, but I don't want to do it full-time. I had that option after I got the Ph.D. I looked at it as a career. I could have gotten an academic job in 1973, but [the job market] was discouraging. I've learned a lot about myself. I'm not much of a publisher. I have published ten to twelve articles in sixteen or seventeen years, and these are policy interpretation stuff. I've lost the cutting edge. I enjoy the teaching, but I don't want the rest of the full-time responsibility.

Another part-time faculty member also currently works as a biochemist for a major corporation. His research, while satisfying, does not fulfill his interests in teaching:

> I love teaching! I work full-time in the private sector for the money and because I have a chance to do research. But I wanted to grow personally and am looking to options for a postretirement career—teaching is high on the list. I love the challenge of dealing with students who aren't intrinsically interested and who are required to be in my class. I feel I can bring real world examples to help motivate and interest them in the study of biology.

Over and over again, we interviewed executives, health care specialists, engineers, artists, public school teachers, and others who teach in addition to their full-time careers. They teach because they love to and are rejuvenated by their students. But they often teach at considerable personal sacrifice.

> When you work full-time, it is hard to find the time to teach. It is hard to juggle the schedule. I teach at most twice a year here. Employers are supportive of the concept [of teaching], but the work doesn't go

away. Employers are expecting nothing in return; they are neutral. It is your choice to teach.

Part-timers in the School of Extended Education at Saint Mary's College whom we interviewed were commuting to off-campus teaching sites from homes and jobs all over the greater San Francisco Bay area, frequently at peak commuting hours.

> My personal life is very scheduled, and my children recognize this. My wife is also in health care. I schedule time with the children. I keep a calendar, and the kids know this. I am working in Pleasanton, living in Richmond, and teaching in San Francisco. But the students are also driving and preparing and they have full-time jobs.

Still, the personal price tends to be worth the costs to those with primary jobs elsewhere. As one part-timer put it:

> Teaching at _____ is the only stable part of my life. CEOs in health care have rapid turnover.

Some careerists mentioned their desire eventually to switch from full-time executive jobs to teaching positions:

> Teaching is very rewarding personally. In five or six years I would like to make a career change to full-time teaching and part-time consulting. Now I have two children.

Aspiring Academics

Aspiring academics include relatively new Ph.D.'s seeking tenure-track appointments and some Ph.D. recipients who have been teaching on a part-time basis for years in the hope of attaining a full-time, tenure-track position. Under better circumstances, they would be part of the tenured faculty. Aspiring academics also include ABD doctoral students who are simultaneously employed as part-timers.

Many of these long-term part-timers, while still retaining a wish that they could be part of the "regular" faculty, have found ways to build academic careers within their part-time status. In the most satisfactory arrangements, they have successfully put together several part-time assignments within their institutions and/or have taken leadership positions in faculty governance.

One part-timer exemplifies this group of individuals. With a Ph.D. from a leading university in 1972, he held a tenure-track position for four years before deciding to return to California. Employed in higher education for several years, he was laid off in the wake of California's Proposition 13. He then took courses in computer science at his local community college. In 1978 he returned to the university in a half-time faculty position in medieval studies and in a staff position created for him because of his knowledge of the use of computers in the humanities. Now he teaches courses in his discipline in three different departments and is also employed as a data base manager. All of his part-time assignments, when put together, are more than full-time. This ability to put together a full-time "position" out of pieces of part-time assignments is characteristic of more than a few of the part-timers we interviewed. While the pieced-together temporary assignments may constitute a full-time work load, they remain without the status, salary, benefits, and security normally associated with full-time or regular employment. At any time one of the part-time assignments can easily "disappear."

For other aspiring academics we interviewed, waiting and hoping had extended for substantial periods of time without bearing fruit. Some of these people realized that they were now falling behind the newer doctoral graduates and had become less attractive as potential full-time faculty. One assessed his situation this way:

> I am ambivalent as to whether part-time faculty should be thankful they've had an opportunity to teach or whether they should be regretful that they've pursued teaching too intensely at the expense of other things. You teach part-time here at the expense of research, and this forecloses opportunities. . . . There

are also psychological issues: part-time faculty sometimes wonder if they are living in an artificial world;
my kids think I'm a professor, but I know nothing is
guaranteed beyond the current semester. I feel I am
under scrutiny all the time. I worry about how I am
doing and am oversensitive to student reactions. Every
year, you are judged. You have to perform all the time
and can't rely on the colleagueship or goodwill of full-
time faculty. I also can't take time to do research. I
teach ten to fifteen hours each semester with hundreds
of papers, and I don't have time for research or even
to prepare properly for class. I know I've devoted too
much energy to teaching and should have done more
research. I deeply regret this choice, but [I] had no
alternative at my age and with my family commitments. I needed to provide a stable income.

This person was acutely conscious that he had essentially
foregone the opportunity for a full-time position and was now
"stuck" in a marginal role in academic life. A major reason for
being stuck is lack of geographical mobility. Another part-timer we
interviewed is teaching at a large comprehensive regional university
in an urban area. She has all her degrees, including her doctorate
from the institution where she is currently employed as a part-timer.
She started teaching part-time as a graduate student in 1978. By the
mid 1980s she had achieved a full-time teaching load while retaining part-time status.

I wanted an academic career, and this is the only way
I could do it. . . . Part-time work was the only route
to go. . . . I am not terribly satisfied. I am paying a
mortgage and am overworked to meet this obligation.
I need to work hard to survive. . . . [There is] not
enough time to do a lot of research. Also, I am committed to one institution. As a part-timer, I basically
have to take the work that is available to me. I want
to teach a philosophy course. I am teaching humanities, social sciences, English, extended education. [I

am] teaching all over the university. . . . Our experience is a mile wide but an inch deep. . . . I can use
my seniority to get part-time positions all over the
university, but I can't use it to get a tenure-stream
appointment.

These two individuals exemplify a small but important and
vocal part of our total sample: those dedicated, well-prepared individuals who still hope to move to tenure-track status but who have
pursued, for whatever reasons, the wrong strategies for achieving
that goal. They feel stuck, and their future prospects are uncertain
at best.

Other aspiring academics are more recent Ph.D.'s. Some
begin teaching part-time immediately after completing the Ph.D.
while they seek tenure-track positions. Others are teaching part-
time because of family responsibilities. While we interviewed several men who are the trailing spouses in dual-career couples (see
Chapter Two), by far the majority are women. These women are
caught in their prime childbearing years in an unresolvable conflict
between their desire to have a family and the lack of alternatives and
flexibility in an academic career. Through its rigidity, this career
system fails to use considerable available talent and also demonstrates a systemic, if not intentional, gender bias. Such bias wreaks
havoc with the lives and plans of superbly well-qualified
individuals:

I came from England where I did my B.A. I came to
_____ on a four-year fellowship to do my Ph.D. I did
not originally plan to stay here. I met someone who
became my husband, and now I'm on my second
child. The first child was born in 1987. The consequence of this decision is that my husband is in his
own business here and I am not mobile. My career
plans changed. I have been working here as a lecturer
since 1987, sometimes full-time, sometimes part-time.
I'm almost forty; my husband is fifty. We did not plan
to have children. I planned to have regional mobility
and come home weekends or whatever. I looked for a

tenure-track position. Then I got pregnant. Having a
child changed my plans. I wasn't willing to commute
long distances. Decisions have come after life changes.
It has been *difficult*. I was always at the top in fellowships, scholarships. For example, I published my honors thesis as an undergraduate student. The institution loses out because I have lots more to offer than
they are taking advantage of. The institution could
gain from accommodating my needs. Until very recently I was not eligible for research grants.

In our interviews we encountered evidence of unused potential over and over again. Many women (and increasingly men, too)
feel exploited by an academic career system that does not adequately
address the interrelationship between the personal and professional
lives of faculty and that takes advantage of their training and talent
without providing rewards and incentives.

A small subset of those we interviewed were doctoral students
close to completion of their Ph.D.'s and employed as part-timers.
Aspiring academics who are also aspiring Ph.D. recipients can lead
very hard lives. The Ph.D. candidates we interviewed had been
struggling for years to earn a living by teaching part-time while
finishing degrees. Said one,

> I came to the University of Minnesota to get a Ph.D.
> I am in my fourth year at _____ . I am also teaching
> at three other institutions. I am primarily here as a
> Ph.D. student. The relationship between jobs is
> rough. I don't like what I am doing. It is hard on me
> and has slowed down my progress on the dissertation.
> I have to work hard to make a minimum income to
> support me and my family. It would be nice to have
> a job in one place so I wouldn't have to run around.
> My wife is not allowed to work because of immigra-
> tion, and we have two children. It is not easy. Our last
> child had major medical problems. I hope to finish
> the Ph.D. in a year and a half.

Another interviewee had been working on her Ph.D. for seven years. She had received her undergraduate degree in 1968, worked as a librarian, had three children, and now is divorced.

> I am going to have to skip doing academic jobs in order to get ahead in my academic career. I need the money. I am a single mother with three teenagers. ABDs teaching part-time are having a real struggle. It's a full-time job just to be employed enough to support myself in getting the Ph.D. Colleges and universities are using us as a cheap source of labor.

A final subgroup of aspiring academics are "freeway fliers," those part-timers who have teaching assignments at several institutions at the same time. They represented a small portion of our total sample of part-timers. Their "packages" of teaching assignments in multiple locations contribute to the marginal nature of their affiliation with each of their institutions and to the little that is known about them by their departments. One young man's situation illustrates the rigors of multiple teaching assignments in different locations:

> I have a lot of roots in [the area]. I don't want to relocate. I wanted to keep a foot in each door as an inroad to a full-time job. . . . I have taught part-time a lot. One year I taught at five colleges simultaneously. Thursdays I started at the university for an 8 A.M. class. Then I went [across town] for a 9:45 A.M. class, which went to 11 A.M., then to [a nearby institution] for early afternoon and to [a fourth institution] for mid afternoon. [Finally, I returned] to the university for an evening extension class. I finished teaching at 9 P.M. I think I taught well. I never sacrificed the classroom. The colleges lost the out-of-class interaction. It really compromised my personal life. But it would be too embarrassing to be unprepared for class.

Another part-timer in a large city had been teaching at three different institutions for the past eleven years, having begun her career as a part-timer more than twenty years ago. During our interview, she said,

> I used to teach seven or eight classes a semester. I'd come home and read *The Faerie Queen, Paradise Lost*, and *The Sun Also Rises* at the same time. I started retrenching. I try to coordinate. Here I have one class and work with the learning-disabled students. I also do tutoring ten hours a week. I have cut down on the work. Now I teach four courses a semester and a bit in the summer. I make $20,000. I don't think about the money. My primary job is at all three places. I am the oldest living adjunct (here). Nasty rule they have here—three-courses-a-year limit. That hurts. I used to teach two each semester and one in the summer. Doing the preparation for one class doesn't pay. But I like the variety. . . . I don't want to spend time on bureaucracy. I don't want committees. I don't like office politics. A number of things that go along with full-time work don't interest me. I would prefer the variety of three schools to the convenience of three composition courses here. I like the sense of freedom I have.

This part-timer is both a freeway flier and a freelancer. While she commented that there are aspects of the academic career she values, she also values her freedom and the variety that a series of part-time positions can offer. Thus, she provides a good introduction to our final employment group, the freelancers.

Freelancers

In our interviews, we encountered as many career profiles as we encountered freelancers. Their reasons for working part-time make sense in the context of their lives. The composite group of freelancers includes homemakers or primary care people; artists and others seeking affiliation with an institution for a variety of reasons; individuals who choose to build their careers around a series of part-time jobs that are generally interrelated but occasionally capitalize on varied skills and talents; and individuals who at the time of our interviews occupied part-time positions for reasons beyond their control. A substantial number of the part-time faculty we interviewed were freelancing to support themselves. They held a variety of "jobs," including writing, consulting, and teaching and preferred not to have ties to any particular institution or position.

One woman we interviewed exemplifies the freelancers. She had moved to a rural area as a "life-style émigré" after her husband left corporate life. She now writes education books and manuals for teachers, offers in-service teacher training as an independent contractor, holds a one-quarter-time position as director of a state energy education program, and teaches part-time at a public institution in her area. Her various jobs and roles reinforce each other; what she learns in one arena she puts to use elsewhere. Her teaching job, for example, serves as a laboratory for new ideas that she can later pass along in her writing and consulting. Although she reported being isolated from the full-time faculty and her department chair, she prefers not to have any greater involvement in the institution because she values the free time she can devote to her other roles and activities.

There are many variations on this theme. Generally speaking, freelancing part-time faculty have much to offer the colleges and universities where they teach. They have varied experiences that they put to good use in the classroom. They tend to be resourceful and are able to use their contacts and connections to benefit the college or university. All in all, they constitute a resource not easily found in other ways. The part-timers who are freelancers are also usually uninterested in tenure-track appointments. They vary in whether or not they are dependent upon their part-time positions for salary or benefits.

Some of the freelancers we interviewed were experimenting at the time. They had not yet found a career that ideally suited their needs. One of the women we interviewed has bachelor's and master's degrees and a teaching credential. She had tried full-time teaching but had not found it a viable career alternative. So she had gone to Maine to write the great American novel and run out of money!

> It took me ten years to pay off the two degrees. I
> worked in a press office for a U.S. senator. He lost. My
> thirtieth birthday was spent in unemployment offices.
> I became the communications director of a company.
> Then I went to Lexington, Kentucky, as a spouse.
> There I taught business writing at the university and
> really liked it. But I hated Kentucky so we moved back.
> I worked for a trade association. I hate office politics,
> working twelve-hour days, feeling out of control of
> my life. So I went to part-time work. The head of my
> department was in a class in Gaelic [with me]. She
> hired me. Now I am putting together a Ph.D. pro-
> gram, teaching three courses, and making money as a
> freelance editor. I take the summers off and work on
> my fiction.

This ability and desire to handle multiple jobs and interests simultaneously was common in our interviews.

Some part-timers have already experimented and, at the time
of our interviews, were quite satisfied with their career choice to be
a freelancer. One of our interviewees had started out with a Ph.D.
in English (Shakespeare). She had gone into publishing and opened
her own consulting firm in textbook development. From there she
had moved into business communication and teaching business
writing. Recently married to a tenured faculty member, she has
continued her consulting business and teaching, in combination
with enjoying a new marriage and stepson. Experiencing a variety
of roles or jobs simultaneously meets her personal needs at this
point in her life.

At most of our site institutions we found a substantial
number of freelance studio artists. One member of the art department at a comprehensive regional university in a large city was
teaching at two other institutions and was also a professional paint-
er when we spoke with her. Because of her financial needs and the
benefits package the university offered, she commuted to the regional campus three days a week, leaving home at 5:30 A.M. and
returning at 7:30 P.M. The other two days she taught at the other
institutions. Another artist whom we interviewed talked about her

commitment to staying in a major city in order to be part of its art world, to retain her affiliations with a gallery and an art institute. She talked about how she was balancing her life between the loneliness of painting in her studio and her teaching:

> I want contact with people. I want to offer people things. It is a thrill to teach people how to draw or to help the advanced people into careers.

A music teacher at an urban community college maintained an intimidatingly energetic schedule, dividing her work among a number of activities. She told us:

> I wanted to teach at the college level and wanted time for composing, arranging, and concertizing. In addition to teaching here, I also teach at [a local] music school, serve as church choir director, give concerts around the country, and provide private music lessons. I like the flexibility part-time teaching allows me.

Conclusion

The profiles of academic and employment experience show that the bifurcated employment system that lumps all tenure-track faculty in one class and all part-time faculty in another does not nearly fit the current realities. Part-time faculty come from enormously varied backgrounds and life situations. They need a far more flexible set of options, rewards, incentives, and recognitions for their work. Some depend almost completely on their part-time teaching to survive, but others are primarily committed to other professional careers in which they are well compensated. Some part-time faculty aspire to academic careers, but others have no interest in them at all. Yet most institutions treat all part-time faculty alike. They see part-timers as marginal, temporary employees with no past and no future beyond the immediate term and give them no incentive to stay and make a commitment.

Institutions should make a greater effort to understand who

is teaching for them, what each person has to offer, and what kind of incentives and support would help part-timers make a greater contribution. For example, are aspiring academics being developed as a legitimate future pool for tenure-bearing appointments? Are career enders seeking part-time employment as an attractive transition to retirement? Are specialists, experts, and professionals recognized as an untapped resource with great potential for enriching academic programs? Could freelancers make more enduring contributions if they enjoyed a more stable employment relationship with their institutions? We found these questions rarely raised and even more rarely addressed because part-timers are treated as an invisible, indistinguishable mass and dealt with arbitrarily.

Four

External Forces
Affecting Part-Time
Employment

Each of the fifty states establishes legal and policy environments that affect part-time employment differently. We asked administrators to discuss the constraints and incentives they face and how public law and policy affect their plans and decisions. We also conducted a survey of state attorneys general, searched current court cases, and studied state laws to identify some of the major external factors that affect the employment of part-time faculty.

The picture is one of great complexity. Judicial precedent, state statutes, custom and common practice, state higher education system policies, funding patterns, labor board decisions, and accrediting standards are all considered in this chapter. We conclude that all of these sources of policy interact in unique ways from state to state and that very little general advice can be offered. However, we can suggest that institutions take a clear and purposeful course in establishing their own policies for part-time faculty employment so that confusion and conflict between unclear laws or state policies do not force them into unanticipated and undesirable commitments.

Because this subject is so complex, we have chosen to highlight some of the principal areas of concern, but we cannot offer definitive legal or policy recommendations. Those who want to test their own policies for legal implications will find that this chapter does not offer technical advice; legal counsel should be sought in such cases. Readers who are not specifically interested in all of these matters are invited to focus on policy topics of particular interest to them or proceed directly to Chapter Five.

The Courts: Judicially Determined "Thresholds" of Employment Rights

Disputes over employment rights often turn on misunderstandings or on ambiguities in the agreements people believe they have about their jobs, their pay, and their benefits. Employment disputes involving part-timers must sometimes be resolved by reliance on common law and on the courts' interpretation of both public and institutional policies because these institutional policies allow for employment based on oral agreements and are themselves unclear or ambiguous. In some cases, the courts have rendered decisions with a "through-the-looking-glass" quality, decisions that appear to give part-time faculty certain rights that institutions did not intend them to have. We will outline both the conventional rights afforded part-time faculty and the employment practices that have, in some jurisdictions, exposed institutions to liability.

The Contract

At the bottom of every employment relationship, whether full- or part-time, is a contractual agreement. The institution offers to pay someone in return for which that person promises to perform work. Although contractual agreements may be—and usually are—reduced to writing, there are several ways in which the contractual relationship may break down.

In the case of part-time faculty, the most serious legal danger we encountered was the lack of written contractual agreements. In most cases, clear, explicit letters of appointment or formal contracts were issued, but an administrator at one institution reported:

> There is no written contract [with part-time faculty]. Everything is oral. Some departments send a letter. There are many different configurations established through these letters. There is no central control.

When an agreement is not put in writing, there is room for misunderstanding and disagreement between the parties.

The legal hazards to the institution were clarified in a case involving a part-time faculty member at a Louisiana business college. The part-timer taught a course during the fall semester for an agreed-upon fee of $200 per month. When he agreed to teach this course again in the spring, he was asked also to teach a section of the next higher level of the subject during the same class period. He assumed that he would receive $400 per month, $200 for each "course." The institution paid him at the $200 rate because he only met one section per week. He resigned after receiving his first paycheck and sued for what he assumed he was entitled to: the other $200 per month for agreeing to teach two courses.

The appeals court, reviewing a lower court decision, found that the institution had no salary policy and that it had never intended to pay the part-timer $400 per month (*Kethley* v. *Draughon Business College*, 1988). On the other hand, the part-timer had never intended to teach two courses at the same rate for which he had taught one course the previous semester. Under these circumstances, the court held, there was no contract in effect because there had been no "meeting of the minds" between the parties (p. 506).

The most important part of the ruling, however, clearly opened the institution to liability. In an equity case, one party might be found to have relied on the other's word and to have suffered damage as a result. This theory of "detrimental reliance" was in effect in this case, the court held, because the part-timer had in good faith prepared to teach and had met his class twice before realizing he was being paid half of what he expected. The court awarded him compensation for his efforts, recognizing that he would not have done as much preparation if he had realized that the institution was not paying him to teach two courses. Under the detrimental reliance theory, the court took into account the part-timer's preparation time, the fact that he met the class twice, and the fact that the institution had not made clear just what it intended to pay him.

The decision highlights several issues that might become matters of contention in employment relations with part-time faculty. Reaching clear expectations about pay and the work to be assigned is essential to the existence of a valid contract and to the avoidance of any misunderstandings. How preparation time will be recognized or compensated is also an area of ambiguity in part-time faculty employment. The *Kethley* decision now makes clear that preparation time may be considered as one element of detrimental reliance when part-timers feel they have suffered some kind of damage by preparing to teach and then not receiving anticipated compensation. Further, either side—the institution or the part-timer—may decide to end the relationship, whether because of insufficient enrollment, because of bumping the part-timer to ensure complete assignment for a full-time faculty member, or because the part-timer does not wish to (or cannot) continue for one reason or another. Detrimental reliance obviously requires the institution to make clear any conditions that are attached to the part-timer's contract, to reserve its right to cancel the contract, and to stipulate under what conditions such cancellation might occur. Without clearly understanding these conditions, part-timers might successfully argue in court that they are entitled to compensation for their efforts to prepare and to meet a class; arguably, they could succeed even if no students were to register.

Renewing Appointments and "de Facto" Tenure

One case has clarified what must be shown by whom when the issue is about renewing appointments and the possibility that part-time faculty will achieve some kind of "de facto" tenure—or right to continued employment without going through the normal peer review (or other prescribed) process for achieving employment security.

Howard University v. *Best* (1988) dealt with the claim of a part-time faculty member who asserted that she was entitled to tenure upon receiving a full-time contract after teaching for ninety days on a part-time contract. She claimed that the full-time appointment was a "reappointment" under the policies of the university and that a reappointment would entitle her to tenure under the rules in force at the time.

Because there was no explicit policy covering this situation, the court was persuaded to examine the "custom and practice" of the university in handling part-time appointments, reappointments of full-time faculty, and tenure decisions. It ruled, however, that it was up to the part-timer to prove that custom and practice supported her claim. The court put the burden of proof on the part-timer because it recognized (from precedents) "public policy concerns that indefinite tenure not occur by default" (p. 154). In other words, the common law assumes that tenure should be granted only by an affirmative decision rather than by a series of omissions, for example, failing to tell part-time faculty that they do not qualify for tenure no matter how long they serve.

In this particular case, however, it was also made clear that misunderstandings about the terms of employment and its continuity (if not its security) can be a source of major liability. The university, the court said, had made a series of technical errors in giving notice at the end of Best's appointment in the full-time position. The remedies included a new three-year contract and payment of $155,000 in damages.

Notwithstanding the seriousness with which the court viewed the damages done to the part-timer, it considerably clarified two issues. Courts may require the part-timer to prove that custom and practice entitle them to tenure (if the formal rules of the institution do not), and tenure is not to be awarded by default without provable reasons for doing so; public policy requires affirmative decisions by those with the authority to award tenure.

Custom and Practice

Saying that the burden of proof lies with part-timers or plaintiffs to show that custom and practice would entitle them to tenure does not mean that they carry the same burden in all other employment situations. In another case, custom and practice were found to entitle a deceased part-time faculty member's estate to compensation from the New Jersey public employees' retirement fund (*Estate of Hagel* v. *Employees' Retirement System,* 1988).

A part-time faculty member had taught one course in three of every four terms for three consecutive years. He usually did not teach during the summer term. At the end of the third year, he was offered a summer course to teach but declined the offer because of ill health. During discussions with the part-timer, the department chair promised to hold open the part-timer's usual teaching assignment in the fall semester.

During the summer, the part-timer's health deteriorated and he died. By law, he had become a participant in the retirement system after two years' employment, but the retirement board declined to pay death benefits on the ground that he was not an employee at the time of his death. The board ruled that as an adjunct faculty member, Hagel was hired only term to term, was neither employed nor on official leave at the time of his death, and was ineligible because he was not an "active employee."

The appellate division of the New Jersey superior court ruled against the retirement board and ordered it to pay death benefits to the part-timer's estate. Custom and practice, as well as public policy issues, were central to the court's reasoning.

In deciding where the burden of proof lay, the court held that the coverage of public employee pension laws must be construed liberally. That is, the laws are intended to protect the security of those who choose public employment, and rights accruing under those laws should not be taken away too readily. Consequently, in looking to see if custom and practice would entitle the employee's estate to the death benefit, the court construed the facts generally in the employee's favor unless the retirement board could prove the opposite. The burden of proof was, in other words, exactly the opposite of that in the tenure case discussed above. The difference lay in what public policy (as interpreted by the court) required. In the former case, the institution was protected; in this one, the part-time faculty member was protected.

The liberal construction of custom and practice in the *Hagel* case shows how readily a part-time faculty member might achieve protection of rights to benefits. Despite the term-by-term employment of the part-timer and the regular lapses in continuity during the summer, the court found that he "had taught semester after semester for years and was told by the professor who supervised [him] that a course would be held open for him in the fall semester. . . . There was no real interruption of his 'active service' " (p. 1013). In addition, the court found that the employer-employee relationship had continued through the summer despite the fact that the part-timer had been offered a summer contract and had declined it. Two elements entered the court's reasoning. First, the part-timer had been promised employment in the fall term, and second, it is common practice for "most teachers at all levels either [to] take actual vacations or [to] find outside summer employment" (p. 1013). As a result, the court said, "since [the instructor] had been specifically notified in May at the end of the winter term that he had a reasonable expectation of teaching his usual course in the fall term, the type of [part-time] employment here . . . should continue to carry with it de facto 'active service' insurance protection over the brief hiatus during the . . . summer term" (p. 1013). The key conclusion behind the court's decision was its finding that the part-timer, "had he survived illness, would have been teaching in the fall" (p. 1012). Coupled with the customs and practices surrounding the employment of part-time faculty and the common breaks in employment over the summer term, this conclusion led the court to order payment of death benefits to the part-timer's estate because the part-timer—although not employed at the time of his death, or in possession of a formal contract for future employment, or formally on a leave of absence—nevertheless had to be considered an eligible employee.

The *Hagel* decision demonstrates how important custom and practice can be in establishing the employment rights of part-time faculty. By long continuity of employment, even if not literally continuous, and by reason of oral promises and understandings, someone who has never taught more than a single course is, according to this case, held to be an "employee" with certain rights secured by law and public policy.

Benefits Provided by State Laws

State law may create substantial liability for institutions that employ part-time faculty. Part-timers in some but not all states are eligible for certain benefits prescribed by law. A case in point is state insurance. Although most private employers are required to contribute to insurance funds created to pay for worker's compensation and unemployment compensation claims, it is possible for public institutions as nonprofit employers to opt for direct payment of these claims by present or former part-timers (instead of making regular contributions to the insurance fund). On occasions when claims for worker's or unemployment compensation are filed and approved, a department or college may suddenly find that the liability for those claims is charged against its budget.

A department chair or dean may have very little control over this sort of hidden liability that sometimes comes with the use of part-time faculty. The central administration would be well advised to make sure its deans and department chairs have a clear summary of the laws under which individuals might successfully file for such benefits and a clear understanding of how payment of successful claims will be made. Institutions may wish to consider the potential costs of exposure to these claims in their own state. If they elect not to contribute to the state insurance fund, institutions should consider the impact of charging full liability for benefits against department budgets. Such payments can mortgage the ability of some programs that may have very marginal budgetary flexibility, especially if a claim is unanticipated.

Worker's Compensation

In general, part-time faculty are considered "employees" for the purposes of worker's compensation claims. Our review of selected state laws suggests that virtually everyone hired "to do work" in a public or private institution of higher education is covered by worker's compensation laws. For example, according to Illinois law, employers are defined as "every person [or corporate enterprise of any kind] who has any person in service or under any contract for hire, express or implied, oral or written" (Illinois Statutes, chap. 48, para. 138.1).

Occasionally, a state will exempt "independent contractors" (see above) from the definition of employees. Moreover, there may be exceptions where part-time work is truly short-term or casual. In Kentucky, one must be employed for twenty days to be considered an employee (Kentucky Revised Statutes, sec. 342.650). Someone hired as a true substitute teacher for one or two class sessions might therefore not be covered by worker's compensation. In general, though, the exceptions are truly marginal, and it is probably safest to assume that part-time faculty are covered *unless* specifically exempted in a particular state.

Unemployment Compensation

The applicability of unemployment compensation laws to part-time faculty is somewhat more complicated. Every state has set its own standards of eligibility for unemployment compensation. In general, states do not recognize claims from someone who became unemployed after completing the terms of a contract limited to a specific period. Maryland, for example, treats employees on a term contract differently from those whose employment continues from year to year or term to term (E. Langrill, Maryland assistant attorney general, personal correspondence, July 30, 1990). Nevertheless, unemployment compensation statutes are sufficiently complex and arcane to warrant caution in offering any rule that might apply to all situations.

With that caveat, there are some common patterns in the standards states have established to determine who is eligible for unemployment compensation. Some laws require a minimum period or amount of employment before an individual is eligible to claim benefits. Wisconsin requires a period of at least seventeen weeks of employment before an individual becomes eligible. The other principal criterion is the amount of pay an individual must have earned before becoming eligible. In North Dakota, for example, individuals must demonstrate that they have earned eight times the weekly unemployment benefit for which they would be eligible before they qualify (North Dakota Century Code Annotated, sec. 52-06-02.1.b).

Many states, recognizing the customs of academic employment, have carefully written their laws to exclude claims by faculty during normal interim periods when they may not be technically employed. A tenured professor, for example, would have difficulty qualifying for unemployment compensation in most states during a summer term when he or she is not teaching. (See, for example, Wisconsin Statutes Annotated, sec. 108.04 [17(a)].)

Unemployment claims appear to be filed with some frequency by part-time faculty, according to those interviewed at our site institutions, but we can offer no general conclusion or advice about eligibility of part-time faculty for unemployment compensation. Each institution—indeed, even separate divisions within institutions—must get a definitive ruling from its own legal counsel about the state law that governs unemployment compensation in its own jurisdiction. It is sufficient to say that some part-time faculty in some states are sometimes eligible, depending on the nature of their contract with the institution, the duration and continuity of their employment, and the amount of money they earn or proportion of time they are employed.

Retirement and Other Benefits

State laws also differ substantially as to whether part-time faculty at public institutions are eligible for participation in state retirement systems or for other benefits, such as medical and dental insurance. These laws differ especially with regard to the criteria used to determine when a part-timer would be eligible to participate.

State benefit programs, including retirement, must address several common problems. They need to maximize contributions, minimize liabilities and payouts, and satisfy public demands for fairness and equity in providing coverage. Public policy in the states is in flux on this issue. Not only are considerations of justice and fairness prompting reexamination of policies that exclude part-time employees from retirement and other benefit programs, but the fact that so many part-time faculty continue in their positions year after year has stretched some policies that exclude "temporary" employees beyond any reasonable meaning.

Florida provides one important example. The policies that determine who is eligible to participate in its state retirement system exclude "temporary" employees of local government entities, a class that covers the state's massive community college system. Temporary employees are defined as those who have no expectation of continued employment beyond a given term (the semester or quarter in the case of part-time faculty). However, state audits of personnel records have shown that very substantial numbers of part-time faculty do, in fact, continue their employment from term to term, often over very long periods of time. They thereby establish de facto continuity that is subject to a court's interpretation in light of custom and common practice. A major policy issue has therefore been raised in Florida about whether part-time faculty should be covered by retirement benefits (and thus whether the community colleges should be contributing premiums as required for full-time employees) (L. T. Vause, Division of Retirement, Florida Department of Administration, personal correspondence, March 1991).

The policies of other states provide a very mixed picture. In Utah, for example, there appears to be no provision for coverage, under the state system of benefits for public employees, of part-time faculty at state institutions. According to that state's assistant attorney general, this exclusion even extends to part-time employees at public colleges and universities who may be working more than forty hours per week (B. H. Cameron, personal correspondence, Feb. 4, 1991).

In Maryland, by contrast, "regular" part-time faculty—those who are not on temporary appointments with a defined term—are eligible for retirement and other benefits on a prorated basis (for example, half benefits for half-time work). Other states set standards that require either a certain level of employment or length of employment over a continuous period of time as the criterion for eligibility (E. Langrill, personal correspondence, July 30, 1990).

Wisconsin's policy is an illustration of how both standards might be used to determine which part-time faculty members are eligible for retirement, disability, health, and other benefits. An employee must work at least one-third time for at least one year in order to be covered by the retirement system. Once employees qualify for participation in the retirement system, they are automatically eligible for other benefits as well (Wisconsin Statutes Annotated, sec. 40.02).

If the Wisconsin policy appears to be relatively liberal, that of New Hampshire is less so. In that state, only persons appointed to full-time positions may participate in retirement and other benefit programs (New Hampshire Revised Statutes Annotated, sec. 100-A:3).

In some states, an individual may be eligible for retirement after accumulating a minimum amount of service. In Oregon, for example, the employer begins making retirement contributions on the employee's behalf after the worker has been paid for six hundred hours of work (Oregon Revised Statutes Annotated, sec. 237.103).

We have discussed the basis for eligibility of part-time faculty for state-funded retirement benefits in some detail because the same state standards usually apply to eligibility for medical, dental, life, and disability insurance coverage. There is equally great variability in the standards for these benefits from state to state.

Eligibility Versus Coverage

While various state laws provide legal eligibility for benefits, in actual fact we found that comparatively few part-time faculty receive coverage of any kind. Even when a state or an institution has established the principle that part-time faculty are eligible to participate in group insurance programs, the standards are set in such a way that relatively few individuals may actually meet them. In some cases, budget constraints are so severe that institutions must actually make decisions about hiring or continuing with part-time faculty on the basis of whether the appointment would trigger additional spending on insurance premiums or retirement contributions. In some cases individual part-time faculty are not retained precisely because doing so would create additional financial obligations. Part-timers themselves recognize the practice and are sometimes aware that they are not rehired in a particular term because they would become eligible for benefits at the institution's expense if employed for one more continuous period.

State System Policies

Policies on the use of part-time faculty are sometimes adopted by legislatures or by statewide systems of public colleges or universities. California, for example, passed a law in 1988 requiring diversion of program improvement funds for creation of full-time faculty positions in the community colleges if fewer than 75 percent of all credit-hour instruction is done by full-time faculty. This policy has affected most community colleges in the state (West's Annotated California Education Code, sec. 87482.6). Although the rationale for such policies is not always made clear, there is usually an implicit concern for quality and a sense that the use of part-time faculty needs to be controlled or limited.

Regulations

Direct regulation of the amount of instruction performed by part-time faculty exists in some states. In our site visits we found one system, for example, where a limit of 40 percent of all instruction is specified. At another, we found that the amount of undergraduate instruction that can be taught by part-time faculty is limited to 33 percent. Some institutions in both systems exceed the specified proportions, at least in certain programs, but they incur the burden of proof when they do so. They must, for example, show that full-time faculty are fully assigned and used efficiently. They must also submit the credentials of all part-time appointments to the system office for a check against the minimum standards for such positions.

Budgetary Limits

One alternative to placing direct limits on the amount of teaching that can be done by part-time faculty is to limit the amount of money that can be spent on their appointment. The Florida community college system, for example, limits the amount of funding for part-time and overload appointments to 40 percent of the total dollars available for all faculty salaries. As in the case of limits on the proportion of instruction provided by part-time faculty, institutions with strong enrollment pressure will seek permission to convert some of the salary money available for full-time faculty to less expensive part-time faculty instead.

Academic Program Reviews

State systems commonly conduct reviews of academic programs, which are used as comprehensive assessments of quality. Faculty quality and performance may be an integral part of such assessments, along with outcome assessments and other productivity measures. While academic program reviews are common in state systems, we use the state of Florida here to illustrate the potential impact of system policies on part-time faculty within institutions.

In Florida, both the state university system and the community college system conduct such program reviews. They identify a selected program area and review all the programs in that area simultaneously. In recent program reviews conducted by each of these systems, we find a continuing concern over the use of part-time faculty and its impact on "quality" of instruction.

A recent review of programs in the arts and sciences in the Florida community colleges, for example, discusses at considerable length the appropriate limits to use of part-time faculty. No conclusion was reached beyond finding a consensus of opinion that 30 percent of the total instructional load is an appropriate target; coincidentally, the reviewers found that just under 30 percent of all instruction in the community colleges is done by part-time faculty!

Another recent program review of all of Florida's state university programs in mathematics and statistics expresses similar concern over the use of part-time faculty and makes strongly worded assertions about the consequent threats to academic quality. Among other points, the report concludes: "Adjuncts never play a full part in the life of the department; typically they arrive on campus to give their courses and then depart. Thus they are not at all involved in other professional activities of the faculty; moreover, they also tend to play no role in the thinking that goes into course improvement, and they are not available to students who wish to consult with their teachers" (Board of Regents, State University System of Florida, 1991, pp. 7–8). On one hand, these program review reports suggest "whistling past the graveyard" in their overly general focus on systemwide proportions of part-time faculty. This approach does little to identify or rectify serious problems that may exist in specific fields or at specific institutions. On the other hand, harsh language criticizing the lack of involvement on the part of adjunct faculty seems to "blame the victims" of a system that makes it very difficult for part-time faculty to participate fully even if they want to do so.

Perhaps most serious, in our view, generalizations at the system level about part-time faculty seem to be based more on common myths than on real evidence. It is gratuitous and arbitrary to suggest that part-time faculty play no role (or can play no role) in curriculum development or course improvement. In many departments, they play very positive roles—but only where the full-time faculty actively include them. The danger we see in program reviews of this type is that they rely on assumptions about part-time faculty that are not reexamined in light of empirical evidence. Such reviews tend to perpetuate an undesirable status quo without examining ways in which institutions could establish a more positive environment to ensure the kinds of contributions of which talented, experienced, and committed part-time faculty are capable. This is particularly unfortunate because academic program reviews are frequently used to present issues to governing and coordinating boards.

Collective Bargaining: Labor Board Decisions and Unit Determinations

When a work force exercises its privileges under law to organize and elect a bargaining agent, one of the first steps is to agree on the appropriate composition of the bargaining unit—in other words, to establish who is collectively within the community of interest and therefore eligible to participate in the election of an agent. Although the parties involved can sometimes come to agreement about the composition of the bargaining unit, the history of academic collective bargaining has often produced disagreement over the involvement of department chairs, part-time faculty, and other groups. Accordingly, the composition of the unit must often be decided by a labor board. We deliberately included among our site institutions a range of different solutions to this perennial problem.

Sometimes a labor board decides that all part-time faculty should be included in a bargaining unit with full-time faculty. Alternatively, a bargaining unit that includes full-time faculty may exclude some or all part-time faculty. Where some part-time faculty are included in the unit, they are most likely to be the part-timers who carry a teaching load of at least half the normal full-time load and who have more than a temporary, term-to-term contract.

In a number of cases, labor boards have decided that part-time faculty should be eligible to form their own bargaining units and elect their own representatives separately from the full-time faculty. At three of our site institutions, such separate unions have been formed and have negotiated contracts with the institutions.

Since special issues arise with each of these approaches to collective bargaining, they will be discussed separately. National data on bargaining by part-time faculty have been compiled by Douglas (1988), but this report deals principally with the establishment of separate units and not with other options.

No Bargaining

The vast majority of part-time faculty are not organized for collective bargaining, and it is unlikely that they could readily organize themselves. At most institutions, the part-time work force is a widely disparate collection of individuals on short-term appointments. They are involved in the institution and with each other in only the most tangential ways, coming to campus primarily to teach classes. Their interests are not especially convergent because many of them are otherwise employed, and a wide variety of other motives and means of support characterizes their situations. They are acutely conscious of their vulnerability, too, as reported by one part-timer who chaired a part-time faculty association:

> The part-timers are "ghettoized"; there is a real fear of a union-busting mentality. We really don't have any rights and are fundamentally unorganized to protect our interests. We are transients, and it is hard to organize transients. We can be retaliated against if we aren't super careful.

Potential militance and motivation to organize are, however, comparatively widespread. Part-timers often feel exploited and are very susceptible to an organizing campaign. Thus, although there may be no visible union activity among part-time faculty on a given campus, such activity may emerge with the slightest of excuses and the coalescing of any reasonably capable group of leaders. For example, at one of our site institutions, a successful unionization campaign was led by two retired business executives who had considerable experience in corporations that were unionized, one in legal affairs and one in human resources. Both individuals knew how to organize and lead a union and how to negotiate a contract, and they felt it was important to do so on behalf of their fellow part-time faculty members.

Partial Inclusion in the Full-Time Faculty Unit

Including some part-time faculty in the bargaining unit but excluding others may appear bizarre. In fact, however, there are meaningful distinctions among part-time faculty members that lead labor boards to draw such lines. The amount of time worked, the length of continuous service, and the nature of the contract under which a part-timer serves have all entered labor board decisions to include (or exclude) some but not all part-time faculty in the bargaining unit of full-time faculty. For example, part-time faculty who have "regular" tenure-track appointments are usually included.

A 1988 decision by the Vermont Supreme Court, for example, allows part-time faculty in the state college system with some continuity of service (three semesters) and a teaching load of at least six hours in the current term to join the bargaining unit of full-time faculty. Other part-time faculty are eligible to form their own unit and have recently elected to do so (*Vermont State Colleges Faculty Federation* v. *Vermont State Colleges*, 1989; J. Crosby, personal telephone conversation, 1991).

At one of the institutions in our study, part-timers teaching at least two courses are included in the bargaining unit. The number who are included varies from semester to semester, however, meaning that the actual bargaining unit composition changes every term.

Full Inclusion in the Full-Time Faculty Unit

Part-time faculty are included in the bargaining unit with full-time faculty in the massive California State University (CSU) system. This system employed 21,290 faculty during the 1990–91 academic year, of whom 41.5 percent were part-time and an additional 6 percent were full-time in nontenure-track positions. In other words, almost half of the voting members of the bargaining unit were in nontenure-track positions. Both full- and part-time faculty are covered by one contract negotiated on their behalf by the California Faculty Association, the recognized bargaining agent. The range of those covered in the 1990–91 academic year included department chairs and all teachers of record for at least one course, regardless of longevity. Although this may produce some predictable conflict within the union on certain issues, it appears that both part- and full-time faculty have adapted to the single union. In fact, one administrator in the CSU system reported that the hotter issues and more politically active people were emerging from the ranks of part-timers. It is not unreasonable to forecast that the union will become increasingly interested in part-time faculty issues in order to satisfy a large portion of the bargaining unit.

Separate Bargaining Unit

Part-time faculty have been mobilized on some campuses and have successfully formed their own unions where they are eligible to do so. In fact, it is reasonable to suggest that part-time faculty may be the next focus of collective negotiations—if there is any resurgence of interest at all. Part-timers are far less likely than full-time faculty to be identified as "management" under the Yeshiva precedent that has so seriously changed the rulings of the National Labor Relations Board in private college and university cases (*National Labor Relations Board* v. *Yeshiva University,* 1980). Conversely, the obvious difference from full-time faculty in their status, pay, security, and access to benefits creates a pattern that labor boards readily recognize as warranting a separate bargaining unit. Decisions of public employment relations boards have now provided for the creation of many such separate units, and an increasing number of contracts are covering these units.

　　Three of the institutions we visited had separate part-time faculty unions. At one, the union is very large and powerful and has a history of militance. This separate bargaining unit provides a particularly rich example of the strength that a union of part-time faculty can bring to the negotiating process. During our interviews, its members discussed their twenty-odd-year history, including several strikes that had virtually paralyzed the university. Each strike had forced the university to cease operations because of the unwillingness of other unions to cross picket lines and because large numbers of courses are taught by part-time faculty at this institution.

At a second institution, on the other hand, the systemwide contract was favorable to management rights, and there was little militant behavior. The third site institution, which has a separate contract for part-time faculty, avoided bargaining for about ten years by bringing several lawsuits contesting part-timers' right to collective negotiations. The union, having recently negotiated a contract, is now viewed by the part-timers on that campus as providing power and protection for their interests and is accepted by the administration.

In sum, the picture we have found with regard to bargaining units is mixed. Labor boards and local campus and union politics seem to mix in various unpredictable ways to determine both the composition of the bargaining unit and the dynamics of labor relations. We do foresee an increase in interest in unionization among part-time faculty and a clear receptivity among labor boards to the establishment of separate, part-time faculty bargaining units. On the other hand, part-timers have fared well when they are included partially or fully in bargaining units with full-time faculty. Impediments notwithstanding, unionized part-timers have been successful in establishing effectively led movements to secure their rights, either in units of their own or in units that also include full-time faculty.

Regional and Professional Accrediting Agencies

The standards of the six voluntary regional accrediting associations vary in the degree of specificity with which they address the use of part-time faculty. The Western, North Central, and New England associations do not have standards on the use of part-time faculty (although the New England group is currently preparing to issue such a standard). The Northwest, Southern, and Middle States associations use various approaches.

Northwest's Standard VII on instructional staff states: "Institutions commonly employ some part-time faculty to achieve various purposes but a core of full-time instructional faculty with major professional commitment to the institution and with appropriate professional qualifications for the programs offered is deemed essential. Where such a core faculty does not exist, the institution must clearly demonstrate and definitively that its students and the institution itself are being well served without it" (Joseph Malik, personal correspondence, Jan. 1, 1991). No specific number or proportion of part-time faculty triggers concern, but the visiting team makes a judgment as to whether the existing staffing pattern provides sufficient coverage of the programs offered by the institution. In correspondence with us, the executive director of the Northwest Association, Joseph Malik, expressed special concern over the use of part-time faculty in off-campus graduate instruction. He reiterated the issues visiting teams in that region face, noting that it is more difficult to involve part-timers in the curriculum and to ensure that they are familiar with the goals of the institution and the content of the program.

The Southern accrediting association also focuses principally on the need for an adequate core of full-time faculty, but it is slightly more restrictive in specifying the conditions under which it is acceptable to rely on part-time faculty. It specifies that certain minimum qualifications for employment need to be met and that orientation, supervision, and evaluation of part-time faculty are required. Key excerpts from the Southern association's handbook, *Criteria for Accreditation* (Southern Association of Colleges and Schools, 1991, p. 28), follow: "The number of part-time faculty members must be properly controlled. Part-time faculty members teaching courses for credit must meet the same requirements for professional, experiential and scholarly preparation as their full-time counterparts teaching in the same disciplines. Each institution must establish and publish comprehensive policies concerning the employment of part-time faculty members. The institution must also provide for appropriate orientation, supervision, and evaluation of all part-time faculty members. Students . . . must have access to them for . . . academic assistance." Site-visit institutions in the Southern region were particularly cognizant of the association's concern with the qualifications of part-timers. Several noted that the association has requested that they supply lists of their part-time faculty members and verify the qualifications of each in his or her teaching field. This was particularly true of the community colleges, where a master's degree in the subject field is considered the minimum requirement.

In 1985, the Middle States association issued a position paper on the use of part-time and adjunct faculty (Commission on Higher Education, Middle States Association of Colleges and Schools, 1985.) It has incorporated the main components of that position paper in its standards handbook, *Characteristics of Excellence in Higher Education* (Commission on Higher Education, Middle States Association of Colleges and Schools, 1990). The policy emphasizes the "essential" contribution of full-time faculty to program "continuity and coherence." The section on part-time faculty states:

> Criteria for the appointment of part-time or adjunct faculty and their supervision should be comparable as far as possible to those for full-time faculty, as should provisions for review of teaching effectiveness. Opportunities for professional development and participation for permanent part-time faculty should also be available. People with unusual talents or experience, or with special qualifications, may be available or needed only on a limited basis, and institutions may enhance the quality and diversity of their programs by employing such people as needed. The employment of part-time or adjunct faculty, however, requires policies as carefully considered and explicated as those for full-time faculty [pp. 25–26].

In sum, the common concerns of the regional accrediting bodies focus on (1) the need for a core of full-time faculty, (2) concern about the indiscriminate use of part-timers (as opposed to use for specific reasons), (3) the need for fully developed policies governing part-time faculty employment, (4) the establishment of minimal qualifications for employment, and (5) the need for orientation, professional development, and evaluation of part-timers.

In addition to the regional accrediting agencies, which accredit entire institutions, numerous professions have their own accrediting bodies that prescribe standards for individual programs in their respective fields. Although professional accreditation is voluntary in some fields, it is an important factor in attracting students and faculty and in ensuring placement of graduates. The professional accrediting body whose standards were most frequently mentioned during our interviews as restraining the employment of part-time faculty was the American Assembly of Collegiate Schools of Business (AACSB).

The AACSB's old standards were perceived as restrictive, but its membership approved changes in the standards at a meeting in April 1991. The new standards appear to be slightly less restrictive in that they provide more flexibility in the definition of "academically qualified" faculty. The new standards permit up to 40 percent of the student credit hours to be taught by part-time faculty, a subject on which the old standards were silent. They also permit variations from the standards, depending upon the institution's mission. A doctoral institution, for example, is expected to exceed the minimum proportion of qualified faculty members (American Assembly of Collegiate Schools of Business, 1991).

Other National Influences on Part-Time Faculty Policies

Court cases, state statutes, collective bargaining, and accrediting agencies can exert a direct influence on colleges and universities. Institutions are also influenced subtly by national policy discussions in various forums. In this section, we briefly discuss the indirect influence exerted by faculty unions, professional associations, federal agencies, and reports from national commissions. Faculty unions and national commission reports take an essentially negative position on the use of part-time faculty. They argue directly or indirectly that the use of part-timers ought to be restricted. Others take what we think is a more realistic stance. The positions of the Modern Language Association (MLA) and the Fund for the Improvement of Postsecondary Education (FIPSE), for example, accept the presence of part-timers and offer constructive views on how to help them become more effective.

Faculty Unions

The National Education Association issued its *Report and Recommendations on Part-Time, Temporary, and Nontenure Track Appointments* in 1988. The overriding theme of the report is that use of part-time faculty has reached excessive levels and should be reduced in favor of hiring full-time faculty. The report advocates better pay, more employment security, and more substantial involvement in governance for part-timers. It includes, as well, a set of "academic due process" rights emphasizing appointment, reappointment, and evaluation procedures.

As one would expect of a national faculty union, the NEA statement advocates reliance on collective bargaining as "the best way to develop comprehensive policies for part-time and temporary faculty employment." In this part of its statement, the NEA seems to lean heavily toward inclusion of part-timers in bargaining units of full-time faculty, citing a readily recognizable "community of interest" at institutions where the prescribed NEA standards are adopted (NEA, 1988, p. 11).

The NEA statement asserts, as have a number of other prominent reports, that "excessive use" of part-time faculty is a threat to quality, noting that it is exploitive of those working part-time, among other things. Calling it a "false economy," the NEA report suggests that the principal motivations for using part-time faculty are reduction of costs and preservation of "administrative 'flexibility.'"

Although the NEA offers advice to individual part-timers in its 1989 *A Survival Handbook for Part-Time and Temporary Faculty*, its reports do not seem to tackle the more substantive questions about how conditions might be improved. It admonishes institutions to limit use, provide better pay, expand rights to participate in governance and to file grievances, and provide facilities and services, but it does not address how to select, orient, monitor, evaluate, and develop the capacities of part-timers. Thus, while influencing opinions of stakeholders within institutions, the NEA offers little pragmatic assistance in resolving issues.

The American Association of University Professors (AAUP), long the principal advocate and proponent of common standards for academic freedom and tenure, has taken a considerably less frontal position on the use of part-time positions. It issued a statement "for the information of the profession" entitled *Senior Appointments with Reduced Loads* in 1987. This statement recommends allowing limited service credit toward tenure for part-time teaching experience, and it also allows for the elective reduction in one's load (for a variety of suggested reasons) while retaining tenure or tenure eligibility. Directed at "senior appointments" and suggesting that "personal responsibilities" or phased-in retirement would be appropriate reasons to use tenure or tenure-track positions for part-time faculty, the AAUP position clearly does not begin to deal with the very large majority of the thousands of part-timers who neither occupy "senior appointments" nor would be hired to do so. We would characterize the AAUP position as a tip-of-the-iceberg position because it deals only with the comparatively minuscule number of already tenured (or tenure-track) faculty who merely wish to modify their present working arrangements. The statement effectively ignores the burgeoning underclass of part-timers and their interests. Like the NEA, the AAUP does not address the fundamental issues of teaching, learning, and staff development that substantial use of part-time faculty raises for the academic community as a whole.

National Commission Reports

American higher education has been the subject of intensive review by an assortment of blue-ribbon commissions for a decade or more. Concerned with "quality" and how to improve it, these review reports have occasionally, but only occasionally, addressed the use of part-time faculty. Among the first and most prominent of these reports was *Involvement in Learning*, issued in 1984 by the National Institute of Education's Study Group on the Conditions of Excellence in American Higher Education. The report states its point of view on part-time faculty very succinctly: "Strong faculty identification with the institution and intense faculty involvement with students require a primary commitment. Part-time faculty have difficulty making such a commitment" (Study Group on the Conditions of Excellence in Higher Education, 1984, p. 36). The report states an assumption that part-timers are primarily commit-ted to other jobs and are not available to serve students through intense extracurricular involvement. The report concludes that "one full-time faculty member is a better investment than three part-timers, largely because the full-time faculty member contrib-utes to the institutional environment in ways that go beyond teach-ing courses" (p. 36). One of the report's major recommendations states: "Academic administrators should consolidate as many part-time teaching lines into as many full-time positions as possible" (p. 36). Although there is perhaps a sound theoretical rationale behind this point of view, namely, that students' growth and devel-opment is enhanced when faculty are intensely involved in the un-dergraduate experience, we continue to underscore the point that there is no reason why part-timers cannot be very effective in this role.

The report seems to us uninformed because it does not ac-knowledge the potential for positive involvement of part-timers. At the institutions we visited, there were obvious situations in which part-timers were making highly substantive and extremely effective contributions to the quality of programs. It does an enormous dis-service to dedicated and thoroughly "involved" part-time faculty to say categorically and without qualification that full-time faculty are "better." This kind of statement issued with the imprimatur of a federal government agency could only have the impact of a sledge-hammer on the morale of part-timers and—like other policy state-ments reviewed in this chapter—directs attention away from fundamental problems that institutions need to address.

Another influential national report, *Transforming the State Role in Undergraduate Education: Time for a Different View* (Work-ing Party on Effective State Action to Improve Undergraduate Ed-ucation), was published in 1986 by the Education Commission of the States. Among the "challenges" to quality of undergraduate educa-tion, it lists the increase in use of part-time faculty and graduate students to teach undergraduate courses. Among its extensive recom-mendations, however, we could find no specific suggestions about how to meet this challenge, about how to enhance the contributions part-timers make, or about how to further develop this important human resource.

The Modern Language Association

The Modern Language Association has twice in the past decade addressed "continuing increase[s] in the use of part-time faculty." The MLA executive council adopted a statement on use of part-time faculty in 1982 (MLA, 1985), and the Association of Departments of Foreign Languages endorsed the statement in 1987 (Association of Departments of Foreign Languages, 1987). The statement asserts that use of part-timers has dramatically increased in English and foreign language departments and that such use has become "excessive [and] unplanned." Guidelines for employing part-time faculty are promulgated as follows: "(1) Each department should develop a long-range plan that clarifies the use of both temporary and permanent part-time teachers in terms of departmental needs and goals. . . . (2) All part-time teachers should be treated as professionals. . . . (3) If there is a recurrent need for the services of part-time teachers, departments should consider establishing a cadre of permanent part-time teachers" (MLA, 1985, pp. 2–3).

The MLA statement specifies what actions should be taken under each of its guidelines quoted above. By setting guidelines with specific recommendations regarding part-time faculty use, employment policies, and professional development, the MLA appears to be recognizing the inevitability of part-time faculty at least in English and foreign language departments. It also decries the consequences of excessive use of part-timers and the lack of planning and control that have led to such use. It clearly points out some of the serious educational consequences that departments invite when they rely heavily on part-time faculty. Overall, the MLA statement is very direct and realistic about existing conditions in English and foreign language departments, and its proposed solutions address the problems we observed in those departments.

Fund for the Improvement of Postsecondary Education

Over the years, the Fund for the Improvement of Postsecondary Education has supported programs that have assisted and supported the professional development of part-time faculty, programs such as those at Vista College (California), Siena Heights College (Michigan), Cuyahoga Community College (Ohio), Eckerd College (Florida), and Burlington College (Vermont) (Gappa, 1984; FIPSE, 1990). These programs help part-timers learn about effective instructional techniques and practices, and they provide mentors or other kinds of support to help in reinforcing the adoption of new pedagogical skills. Similar initiatives have been undertaken by the New Jersey Institute for Collegiate Teaching and Learning. While we applaud the efforts of FIPSE and other agencies to provide direct assistance in the professional development of part-timers, we believe that many more small investments in such programs could do much to offset the broadly expressed concerns over quality that have animated so much of the public discussion about the use of part-time faculty.

Conclusion

As this chapter has shown, court decisions, state laws affecting employees' rights to benefits, and collective bargaining contracts are, to some extent, dictating how part-timers will be used and treated. Accrediting agencies, state boards with planning and budgeting responsibilities, internal and external program reviewers, and national faculty unions all take positions in favor of controlling the level of part-time faculty employment. However, budgetary and planning realities in most states have created an environment in which institutions are being forced to use substantial numbers of part-timers, educational policy notwithstanding. Institutions are put in a double bind—damned if they do and damned if they do not. One consequence is that they find it difficult to address their own policies, practices, and situations openly and candidly.

It is time to admit that part-timers are a substantial and permanent part of the academic profession and should be treated as such. We do not foresee any real aggregate diminution in their use, and we advocate the adoption of fair and equitable policies that will help them play constructive roles in providing quality education.

Five

Money and the Use of Part-Time Faculty

Fiscal pressures of varying severity have affected the use of part-time faculty at our site institutions. No two institutions have experienced identical situations, but overall, the variety of pressures has closely paralleled those reported by Mortimer, Bagshaw, and Masland (1985). We found, as these authors did, that using part-time faculty is one important means of achieving "flexibility," a frequently used euphemism for saving money.

One department chair responded incredulously, "Come on, it's all money!" to our question about why part-time faculty were used. There is no doubt that cash savings are achieved when fewer salary dollars stretch to cover more sections of more courses. Some institutions candidly acknowledge that use of part-timers serves as a fiscal buffer to protect the salaries, work load, and tenure of full-time faculty. At other institutions, particularly public ones, enroll-ment pressures sometimes outstrip the available salary dollars. These institutions have few options but to convert dollars provided for full-time faculty lines into salaries for part-time faculty to cover the sections of courses demanded by new students.

We have found that fiscal conditions both constrain and en-courage the use of part-time faculty. We begin this chapter with an overview of how state budgeting processes may affect staffing deci-sions and then examine how fiscal pressures may lead institutions to adopt a variety of staffing solutions. We use a case study to show

how administrators at one institution feel that they have lost a significant amount of control over their own staffing options. To illustrate how merely saving cash may not improve overall efficiency, we also discuss what we call the "false economies" of using part-time faculty. Finally, we look at the human consequences of fiscally driven policies.

State Budgeting Processes and Employment of Part-Time Faculty

In the public sector, ad hoc expansion in the employment of part-time faculty is neither a product of rational strategic planning nor the preferred solution on campuses. Instead, it is partly the result of the normal incremental (or decremental) process of annual state appropriations. While we cannot claim to have made a formal inquiry into how state appropriations may cause direct substitution of more part-time and temporary faculty for full-time faculty, it is our impression that the annual cycle of building budgets and the waiting for states and systems to act upon them create pressure to react in the short term rather than to plan for the long term.

Formulas, student-faculty ratios, and plans for program enhancements or additions are all part of the annual or biannual ritual. Budget requests for the following fiscal year usually come forward from institutions in the fall and wend their way through the Byzantine bureaucracies of state systems, governors' budget offices, and legislative committee staffs by the end of the fall term.

Unfortunately, the actual appropriations for the current fiscal year often do not reach the institution's budget office until shortly before the beginning of the fall term. The institution must implement this new budget as the fall semester begins. More frequently than not, appropriations for the current year fall considerably short of plans. A mini-crisis therefore occurs internally at many institutions right at the opening of the academic year. Plans and commitments made a year earlier are adjusted as a minor emergency is declared after the legislature has completed its work. Hasty decisions are made in an effort to protect the institution's fiscal (and political) integrity.

Most public institutions have grown quite sophisticated

about how this game is played. Since the news at appropriations time is almost always in shades of "bad," they have learned to preserve flexibility in the budget at this time of year. Much of that "wiggle room" is in the form of vacant faculty lines and other reserved funds that go to departments for hiring part-time and temporary faculty.

The problem with this common scenario is that it has become an acceptable ritual in playing the annual budget game. It has led many institutions unwittingly (or unwillingly) to allow an insidious decremental erosion of their full-time faculty base and to maximize enrollment by loading up with market-responsive curricula.

The increase of part-time faculty employment as a result of budget-cycle overlap leads directly to some undesirable consequences. At precisely the time when bad budget news is almost ritually forcing institutions to substitute part-time faculty for full-time faculty—the beginning of the fall semester—the next year's budget planning cycle virtually dictates that enrollment be at its peak. Fall enrollment numbers are fed directly into the state formulas (or other persuasive media, such as the press) that help planners and legislative and agency staffs generate the target numbers for the following fiscal year's budget. It would be fiscally irrational (and politically shortsighted) for an institution to cap its enrollment in the face of a routine budget shortfall. Instead, an institution will usually calculate that increasing enrollment—and stretching scarce dollars further through the use of part-time faculty—can only help next year. In the worst case, an institution will become addicted to the last-minute hiring of part-time faculty to cover the proliferation of popular programs and courses.

This annual pattern has been repeated for a decade or more at some institutions. Some of the most harmful effects are felt most severely by the full-time faculty. Annual budget cycles and shortfalls have led to attrition of full-time faculty positions. In a number of cases, departments are left with aging cohorts of senior professors who have no apprentices. Furthermore, at some institutions the pattern has resulted in programs that are staffed only with the most minimal core of full-time faculty. Letting attrition of full-time faculty be driven by budget stringency forces de facto decisions about what work will be done and what work—advising, program development, and governance, for example—will not be done.

It is our impression that these pressures toward greater fiscal constraint at state and system levels and the concomitant shortened planning horizons are worsening at most public institutions. One consequence for the institutions we visited is that they have somewhat less discretion in how they use their faculty positions. Long-term commitments to building programs of excellence tend to be shelved because these programs cannot be built under conditions of steadily tightening resources.

However, we hasten to point out that state appropriations are only one reason behind the declining number of full-time faculty in some institutions or departments. The declining supply of faculty in the arts and sciences documented by Bowen and Sosa (1989) is already being felt at institutions where retirements are outstripping new hires.

Fiscal pressures brought on by the state appropriations cycles, as well as pressures from impending shortages in the supply of faculty, reduce the degree to which colleges and universities can control their own planning and staffing. Some institutions have lost effective control over their staffing and now use part-time faculty indiscriminately. Although saving money is part of the motive, it is neither the central issue nor the issue that we think should be of the most concern. We are most concerned with the general loss of control and the inability of institutions to staff their programs with the faculty best able to accomplish the institution's goals.

Impact of Fiscal Stress on Institutions

State budgeting issues aside, most of our site institutions were experiencing (or had recently experienced) one or another variety of fiscal pressure at the time of our site visit. Two typical patterns had an impact on the employment of part-time faculty: (1) using part-time faculty as a buffer led to a reduction in their numbers or (2) expanding enrollments led to the substitution of part-time for full-time faculty.

Using Part-Time Faculty as a Buffer Against Hard Times

Some institutions under fiscal pressure reduce the number of part-time faculty to protect the tenure rights of full-timers. Part-timers commonly have no protected rights to continued employment and can be "not rehired" at the end of any given academic term. An institution in acute fiscal difficulty, that is, a cash-flow crisis, will sometimes choose not to reemploy part-time faculty as its first line of response.

Institutions facing enrollment declines or fiscal retrenchment often use part-time faculty to absorb anticipated shortfalls. They control the number of tenured faculty and distribute the remaining pool of instructional assignments among temporary and part-time faculty. They can save cash and avoid fiscal exigency in this way. They also preserve the flexibility to hold full-time faculty teaching loads constant against fluctuating enrollments. When stringency compels them to do so, they can release part-time faculty who are on one-term contracts simply by not rehiring them.

One of our site institutions was in the process of cutting back its part-time faculty when we visited it. We were told:

> We met with the department chairs one by one and came to an agreement on what the curriculum needs were. We did this all fall semester. We have now cut thirty sections. We got rid of low-enrolled courses and told chairs to offer the courses in alternate years. This impacted the number of part-timers. Part-time people went down in their time bases. Next year we will have two part-time people with four courses each, and everyone else is under this. _____ was teaching four or five courses. We reorganized the area and eliminated the position. What we have left are basic English and sabbatical replacements. We are at bare bones.

Such a strategy has immediate and obvious negative consequences. Full-time faculty, for example, must accept heavier teaching loads and teach more introductory and lower-division courses.

Section sizes may increase, and the availability of faculty for individual contact with students may be constrained. Furthermore, the range of expertise in the faculty is reduced, particularly in programs that rely on part-timers to round out highly specialized programs.

Part-time faculty in this situation serve collectively as a buffer against economic hard times. Tenured faculty do not have to be dismissed when a disposable work force is there to be expanded and contracted according to the fiscal situation in which the institution finds itself.

Dismissing (or not rehiring) part-time faculty under these conditions probably creates illusory savings at best. (Certainly, an institution with a cash flow problem may have no short-term alternative.) The net amount of work to be produced remains the same. The quality of the product, however, may be diminished by overworked faculty who cannot prepare properly, who may be teaching outside their field of interest and competence, and who have less time to work individually with students. Morale diminishes because those with increased work loads feel that the social contract (if not the legal one) has been violated. Scheduling difficulties are increased, and potential new "markets" may have to be overlooked as a result. Finally, part-timers themselves are less willing to work for an institution that is perceived as being an erratic employer. They are quick to understand that they are being treated as disposable people. In these ways, the reduction of part-time faculty can be damaging to the institution's long-term welfare; it may be penny wise and pound foolish.

Expanding Enrollments and the Substitution of Part-Time for Full-Time Faculty

Chronic fiscal stringency, as well as the demand for more and different "output" in the form of more courses and sections, new programs, and schedules that are more adapted to the needs of working students (evening and weekend classes), have simply outstripped the financial ability of institutions to meet enrollment increases with full-time faculty employed according to the traditional model. Apparently sensing that tighter budgets will require faculty members to work harder, a number of states have initiated inquiries into whether full-time faculty are "productive" enough (usually a thinly disguised way of delivering a message that they should be teaching more) (Cage, 1991).

Two of our site institutions, both community colleges, reported that their budgets were based on unrealistically low enrollment projections. Limiting enrollment had been neither politically nor fiscally rational for these institutions at the time of our site visits. They find it necessary to live with the fictional expectation from one budget year to the next that they will actually receive appropriated salary dollars commensurate with their real enrollment levels. One provost said,

> We want as a matter of policy to hold our overall teaching ratio to 60 percent by full-time and 40 percent by part-time. But we have budget constraints. Funding in _____ community colleges lags behind enrollment because we use a three-year moving average. So we almost never do better than 50 percent [full-time]. It is not a desirable situation, and it is not getting better because we have very, very strong enrollment growth.

A similar scenario had unfolded at a comprehensive regional institution in another state. A policy limiting the use of part-time faculty was rendered meaningless by a set of interacting issues rooted in chronic fiscal difficulty. Systemwide board of trustees' policy mandated that no more than 33 percent of the total course offerings be taught by part-time faculty. The faculty union contract, however, limited section size and required a seventeen-to-one student-faculty ratio for the institution as a whole. Furthermore, no classroom at this particular campus accommodated more than twenty-five students.

The number of faculty positions authorized in the budget is based on a three-year moving average of enrollment, just as provided in the budgeting process for the aforementioned community colleges. When the college is growing in enrollment, the moving average does not catch up and additional part-time faculty *must* be employed to cover any excess enrollment over the effective limit of twenty-five students per course.

This institution is caught between tight money and what its formula for faculty staffing defines as good education. The institution has open admissions and no effective controls on the number of students who register, and it has experienced substantial overall growth that is uneven from one field to another. For example, some of the more recently developed degree programs in areas such as mass communication and outdoor recreation have proved popular, perhaps at the expense of some of the more traditional disciplines. At the same time, state appropriations have not kept pace with these trends and now lag behind the level of funding that the system's policies and the collective bargaining agreement require. So unless the institution is prepared to limit enrollment, it is almost forced to employ more part-time faculty than the state policy of 33 percent allows.

A Case Study in Fiscal Stringency

At one of our site institutions, chronic fiscal stress has led to steadily increasing dependence on part-time faculty with predictable consequences. This institution is conscientiously working against those consequences on a variety of fronts, but it is doing so under increasingly difficult conditions.

Administrators at the campus virtually all agree that employment of part-time faculty, already comparatively high, will increase in the foreseeable future. This is not the preferred strategy, and they are working to reduce the percentage of course sections part-timers teach. Over the last ten years, however, the institution has experienced a decrease in the absolute number of full-time faculty and a 30 percent increase in the number of students. During the fiscal year in which we conducted our site visit, it was functioning under a state-imposed budget freeze on full-time positions.

Past budget problems led the institution to the beginning of the 1990–91 fiscal year underfunded by roughly 20 percent, according to the state formula. In addition to a freeze on full-time positions ordered at the beginning of the year as a result of anticipated budget stringency, the state rescinded 5 percent of the institution's budget in the middle of the year. Therefore, the institution anticipated beginning the next fiscal year without any hope that it would be able to escape the fiscal pressures that lead to heavy utilization of part-time faculty.

Compounding the immediate fiscal problem, the institution knows its faculty members are aging and that between one-third and one-half of its tenured people in some traditional fields will have to be replaced over the next five years. Funding for the replacement positions will almost certainly not keep pace with the need unless two important changes happen: the state's economy improves, and the tax base is strengthened. Neither of these was even a remote prospect one year after our site visit; in fact, the economic situation had worsened, and the state's governor had publicly refused to consider a strengthening of the tax base in the foreseeable future.

One further trend reinforces the increasing reliance on part-time faculty at this same institution. Increasingly poor preparation of entering students requires more college preparatory (remedial) instruction. Not only is it difficult to find full-time faculty with the preparation and interest to do this kind of teaching, but it is state policy that the cost of remedial instruction should not be borne by postsecondary institutions. Enrollment in remedial courses is therefore not fully funded, and institutions do not have full-time positions they can dedicate to remedial instruction. On the other hand, remedial instruction is something that moonlighting high school teachers can do particularly well, so they are hired in substantial numbers for part-time assignments to staff remedial courses.

For all these reasons, this institution faces pressures to use part-time faculty in ever-escalating numbers. It has reached a point, though, at which it has recognized the need to respond. At the time of our site visit, fiscal pressures had led to a cap on the number of sections offered, an unprecedented action in an institution and state with a policy of open access. Although the institution felt the strong temptation to continue to add sections to meet enrollment demand and to maximize its advantage under a state formula that allocates budgets on the basis of enrollment, the ultimate consequences of this cycle had begun to hurt both the quality of education and the quality of life in the institution.

Hiring a part-timer to teach one section could be absorbed

easily because tuition receipts almost always paid more than the part-timer's salary. But indiscriminate enrollment "growth" without compensating new resources had put the rest of the institution's programs, facilities, and services under more stress than it was willing to allow. Because funds had not kept pace with enrollment, the increased number of students did not generate more support staff, supplies, equipment, or office and classroom space. Students were overwhelming the institution's infrastructure. In sum, the situation at our case study institution was similar to that at another campus, where one interviewee, in a comment about budget formulas, remarked:

> The students may be part-time, but they all still use the bathrooms.

They also use parking space, advising services, faculty time, computers, recreational and food service facilities, and all other forms of support budgeted for far fewer students.

In addition to the tangible evidence of erosion of the infrastructure in the face of under- or unfunded enrollment increases, deans and vice presidents at our case study campus readily noted that the institution was in danger of losing its sense of community and values. To preserve institutional values, they felt a responsibility to help the increasing number of part-time faculty become an integral part of the academic life of the college. They initiated an institutionwide program to provide these part-timers with assistance and support in their development and performance as teachers. The vice president summarized the initiative this way:

> Part-time faculty don't have the institution's mission in focus. They do not know as much about the "open-door" student body as the full-time faculty know. They probably aren't as ready to diagnose problems and give individual help. Part-time faculty don't know where to send students who need help, where to get assistance themselves, or other avenues to help, and so on. . . . We have put together our teaching/learning project, which includes a special committee

on issues affecting part-time faculty, to try to preserve
the special values we have built [here] and to translate
those values into teacher behaviors for the next generation of faculty.

But this initiative will take time and money, and—of course—its
ultimate payoff is years in the future.

False Economies of Part-Time Faculty Employment

Immediate cash savings notwithstanding, it is abundantly clear that
using part-time faculty does not always improve the efficiency of an
institution's educational programs. In fact, we question whether
any net improvement in efficiency can really be associated with the
employment of part-time faculty. As much as it may appear that
employing part-timers who are paid low wages will save money, we
think this is far too simplistic a way to calculate cost-effectiveness,
and it leads to using part-timers for the wrong reasons. At some
indeterminate point, adding part-timers creates substantial hidden
costs to the institution. These hidden costs are behind the concerns
about whether quality can be sustained when part-time faculty are
employed in substantial numbers.

Where proportionally large numbers of part-time faculty are
used, many noninstructional responsibilities must be performed by
comparatively few full-time faculty or may be neglected altogether.
As a department's enrollment expands with the consequent addition of more part-timers, relatively fewer full-timers remain to take
on departmental work. The full-time faculty are progressively
drawn away from their teaching assignments to handle advising,
curriculum development, and program coordination, if these functions are handled at all. In addition, they are needed to assist with
the supervision and evaluation of part-timers and even the recruitment and hiring of part-time faculty. Moreover, time-consuming
bureaucratic burdens fall heavily on department chairs. There is
more paperwork, more time needed for recruiting and interviewing,
more mentoring and supervising, and more counseling of both faculty and students.

Perhaps less visible is the attrition of faculty involvement in governance, which is particularly obvious where part-timers are the most numerous. Not only are part-time faculty commonly excluded from voting privileges in standing governance bodies, but they are routinely reported to be unavailable for the deliberative work of committees and departments. This leaves the remaining full-time faculty and the institution's administration with the distinct feeling that there is not a sufficient and definable core of people devoted to institutional maintenance and improvement. It also leaves part-timers feeling that they work in isolation and that they have been disconnected from the mission and the spirit of the institution.

Again, quality suffers—not because the part-time faculty cannot teach well but because the department or the institution becomes less able to carry out the infrastructure work. People simply do not have enough time to maintain themselves, the institution, and the educational process.

While institutions may calculate efficiency by focusing on how to get the most instruction done for the least money within a given fiscal year, what they often overlook is that full-time faculty have very broad roles to play in the operation of high-quality academic programs. These roles consume significant portions of their time, and that time costs money.

For example, an associate professor making $40,000 a year may have a half-time teaching assignment (meaning $20,000 is accountable to other work) and teach four courses a year. With $20,000 of her salary assigned to teaching, some of which is "indirect" (including advising and related duties), a full-time associate professor may be producing a three-credit course for somewhat less than $5,000. Although a part-timer may teach a course for about one-third of that, say $1,500, the part-timer has to be hired, oriented, supervised, and evaluated to a greater extent than the full-timer. Space, equipment, and support services must be provided for each part-timer as an individual, not as a full-time-equivalent member of the faculty. The inefficiencies involved in using many part-timers who teach only one or two courses are most keenly felt, perhaps, in the paperwork generated to continuously reappoint them. After all this effort (and cost), the part-timer does not always stay long enough to accumulate valuable experience. Consequently, the salary expenditure bears little return on the investment, as it would in the case of a full-timer, who becomes more valuable with years of experience. For all these reasons, the direct dollar savings per course are not as dramatic as they appear when the only variable being examined is the actual salary paid per course.

The immediate cash outlay associated with direct instruction will be lower as the proportion of part-timers increases. However, as we have seen, the proportion of nonteaching activity borne by full-time faculty increases. At some point, the amount of full-time faculty time and effort available to perform the required work simply runs out. Things that should be done, like advising students, can no longer be done effectively or even at all. The same kind of calculation can be applied to the support infrastructure. At some point, course materials cannot be copied, and the coffee shop becomes the advising or counseling center because that is the only place to meet. (We interviewed one part-timer who was meeting students in her car in the parking lot until she concluded it was unsafe.) Although direct salary costs continue to decline, these scenarios illustrate how effectiveness reaches a point where it also declines.

Some of this may be mitigated by tight management. Careful scheduling, supervision, and control of support services, for example, can squeeze the last bit of efficiency out of a tight situation. But at some point, no amount of management intervention is going to turn around the loss of effectiveness. Unfortunately, there is no easily derived formula to use in deciding when this point has been reached. It is, however, a point that may be felt subjectively by students, faculty, and administrators. Indicators, even subjective ones, can help identify symptoms of stress and declining effectiveness.

In our interviews we found little to suggest that such indicators were being developed. Administrators' comments about salary tended simply to compare full-time and part-time faculty. At one institution where 492 part-timers were teaching 547 courses, the starting salary per course was about $1,200. As one chair commented:

> The salary is totally inadequate. It is very difficult to recruit for $1,300 [when the part-timer is] teaching thirty students who are paying $1,000 per course.

Another administrator at the same institution asked,

> What does it look like if you have a full-time faculty
> teaching four courses a year for $65,000 and an adjunct
> teaching four courses for $6,000?

While this situation is clearly "making money" on part-time faculty salaries, it is not taking into account the total "costs" involved in part-time faculty employment. We submit that institutions simply do not know the real costs and benefits of using part-time faculty. We speculate that some institutions are probably actually making a small amount of money, some institutions are probably coming out about even, and some institutions are probably actually losing money over the long range.

We have described a case study and highlighted the false economies of part-time faculty employment not because we are arguing that the use of part-time faculty should be universally limited to some magical percentage of the total faculty. Quite to the contrary, we strongly believe that part-time faculty members have much to offer institutions of higher education. We will argue in subsequent chapters that decisions regarding the use of part-time faculty should be made for educational rather than fiscal reasons and that salaries of part-timers should be based upon carefully thought-out salary policies and concepts of equity or fairness. Here we simply point out that fiscally driven motives for using part-time faculty may, in fact, be based on very erroneous assumptions about their real costs.

Human Consequences of Fiscally Driven Policies

Perhaps without intending to do so, institutions have created a substantial secondary work force. This has now become such an important element of short-term planning and budgeting that we foresee continued reliance on part-timers to do many of the things that full-time faculty might once have done in a different era. What was once thought to be a temporary solution to temporary problems has become a more or less permanent solution to serious and worsening fiscal problems. Once part-timers are employed to absorb new enrollment without commensurate budget increments, it becomes more difficult in future budget cycles to recoup the lost funding—while pressure to accommodate more new students with less expensive faculty continues to build. This practice raises concerns about the integrity of academic programs.

Of greatest concern to us during our site visits, however, was the extent to which we observed the bifurcation of the work force into haves and have-nots. The fiscal strategies of the institutions we visited often help create and reinforce this bifurcation. As the provost at our case study campus put it:

> There is a whole new category of permanent part-time
> faculty emerging who need to be treated better than an
> academic underclass. We can't increase their rate of
> pay, inflation notwithstanding.

A dean at this institution illustrated the extent to which the institution has become dependent on part-timers to stretch its increasingly stressed budget to meet escalating demands:

> Not only are are full-time faculty maxed out [teaching
> their maximum load], but some part-time faculty are
> teaching five courses now.

There is, of course, a good deal more than mere fiscal crisis implied in this statement. An enormous ethical (and potential legal) question arises around the assignment of full-time work to people paid at part-time rates.

This condition existed at most institutions in our study, although it is difficult to estimate how many part-timers shared the experience of this person:

> For a long time, I have been teaching [a full-time load]
> for part-time pay.

The real consequences of institutions' heavy reliance on part-timers are borne by the part-timers themselves. They have to rationalize why they allow themselves to play along with obviously exploitive practices. Some are vulnerable and desperate. They will work where there is an opportunity and not ask questions. Some have intrinsic reasons for working. They do not need the money or benefits but teach to satisfy an interest or need to be involved. Yet others can easily see how they have been put in a compromised position and are openly resentful that the pay is not calibrated to any measure of objective worth:

> They are not paying you for your training and experience.

Administrators agree with part-timers. An administrator at one institution characterized the rates at which part-timers are paid as not only low but "capricious." Several others echoed the theme struck by another administrator:

> You start at whatever rate you and the chairman agree to.

At many institutions, it was clearly recognized that the pay for part-time teaching is far below any equitable compensation for the kind of commitment required:

> The pay is not enough to buy an appropriate level of commitment to the work or the institution.

At another institution, it was noted that the pay is so low that the only people who continue to teach part-time are those for whom the intrinsic satisfaction is paramount.

For some part-timers, the salary issue has more symbolic implications:

> [I am] angry at my salary because it is a recognition of my worth. . . . I need recognition and appreciation. [The institution is] . . . embarrassed because they don't pay well.

The sense of deprivation and injustice among part-timers is almost palpable. Although some do not truly need or want pro rata pay and benefits or even roughly equitable compensation, they nevertheless resent the apparent disregard implied by the institution's practices. One part-timer who had previously worked for the same institution in a staff capacity was perhaps more hurt by the loss of status than by the actual economic impact. Another suggested that it is not so much the deprivation of pay and benefits but the demeaning symbolism involved in being denied the right to use university facilities that makes such a difference in how one feels.

Conclusion

Varying fiscal circumstances that institutions face have affected their use of part-time faculty. In some instances, crises force institutions to reduce the part-time work force in order to protect their full-time faculty. On the other hand, constantly inadequate state budget appropriations and formulas for allocation of resources that reward expanding enrollments have forced other institutions to rely on increasing numbers of part-timers. In these situations, enrollments can exceed the fiscal capacity of the institution to provide appropriate faculty staffing and infrastructure support to accommodate burgeoning enrollments. Although there are no simple rules, each institution has certain working (or formal) assumptions about class size, quality of instruction, work loads, and related factors that impose limits on how much discretion a dean or a chairperson can exercise. For most of the people we interviewed, there is too much teaching to be done with too little money. Hiring part-time faculty is one immediate solution to a pressing problem.

Certainly direct savings in instruction are obtained over the short term with the increased use of part-time faculty. However, over the long term, the magnitude, if any, of real savings becomes highly questionable. Institutions generally have not undertaken cost-effectiveness studies that would illuminate the real costs associated with the use of increasing numbers of part-time faculty to handle inadequately funded enrollment growth or market-driven curricula.

Institutions are not always able to control their own destinies. Fiscal crises force them to do things they might prefer not to do. One of the consequences is the widely lamented insecurity that part-timers feel. They are usually the first to suffer in periods of fiscal stringency, and their employment is contingent on many uncontrollable and unforeseeable conditions. However, budgeting cycles, particularly for public institutions, are often behind a series of decisions in which institutions are as much the victims as the part-timers themselves. The large question that needs addressing is whether states can continue to guarantee access to high-quality postsecondary education without making the commensurate fiscal commitments to faculty (full- and part-time) who must produce that education.

We see a great need to bring the consequences of such unplanned staffing into the open and to set out much more clearly defined strategies and operating policies. If, for example, part-time faculty are going to be hired in large numbers for the foreseeable future, what will be required to ensure that they have the support they need and the opportunities to participate in the coordination of instruction? Will long-term commitments be made to part-timers who teach critical parts of the curriculum? What kinds of options will be made available to attract the best part-time teachers? Who needs to be involved in making strategic decisions about these matters?

Six

When and Why Institutions Employ Part-Timers

For at least twenty years, colleges and universities have been employing an increasing number of part-time faculty. Although great concern has been expressed over the number of part-timers employed nationally (now about 270,000), there has been no decline in this number and we do not project any. While individual part-time faculty members come and go, part-timers as a group constitute a permanent part of the faculty work force in every type of institution of higher learning. As one part-time faculty union leader expressed it:

> Part-time faculty are a modern fact of life and a useful flexible resource. They are emerging as a rational alternative to the elite institutions in a different kind of university that can extend itself in less expensive ways to a greater segment of society. Without part-time faculty, we would still be an elite organization. If you want mass education and modern access, the use of part-time faculty is the model for how to do it.

In preceding chapters we have shown that part-time faculty are well qualified for the assignments they hold and highly motivated to teach. Why, then, is there so much institutional concern about part-time faculty? We submit that this concern derives from

110

when and why institutions employ part-time faculty, not from the performance of the part-timers themselves.

This chapter discusses when and why part-time faculty are employed and what impact their employment has on academic quality. We will look at the extent and patterns of employment within different types of institutions and different disciplines and at the institutional and educational reasons for these varying patterns. We will then explore whether the increased use of part-time faculty results in a deterioration of academic quality. Finally, we will look at planned and unplanned use of part-time faculty. We will examine situations or circumstances that lead to unplanned or out-of-control use and planned or in-control use and the consequences of both.

Extent of Employment of Part-Timers

While virtually all institutions employ some part-time faculty, there is significant variation in their use by type of institution. Across all institutions, the ratio of part-time to full-time faculty is 35 percent. Public and private research and doctorate-granting universities, on average, employ considerably fewer part-time faculty members (from 15 percent to 24 percent of their faculty total), whereas public two-year colleges use considerably more (an average of 54 percent of their total faculty). Use of part-timers in public and private comprehensive colleges and universities and liberal arts colleges varies but falls in between these extremes (26 percent to 42 percent) on average (NSOPF '88).

Part-timers also teach in all disciplines. They are most commonly found in the fine arts (40 percent of the total faculty), business (30 percent), and education and the humanities (26 percent). They are less commonly found in agriculture and home economics (14 percent), the social sciences (19 percent), and the natural and health sciences and engineering (all averaging about 22 percent) (NSOPF '88).

National data are helpful in demonstrating that employment of part-time faculty is widespread, but national averages mask the variety in employment we found at our site institutions. We asked the chief academic personnel officers, deans, and department chairs this question: What portion of total instruction is provided by part-time faculty? Their responses show the enormous variation in patterns of use within and among the institutions we visited and, similarly, within and among the academic disciplines.

Community Colleges

Clearly the community colleges employ by far the greatest overall number and percentage of part-time faculty. As many as 60 percent of all faculty members in some community colleges have been reported to be part-time (Palmer, 1987.) At one large community college campus during the time of our study, well over half of the faculty in every discipline were part-timers. Business, math, and technologies (a single division encompassing sixteen separate fields) had 50 full-time faculty members and 120 part-timers; health careers and natural sciences had 7 full-time faculty members and 15 to 20 part-timers; and humanities and communications (twenty-seven program areas) had 31 full-timers and 130 part-timers. The profiles of the other community colleges we visited were similar.

Research, Doctorate-Granting, and Comprehensive Colleges and Universities

The community colleges are not alone. Among research and doctorate-granting universities, we also encountered extensive employment of part-time faculty, though not across all disciplines. One of our site universities had 492 part-time faculty members teaching 547 courses at the time of our visit. Another had 550 full-time faculty and 400 part-timers composing approximately 25 percent of the total full-time-equivalent faculty positions. At one research university, part-timers taught about 40 percent of the undergraduate English courses, the tenure-track faculty taught 23 percent, and graduate teaching assistants taught the rest. In the mathematics department of the same university, 75 percent of lower-division and 25 percent of upper-division undergraduate courses were taught by part-time faculty.

This pattern of extensive use of part-time faculty in certain departments and for undergraduate teaching was common at all our research, doctorate-granting, and comprehensive colleges and universities, regardless of control or location and contrasted with the tendency of community colleges to use part-timers extensively in all fields. The more an institution "looked like" a community college, the more likely it was to make extensive use of part-timers. For example, part-timers were commonly used to staff evening divisions and extended education programs.

Liberal Arts Colleges

Only in the small liberal arts colleges did we find limited use of part-time faculty. These institutions pride themselves on their excellent undergraduate teaching, which is the primary function of the tenure-track faculty. Part-timers in these institutions supplement and enhance the teaching of the full-time faculty. We did not find excessive use of part-time faculty in any disciplines in our sample of small, private liberal arts colleges. As one former provost said:

> We see ourselves as an institution with a strong core of full-time faculty. Part-time faculty have [played] and continue to play a very important role. We are lucky to be in [a major city]. There are lots of first-rate people around. Most of our departments are enhanced through continuing part-time faculty arrangements. We have about 120 to 130 tenure-track faculty, and about 20 continuing part-time faculty.

Institutions' Reasons for Employing Part-Timers

We also asked vice presidents, deans, and department chairs why they use part-time faculty. Motives are varied. Each institution and each academic or professional field operates in a virtually unique context or tradition. However, in addition to the fiscal reasons for using part-timers explored in depth in Chapter Five, our interviewees cited strong institutional and educational reasons for employing part-timers. In this section, we explore institutional reasons; in the next section we look at educational reasons.

Institutional Policy, Perspectives, and Values

Choices about whether or not to employ part-time faculty may be affected by policies, perspectives, and institutional values. Some institutions operate with virtually no policy regarding faculty staffing options, and some operate within strict guidelines. At one small liberal arts college, we were told that faculty staffing is at the total discretion of the academic vice president. Yet at a similar institution, the board of trustees' policy requires that 90 percent of all faculty appointments be tenured or tenure-track, thus severely limiting the number of part-time or temporary appointments. The first of these institutions used more part-timers, 20 percent by head count at the time of our study, while the second was firmly constrained to the limit of not more than 10 percent. Perhaps coincidentally but perhaps not, the first institution reported a broader range of reasons why part-timers were employed (including opportunities for spousal employment), while the second institution, consistent with its more restrictive outlook, reported doubts about the impact of part-timers on "quality." At the time of our site visits, the institution with the more restrictive policy also had a more optimistic financial outlook than did the one with the more liberal approach.

We cannot force this simple illustration into any kind of cause-and-effect explanation. We can, however, point out how two institutions with otherwise similar characteristics differ substantially in their reasons for using or controlling the use of part-time faculty. Whether policy follows fiscal condition, or whether conceptions of quality precede policy, or whether everything follows some traditional pattern of employing part-time faculty, we cannot tell. Each of these two institutions, however, has contrived its own very distinct rationale (or rationalization) for what it is doing and is able to provide a clear and logical explanation of its position.

Control of Work Load

Some institutions have very explicit policies about permissible work loads for part-time faculty. For example, at the time of our interviews, the limit on part-timers' teaching at one site institution was 12 credit hours per quarter (versus 15 hours per quarter for a

full-time faculty load) if a part-time faculty member was not otherwise employed, and 7.2 credit hours per quarter if a part-time faculty member was employed elsewhere.

Policies for controlling part-time faculty work load are developed for a variety of reasons. For example, some institutions
make decisions about the use of part-timers on the basis of efforts
to change full-time teaching loads. Several of our site institutions
were attempting to reduce full-time faculty teaching loads through
a variety of strategies, one of which was a concomitant increase in
the number of part-time faculty employed.

Other institutions control the use of part-time faculty work
load through policy limits on the number of courses they can teach.
Institutions do this because they want to be careful about allowing
individual part-timers to carry too many courses or to work continuously for long enough to qualify for benefits. Almost always, some
limits were being placed on work load or length of time of appointment to avoid liability for benefits. Another reason expressed by
interviewees for limiting work load is recognition of the political
implications of allowing part-timers to teach the equivalent of a
full load while accepting much lower compensation than would be
paid to a full-time faculty member for the same work.

Occasionally, guidelines regarding the use of part-timers are
the product of collective bargaining agreements that specify what
kind of work load part-time faculty can have. At one institution
where faculty have long had a collective bargaining agreement, all
part-timers who teach more than two courses are members of the
unit. However, the contract specifies that no part-timer may teach
more than three courses. The National Education Association
union wanted this provision written into the contract because it did
not want the college to substitute part-time or temporary faculty for
full-time faculty. Such contract provisions set up a potential conflict between part- and full-time faculty. Full-timers have the right
to "bump" part-timers from preferred teaching assignments or to
supersede part-timers' access to employment if their own load is
below a specified minimum.

Collective bargaining contracts affect the rules governing
who teaches and who decides who teaches, as well as how much any
one person can teach. Where the rules about work load are specific,

as in the preceding example, the resulting patterns of use seem to us to reflect less any particular educational logic than the power equation established by the contracts and the political scripts each side follows in defending its own interests.

Rules about part-time faculty work load, developed for whatever reasons, can have unintended effects. Arbitrary limits on part-time faculty work load can interfere with academic decisions at the department level. A chair at a small private college commented:

> The provost has a limit of four courses. Next year I have one extra course. _____ wants to teach it. I want her to teach it. It is silly for me to go find someone new to teach one course one time. I suggested [she] go and talk to the provost.

Market Factors

The part-time work force is almost exclusively drawn from a local pool. This means that there is extraordinary variability from one location to another, as well as from one discipline or field to another. The dynamics of part-time faculty employment differ from institution to institution, depending in substantial part on where the institutions are located in relation to the available talent.

Institutions in urban areas benefit from a surplus of available talent. We saw many examples of entrepreneurial use of local talent in our urban institutions. American University's schools of public administration and international studies recruit a wide array of scholars and experts from the federal government, embassies, and satellite organizations and agencies. San Jose State University is in proximity to Silicon Valley, a "gold mine" of talented faculty, according to the dean of engineering.

A considerably different set of market factors emerges at institutions in rural locations. The talent pool is much "thinner" than in urban areas, and it is more difficult to supply what is needed at the time it is needed. "Thin," however, does not mean nonexistent. Chairs at rural institutions have their own networks and frequently tap nearby universities with promising graduate students for part-time faculty. When they must go farther afield geographically, they sometimes resort to various incentives, such as paying some of the expenses of commuting. Occasionally, rural institutions use local high school teachers, some of whom do not have master's degrees.

In some ways, part-time faculty play a more critical role in small, rural institutions. Most of these institutions need to staff courses in major fields that do not fall within the expertise shared by full-time faculty. In other cases, enrollments in certain courses— albeit courses that are required in certain majors or specialties—are neither large enough nor continuous enough to warrant keeping full-time positions in those specialties. Part-time and/or temporary appointments can help fill these gaps.

Rural institutions often have their own unique reasons for employing part-time faculty. For example, one of our site institutions uses part-time employment in conjunction with a tenure-track offer to recruit dual-career couples. Some institutions are responsible for offering courses in remote regions of a state otherwise unserved by higher education. They rely on "off-campus centers" where courses can be taught in locations convenient to the local population. Although the institutions we visited make an attempt to provide at least some instruction at these sites by regular full-time faculty, they also rely on part-timers to staff many courses. Some rural institutions have a particular niche. In order to broaden their appeal and/or to meet objectives of a statewide plan, these institutions develop programs with special attractions that capitalize on the institution's location and require specialized courses taught by part-time people with unusual qualifications. A program in parks and recreation, for example, might offer a special skill course in whitewater rafting because the institution is located in a region where this is a popular activity.

In some disciplines, the market is notoriously abundant. English and other humanities fields were repeatedly cited as having more people seeking work than there are jobs available. Most department chairs, regardless of discipline, noted that they field inquiries from large number of potential part-time faculty. One reported that he keeps a "need-to-teach" file of inquiries from people who have expressed an interest in teaching at the college level. Surpluses of candidates, many superbly qualified, are more common in urban areas and in areas popular with retirees, but nearly every institution reported the pool of "need-to-teach" candidates was far larger than the number of opportunities available. This surplus has a clear impact on the economics of part-time faculty employment (see Chapter Five). It allows institutions to keep rates of pay low and lagging behind rates of increase recently granted to full-time faculty.

One final market factor deserves mention. Tenured faculty in some fields have aged together since the expansion years of the 1960s. At some institutions, departments that were built rapidly to accommodate student interests or curricular emphases are now fully "tenured in" with faculty at senior ranks. In some cases, these departments will experience the virtually simultaneous retirement of most of their faculty. This phenomenon has been well described elsewhere (Bowen & Schuster, 1986; Bowen & Sosa, 1989), and it was observed at our site institutions, too. As the demand for new faculty exceeds the supply of available talent in some fields over the next several decades, part-time faculty will help fill the gap.

Educational Reasons for Employing Part-Timers

In our interviews, deans and department chairs frequently referred to educational reasons to justify their employment of part-time faculty.

Teaching the Basic Undergraduate Curriculum

One of the most common reasons given for employing part-timers is the need for teachers in the basic, lower-division core courses of the undergraduate curriculum. This reason is frequently stated in terms of a need to keep section sizes small in such courses as lower-division English and mathematics. Florida institutions, for example, are actually faced with statutory limits on how many students can be registered for individual course sections in basic English composition and mathematics, and thus there is pressure on those institutions to staff these sections with part-timers.

As with every other reason for employment, how departments within institutions cope with teaching basic courses varies a great deal among our site institutions. Some departments have strong commitments to having their tenured faculty teach the undergraduate curriculum, particularly the basic courses. A department chair in mathematics in a small college feels strongly about part-timers:

> Three years ago 40 percent of our courses were taught by part-timers. We had four faculty positions in temporary people out of eleven faculty positions total. By next year we will have only one full-time temporary person, who will be here to replace a retiring person. This position will be filled. Then we will have *no* temps. . . . I'm very proud of what we have done here. The optimal mix of part-time to full-time is *zero*. If I have eleven positions, I'll hire twelve tenure-track people and count on one being on leave. . . . I only want part-time faculty for contingencies and leave replacements. I don't like this cycle of people coming and being here a year or two and leaving. It *kills* the program. It requires enormous effort from the tenure-track people.

Some department chairs in other disciplines echoed these sentiments. Others use part-timers extensively for this purpose, and stated that they obtain excellent results. Still others, concerned about the numbers of part-timers being used for basic courses, are experimenting with a variety of nontenurable, limited-contract full-time positions.

Those interviewed during our site visits reported their perception that senior faculty are commonly uninterested in teaching lower-division undergraduate courses, particularly at institutions with a strong research orientation and large graduate programs. At these institutions, lower-division courses are largely taught by part-time faculty and graduate teaching assistants. However, the same courses are also largely taught by part-time faculty at community colleges, so it is not only a matter of the commitment of the institution to graduate studies and research that leads to this practice. To accommodate large numbers of students, there is simply too much teaching to be done within the bounds of an acceptable work load for tenured and tenure-track faculty at most institutions. Budget restraints may also be directly responsible in many cases; just as likely, however, is the continuing shift in faculty attention to nonteaching activities and to teaching in the more attractive and intellectually challenging specialty courses offered to majors and graduate students. Whatever the reason, part-timers are frequently hired to teach lower-division introductory courses.

Teaching Ability

Many of the part-time faculty members we interviewed had gained their teaching experience from years of part-time employment in colleges and universities and are highly valued by their department colleagues for their teaching excellence. Some of these people are aspiring academics who teach part time in the hope of eventually working their way into a full-time position, but many are part-timers by choice, often with full-time positions elsewhere.

A major source of part-time faculty for the community colleges is experienced teachers at the high school level. (A survey by Lowther, Stark, Genthon, and Bentley, 1990, confirms that part-timers have more high school teaching experience than do full-time faculty.) Many talented high school teachers moonlight for the satisfaction of teaching their subject at the college level. Not only are they experienced teachers, but they find great satisfaction in the more highly motivated, purposeful, and focused efforts of the students attending the community college.

Expertise

Part-time faculty provide most institutions with an extraordinary array of expertise. Instructional programs are vastly enriched by the contributions of professional people with outstanding academic credentials and experience. Every institution we visited provided examples of how it is able to broaden and deepen its programs with part-time faculty. Architecture programs rely on practitioners from major firms; dental hygiene programs rely on dentists; accounting programs employ partners in accounting firms; education programs employ retired school superintendents; symphony orchestra members teach instrumental lessons; government officials, elected and appointed, teach public administration courses; research chemists teach their specialty; corporate executives teach management; diplomats teach foreign relations. The level of experience part-time faculty have can be impressive. Retired executives from Fortune 500 companies, judges, directors of federal and state agencies, members of the foreign service, entrepreneurs and small-business owners, poets and authors, and research scientists in government, business, and industry were among those identified at institutions we visited.

These experts are mature, experienced, insightful, and sophisticated in the practice of their art or profession; they are able to relate theory to practice in unusually credible fashion. Adult students, in particular, consistently express appreciation for the ability of part-time faculty to bring concrete examples and vignettes from their own experience to class.

Changing Nature of Student Preparation for College

Pressures to improve the quality of undergraduate education and changes in the nature of students entering higher education have generated incentives to employ part-time faculty. As internal and external factors increasingly concentrate attention on teaching, learning, and assessment, more pressure is placed on institutions to engage students individually and to provide for an environment in which opportunities to learn are designed to accommodate widely varying styles and needs.

Substantial numbers of the part-timers we interviewed have specifically elected to teach part-time because they take considerable interest in the challenges of teaching undergraduates, particularly those who may enter college with less than adequate preparation. Part-timers, who seem to be more student-centered than subject- or theory-centered in their approach to teaching, often prove highly effective in classes that are heavily populated with adults returning to college, underprepared high school graduates, those from culturally different backgrounds, and students with learning problems. Many part-timers find working with students—especially the less able and prepared—to be the most rewarding aspect of their work and acknowledge that the intrinsic satisfaction of close contact and involvement with their students is at the heart of their motivation to teach. This valuable source of dedication and commitment is recognized as such at many of the institutions we visited, but it is not often rewarded.

Connections to the Community

Part-time faculty with full-time jobs and/or professional ties in the "real" world are valuable to programs that need sites where students can get clinical experience. Such part-timers are also valuable to programs that require access to state-of-the-art equipment or front-of-the-curve ideas and practices.

In certain fields, institutions simply cannot keep up with changes in either professional practice or the technology involved in that practice. Many institutions in our sample noted that their capital budgets were so inadequate that their laboratories and workshops had fallen years behind. Part-time faculty with the right connections, however, have been able to provide students with access to the latest generation of computer technology, to new concepts in the art and design fields, and to clinical internships in professional settings in which the state of practice is moving ahead more rapidly than the standard texts and traditionally trained faculty.

Phelan (1986) contributes the notion of "boundary spanning" to our understanding of how part-time faculty enrich academic preparation for the professions. Citing the experience of the Pratt Institute, he notes the extensive use of practicing professionals to teach in fields such as architecture and engineering. Their particular contribution is seen in the following terms: "The value and value-adding roles of professionals who are part-time faculty are most apparent when it is understood that they are a primary source by which appropriate norms, values, and information are inserted directly into the curriculum" (p. 8). By bringing professionals into teaching roles, Phelan notes, the Pratt Institute has eased the transition of its students into the world of practice.

Articulation

As mentioned earlier, the community colleges we visited all employ substantial numbers of moonlighting high school teachers as part-time faculty. According to those we interviewed, this dual employment has several positive, if unsystematic, effects on articulation between high school and college. High school teachers can gain a more complete sense of the curricular requirements and performance standards of the college. That information can help the local schools in their own curriculum development and in advising students. These same part-time faculty members can also help the college better adapt its curriculum to the needs and preparation level of the local student population. High school teachers moonlighting at community colleges are also well aware of the strengths and weaknesses of the preparation local students have in their subject fields. These teachers can tailor their instruction to help students compensate for weaknesses and capitalize on strengths.

Substantial numbers of part-time faculty at some community colleges are also moonlighting faculty or graduate students from local four-year colleges or universities—principal transfer institutions for the community college's graduates. They bring with them an orientation to the senior institution's expectations, its focus or emphasis, and a practical knowledge of the other institution's ways of doing business. This information is valuable to potential transfer students and can be valuable as well to academic leaders at both institutions. Typically, there is little routine intelligence sharing beyond the close circle of departmental colleagues, and that is distinctly informal. Part-timers with appointments at two institutions that share a substantial transfer population can offer a great deal as members of an articulation task force.

Part-time faculty are usually more connected to the community, to students, and to other postsecondary institutions than is generally appreciated. Their prospective role in boundary spanning among institutions can be substantial, and the potential fruitfulness of employing part-time faculty to achieve better articulation has yet to be acknowledged or explored in most cases.

Venture Capital

Part-time faculty may be used to minimize the risks of starting new programs. By hedging on long-term commitments to a permanent faculty, institutions can explore markets for new programs, expand markets for existing programs, refine programs to include new specialties, experiment in the development of courses, limit costs, and generally control risk. Where demand is not clear or not easily established, institutions can start with small investments and tentative commitments by employing part-time faculty. Several of our site institutions have followed this pattern in setting up new or experimental programs. In other cases, they have experimented in offering existing programs to different populations. Part-time faculty were hired to teach the required courses off-campus or at off-hours. A few semesters' enrollment experience allowed the institutions to gauge the level of continuing interest and commitment in the target population—without having hired tenured or tenure-track faculty. One commented,

> [We] can offer experimental courses at a minimum of risk to the institution and help create new program niches.

Some of the program initiatives conducted in this "experimental" mode of staffing principally with part-time faculty to avoid risk are impressive in the quality of the part-timers hired. One of the universities we visited had recently initiated a program to train corporate managers. The credibility of the program depended heavily on the reputation of the faculty, who were described as almost exclusively high-level, fast-track practitioners in their specialties. Students were drawn from the local population and were themselves junior-level practitioners with some knowledge and sophistication about the quality of those selected to serve as faculty. In the judgment of those who initiated the program at the university, using part-timers with high visibility and legitimacy in the field solidly established their niche and gave them a competitive edge. In this case, the low risk associated with nontenure-track appointments was actually a secondary benefit, although certainly one that figured in the institution's decision to proceed with the new program.

The Myth of Unequal Quality

We have cited a number of important educational reasons why institutions are choosing to employ part-timers as an integral part of their teaching faculty. But a major factor in using part-time faculty is the institution's or department's perception of the quality of part-timers' teaching. At each of our site institutions, we asked department chairs, deans, and vice presidents or provosts whether they had evidence to support the common myth that part-time faculty are poorer teachers than full-time faculty. Responses to this bottom-line question were wide-ranging.

Before answering, almost all those interviewed qualified their responses by saying that they had no hard evidence on which to make any judgment at all. We also found a virtually universal belief that part-timers who do not measure up to expectations are not reappointed. Although an institution might make a strategic mistake by granting tenure to a full-time faculty member who is a poor teacher, it almost never retains a part-time faculty member who has difficulty in the classroom. In a sense, then, part-timers may be held to a higher standard of teaching performance on the average.

We found only one department chair who, as part of his academic review, had systematically compared the teaching evaluations of full-time and part-time faculty course by course to determine whether there was any difference in their teaching performance as evaluated by students. Looking at the ratings over a two-year period, he found that the first year, when more than 50 percent of the undergraduate courses were taught by part-timers, their overall ratings were slightly lower than those of the full-time faculty. The following year, when the number of part-timers had been reduced and the number of undergraduate courses taught by them was 45 percent of the total, the average ratings of the part-time faculty were higher than those of the full-time faculty. He planned to continue these comparisons as an important component of his measurement of the overall quality of the department.

Lowther et al. (1990) confirm with empirical data that there is very little difference between how part- and full-time faculty prepare for courses. This finding leads them to conclude that "administrators and policy makers [should] be cautious in assuming that instructional practices of part-time faculty are inferior to those of full-time faculty in the same field" (p. 514).

On the whole, our respondents agreed that the teaching performance of part-timers apparently covers a broader range of "quality" than does that of full-time faculty. Beyond this common ground, our respondents split into two groups, each with its own theme. At the risk of overgeneralizing, we suggest that both themes represent valid answers to our question, depending upon one's own perspective of the issue.

Theme 1: Part-time faculty are not as effective teachers as full-time faculty. Department chairs, deans, and vice presidents are sensitive to the inadequacy of their own search, screening, and hiring practices. They are appropriately worried by the pattern of last-minute appointments that results in "putting warm bodies right off the street" into the classroom. Lack of control at the front end of the selection of part-timers almost inevitably results in a few catastrophic failures every year. Although the number of such failures appears to be small, the trauma to the students and to the institution of even one such event can be very great. In public image terms, it is not unlike the automobile that explodes when hit from behind or the airplane prone to losing one of its engines. Recovery is costly, and the episode tends to take on the flavor of a legend.

Department chairs also worry that courses taught by part-time faculty may be asynchronous with the rest of the curriculum. Sections of their courses may be taught at a different pace, with a different emphasis, and with different overall results than are other sections of the same courses. Although many departments make a serious effort to coordinate the pacing and direction of instruction, it is often difficult to keep part-timers "on the same page." It is simply more difficult to communicate with them, and it is sometimes difficult to monitor what they are doing.

Part-time faculty are also seen as being more fluent in applications and practice than in the articulation of theory. The danger, of course, is that despite the virtues of bringing experiences and examples to their teaching, part-time faculty may merely be entertaining students with "war stories." Although faculty with broad and sophisticated practitioner skills are valued, some teaching assignments require faculty to be up-to-date on the theoretical and research aspects of a discipline. It is, of course, impossible to generalize about the diverse population of part-timers, but some department chairs shared with us their concerns about how they could ensure that part-timers stayed current when they were not routinely doing research and disseminating the results.

We stress that for the most part department chairs' comments in this regard were generalized, comparing the virtues of full-timers and part-timers, and not directed at specific individuals. We also note that the evidence is almost entirely anecdotal or speculative.

Theme 2: Part-time faculty are at least as effective teachers as full-time faculty. Part-timers are viewed as bringing a freshness and enthusiasm to their teaching that full-time faculty often have lost. Many part-timers are new to teaching and dedicate great energy and creativity to their work.

On the whole, part-time faculty are younger and have more recent graduate education than full-time faculty. They are in closer touch with the emerging intellectual currents of their fields, with the latest thinking and writing, and with the trends their students will experience after transfer or entry to graduate school.

Substantial numbers of part-time faculty members are employed in business, government, or a profession. They are in active touch with trends in practice and in some cases have an enormous fund of practical wisdom with which to enliven their instruction. They can engage the interest of nontraditional students by providing a variety of perspectives on their subject matter. They are particularly effective in helping students develop clinical sophistication. Higher-level intellectual skills may be learned more effectively by beginning with the kinds of concrete instruction at which part-time faculty are often particularly good.

Since the responses we received to our question about teaching quality revolved around factors external to the classroom, we probed further in our interviews. Although our interviewees had little hard evidence about differences in the quality of classroom performance between full- and part-time faculty, deans and department chairs (with the one exception mentioned earlier) almost uniformly agreed that they could observe no practical difference on the average. To the extent that we could get people to suggest any distinction at all, some responded that the range of teaching performance might be slightly greater among the part-timers, with some cases of outstanding teaching and perhaps a few more problem cases. However, most pointed out that those who turn up at the low end of the performance spectrum are ordinarily not renewed, so chronic problems are eliminated. Although there may be no consistent difference, it is also clear that part-timers enrich the mix of backgrounds, interests, experience, teaching styles, enthusiasm, and breadth of expertise available in the faculty as a whole. In our view, this means that part-timers contribute to making the faculty as a whole a stronger resource and that the instructional program is both broader and deeper as a result.

Planned Versus Unplanned Use of Part-Time Faculty

Why do institutions plan or not plan for the use of part-time faculty? To some degree, unplanned use results from an institution's view that the very nature of part-time faculty employment as an adjunct, last-minute, expendable resource requires no planning. We submit that this philosophy is expensive and reactive.

Generally speaking, our site institutions did or did not plan their use of part-time faculty because of their reaction to external variables. For example, community colleges, overwhelmed by growing enrollments and diminishing budgets, and remaining faithful to a tradition of open access, were forced into increasing use of part-time faculty beyond any reasonable limit or plan they might have had. Other institutions were forced to work with policies set by boards of trustees or system formulas. Collective bargaining contracts governing certain aspects of part-time faculty employment generally produced a planned approach to part-time faculty employment.

Yet our principle of variability holds true here because of the highly individual mix of circumstances, traditions, and cultures at each institution we visited. We found very different profiles of planning and use at institutions falling under the same system formulas or the same collective bargaining agreements! Located in one place, operating within the constraints of a particular mission, burdened with past decisions and policies, offering a particular mix of programs to a specific population served in the same way by no other institution, and financed more or less adequately, each institution's faculty staffing profile is a product of an idiosyncratic history.

In our interviews, when we asked about the employment of part-timers, some chief academic personnel officers, deans, or chairs were immediately able to articulate the reasons why they used part-time faculty and the exact numbers of part-time faculty members and full-time equivalents they employed at the time. Generally, these institutions have automated systems for tracking this information and readily supplied us with facts, figures, and computer reports.

_____ has 1,568.24 FTEF [full-time-equivalent faculty] positions total; 1,021.6 are tenure-track/tenured; 119.88 are full-time temporaries; 242.08 are part-time faculty; and 183.68 FTEF are in graduate assistant time. The total nontenure-track FTEF is 546.64 out of 1,568.24 FTEF positions—about one-third.

Smaller institutions may have had no need for the sophisticated systems, but at some of them administrators "knew the numbers" and the reasons underlying them, and it was obvious that they monitored employment carefully. Chief academic personnel officers or deans at other institutions, both large and small, had no grasp of the extent of use of part-time faculty and were unable to respond to our interview question.

Institutional planning efforts filtered down to department chairs with varying results. Some chief academic officers would allocate the resources in dollars to deans or chairs and leave their use, in terms of faculty staffing, up to the chairs. Some chairs would prepare exact counts and know their "budgets" to the last penny; other chairs would not have thought about faculty staffing patterns in their departments. At other institutions, tight central control was exercised by a provost or similar officer. In these institutions, general limits were usually established on how many part-timers could be employed or how much of the overall teaching load could be assigned to part-timers. Similarly, controls might be placed on the amount of work an individual part-timer could be assigned in any given term. "Control" was not literally exercised in most cases, although some measures were often taken to monitor the implementation of policies. In a few cases, relatively tight control was exercised over approval of exceptions—for example, in assigning an individual part-timer more than the allowable number of sections.

Unplanned use is generally the result of a fiscal or enrollment situation and is viewed by the institution as departing from its view of "optimal" use.

> We have too many part-timers. Our new full-time position was recently frozen before we could fill it. We have had too many adjuncts for ten years. Students could go all the way through _____ and never see a full-time faculty member. In math, over half of our sections are taught by adjuncts. It should be 40 percent max. But we can't get the full-time faculty. We need more adjuncts to help handle our daytime sections. We just can't keep up with the enrollment; we are able to offer only one section of calculus [and a multilevel one at that], and it has forty-two students. It is being taught by an adjunct faculty member who has never taught before.

However, another institution, in a happier situation at the time of our visit, did not find it particularly necessary to plan for part-time faculty use. The chair of the English Department described the institution's situation well:

> It depends on the quality of the part-time faculty available. We haven't had to think about it much. We have well-qualified and trained people who have been with us a long time. The department is happy to have

> them and we're comfortable. We are fortunate to have
> [part-timers serving as] a semipermanent staff.

Other institutions deemphasize planning because of their traditions or history. Some have strong traditions of decentralized decision making, leaving departments "free" to staff their courses as they see fit. This is frequently combined with a philosophical position that full-time faculty are the only "real" faculty; part-timers are the invisible household staff hired to serve unobtrusively the needs of "the faculty."

In some cases, lack of planning stems from historical acquiescence to necessity and accommodation to a common and comfortable practice.

> The vast majority of teaching should be done by full-
> time faculty—80 percent. There will always be room
> for part-time teaching to obtain certain kinds of scarce
> expertise, take advantage of the community and other
> institutions, or have flexibility to deal with fluctua-
> tions in enrollments. What has happened here is part-
> time faculty have made it their careers, and because it
> is cheaper, the university condones it.

Examples of Planned Use

We found substantial evidence of planned use of part-time faculty within departments and schools, and within entire institutions. Generally speaking, planning occurs when institutions, schools, or departments have a very clear sense of their mission and long-range goals and where there is strong leadership from chief academic officers, deans, or chairs. However, even careful planning may result in unintentional educational consequences, especially when implementation of the plan is not consistent throughout an institution. Examples of planned use are described in the rest of this section.

Aspiring Research University

One institution we visited has based its plan for use of part-time faculty on a clearly defined and widely articulated mission that has been accepted and implemented throughout the institution. This comprehensive regional university is striving to become more research-oriented within the constraints of state funding for its teaching mission. It perceives itself as able to achieve this goal through careful budget management and use of part-time faculty. Part-time faculty are also seen as providing a buffer for the tenure-track faculty during budget crises. Decentralized planning and control of resources, with delegation of authority to deans and chairs to achieve institutional goals, enable the institution to accomplish the mission it has set for itself.

In accord with the institution's mission and budget plan, department chairs are given a dollar budget and a full-time-equivalent student (FTES) enrollment target. As long as they stay within the budget and meet the target, no questions are asked.

> We don't see an issue [in the use of part-time faculty].
> We build the target student enrollment for each col-
> lege and then decide how many faculty positions the
> colleges need to support the FTES target. Then the
> deans get the dollars. The deans tell the chairs their
> allocation. . . . A tenure-track person teaches three
> courses a semester and has release time for research.
> Basically, [chairs] can replace this person in teaching
> with a .60 part-time faculty [member]. [This part-time
> faculty member] can be on a three-course load and still
> teach the same number of students, too.

There is strong sentiment at all levels of this institution that to exercise central control over use of part-time faculty or resources would not "be the right way to go." Deans and chairs are trusted to run the academic programs and handle the resources the "right way." At the departmental level, the number of part-time faculty members varies considerably, but all the chairs and deans know the numbers. The intense preoccupation with the budget at this institution has no doubt been heightened by a fiscal crisis. The institution's resources are severely strained as it attempts to carry out its research mission. Departments adopt the institution's mission and budget philosophy, but because of the financial pressures, methods of implementation occasionally go far beyond what the central administration has envisioned.

Comments by department chairs echo the university's mission while simultaneously reflecting differences in implementation strategies:

> Why are we so complex? _____ wants to be *different.* We are paid to be a teaching institution, but we want to be a research university. _____ uses part-time faculty to accomplish this. The quality of instruction hangs on the part-time faculty.

Another chair emphasized the budget problem more than research productivity, while repeating the university's mission:

> Part-time faculty arc the protection for the university. The tenured faculty can't be removed. The budget is fluctuating up and down. Therefore, the part-time faculty are the buffer. Part-time faculty are an important reality around here. They take care of the budget surges and shortages. The extent of the budget fluctuations requires part-time faculty.

And from another chair who was responding to our question about optimal mix of part-time faculty to tenured or tenure-track faculty:

> The current mix is optimal. We hire part-time faculty to give us a buffer. They are inexpensive. [They have a] different salary and teach five courses for a full-time load. That is a 40 percent saving right off the bat. We buy cheap labor and get what we pay for.

This comprehensive institution clearly articulates its reasons for employing part-time faculty. They are hired to provide a buffer for tenure-track faculty and to support them in their pursuit of research. Communication of this understanding is consistent throughout the institution, and faculty staffing practices uniformly serve to implement these reasons for using part-time faculty.

High-Tech University

At another institution similar in size and urban location, operating
in a policy and collective bargaining context similar to the one just
described, the use of part-time faculty is again carefully planned and
monitored but for very different reasons.

As in our first example of planned use, at this institution
there is clarity in the mission and in its implementation at the
central administrative, school, and departmental levels. However, at
this institution the mission is excellence of instruction, and part-
time faculty are employed for the contributions they can make to
the quality of instruction. Part-time faculty are valued for their
scarce expertise and the quality of instruction they provide. To
ensure that part-time faculty enhance the quality of instruction, the
central administration is committed to achieving an 80 percent to
20 percent ratio of tenure-track faculty to part-time faculty. This
ratio is viewed as assuring continuity of instruction and attention
to student advising while allowing for the influx of extraordinary
talent to contribute to the richness of the curriculum through the
use of part-time faculty. As one administrator said,

> A target 80 to 20 percent ratio provides for a solid
> helping of meat and potatoes balanced with an ap-
> propriately sized dessert.

At this institution, there were 916 tenured and tenure-track
faculty and 1,099 part- and full-time temporary faculty who filled
a total of 447 full-time-equivalent positions at the time of our site
visit. While the number of part-timers was high, this university
managed them through a well-understood and accepted mission
and careful attention to policies promulgated to achieve the university's goals.

The first policy pertains to the hiring of part-time faculty.
Regional advertising of part-time positions is required. In addition,
the university has a policy that delineates the terminal degree required for appointment to tenured, tenure-track, and part-time or
temporary positions for each academic department and discipline.
Clarity in qualifications helps ensure the hiring of part-timers with

the appropriate skills for their teaching assignments. As one chair described it:

> We are not using part-timers as a contingency faculty for emergencies. We are using part-timers to teach what they know well. If they are inappropriately assigned, then we do a disservice to both the part-time faculty member and the students. [Teaching] quality depends on *matching* teaching assignment to qualifications. For example, part-timers having a master's degree and extensive experience are assigned to methods courses and supervision but not to foundations courses.

Equally important to the enhancement of academic quality is the evaluation of the teaching performance of the part-timers. Again, university policy specifies the type and frequency of the evaluations, and most chairs we interviewed stated that the evaluation methodology for teaching performance was the same for tenure-track and part-time faculty.

Department chairs we interviewed at this institution echoed the central administrative view in their concern about the screening, hiring, and assignment of part-timers and the monitoring of their teaching performance through rigorous evaluation. For example, the mathematics department has a unique structure for its use of part-time faculty. It has a special program to hire people with bachelor's degrees who are graduate students in the department. Only twelve are chosen each year, and they teach highly structured remedial courses. An internship adviser supervises their teaching and evaluates them extensively. This program benefits the students who need the remedial math courses and the graduate students who get training in teaching. In the next tier of part-timers are the people with master's degrees and high school or community college teaching experience. They are assigned to teach the basic lower-division required math courses. At the third tier of part-timers are the Ph.D.'s, who teach upper-division and graduate courses. These part-timers tend to be relatively long-term employees with full-time positions in industry.

The school of engineering perhaps best exemplifies the implementation of the university's mission and policies. Part-time faculty are used for their expertise and experience in industry. Within the school of engineering, the current ratio of part-time to tenured faculty is 40 percent to 60 percent. The dean's goal is to achieve a ratio of 20 percent to 80 percent in faculty staffing in conformity with the university's goal. When this goal is achieved, the dean foresees that two-thirds of the curriculum will be taught by the tenure-track faculty, with the remainder of their time devoted to research and service, and one-third of the curriculum will be taught by part-timers. To ensure quality of teaching performance, the dean has limited the teaching load of part-timers, who are largely specialists with full-time positions in industry, to one course each semester. Because of the partnerships he has built with local engineering firms, part-time faculty come and go at the campus as a regular part of their primary job in local industry. According to the dean:

> A major strength is part-time faculty. They add quality. They are much stronger teachers/experts than those [found in] institutions that use foreign-national graduate students to teach engineering and science. These part-time temporary faculty are experienced. We have a world center in engineering in our community. . . . We have a rich, rich pool. People who would never take a teaching job are teaching for us— presidents of companies, all kinds of expertise. [They have] outstanding peer and student evaluations. Many are teaching at upper-division and graduate levels. They are better than the tenured faculty in some cases. Accrediting association teams made up of people from the research universities decry our use of part-time faculty, but they are using foreign-national graduate students!

Within the school of engineering, quality of instruction is also achieved through departmental organization. Each department has areas of concentration. Each area is headed by a tenured faculty member who oversees the curriculum for that area as it is taught by tenure-track and part-time faculty. All faculty members relate to each other through these areas of concentration, which helps break down barriers between part-timers and tenure-track faculty and encourages communication. One department chair echoed the dean's philosophy:

> All part-time faculty have strong backgrounds in industry. They are at the master's or Ph.D. level. More than 50 percent have Ph.D.'s. We use them strictly for teaching courses in their areas of expertise. We hire graduate students to help in the labs.

Urban University

A similar situation exists at yet another university in a major urban setting. At this institution there is universal concern about the quality of teaching as an important factor in student recruitment and retention. While there is no universitywide policy regarding the appropriate number of part-time faculty, there is careful monitoring of appointments and an annual review of all part-time faculty members for merit raises and promotions. Within this university, several deans have capitalized on the rich resources available to them in the urban area and manage their part-time faculty work force carefully.

> We have 20 percent of the students, 9 percent of the faculty, and 6.7 percent of the budget at _____ in our school. In spite of this budget profile, we have the smallest number of part-time faculty of any school [within the institution]. We make sure every class is filled in this school. The situation I came into was chaos. Some of the use of adjuncts at the university comes from the failure to manage resources. [But I manage adjuncts according to] my management model: *Figure out the curriculum. Then figure out how the curriculum should be staffed. Then manage who teaches what course* [italics added]. Adjuncts used

at 10 percent of the total [faculty] can be a tremen-
dously valuable asset. It is a real management challenge
to use them, but it is doable. [It] requires the dean's
management. I don't give course releases; our tenured
faculty teach a full load of five or six classes [a year];
there are no little "side deals"; there are no low-
enrolled classes. I don't let these things happen. You
have to eliminate all the special deals of the senior faculty. You do it by making everything equitable.

This dean continued the interview by tracing the history of
employment of part-time faculty in his school:

In 1986 we had 800 students. Now, in 1991, we have
2,100 students. We offer 130 courses a semester; 25 are
taught by adjuncts. Five years ago one-half of the
courses were taught by adjuncts and one-half of them
were [our] ABDs. . . . Today, 15 percent [of our
courses] are taught by adjuncts, and they are taught by
outstanding people from downtown. [We allow] some
teaching by ABDs to help them get the experience.
Two-thirds of the adjuncts are downtown people, and
one-third are ABDs. [They teach] an average of two
courses a year. Fifteen to 20 percent is about right for
adjunct faculty. We have achieved our goal.

Another dean, also capitalizing on the rich resources of the
metropolitan area, exercises tight control over use of part-time faculty within his school:

We have 50 tenure-track faculty, 900 undergraduate
majors, 400 graduate students, and 40 full-time doctoral students in the school. We have very limited use
of adjuncts in the graduate program. We use "distinguished adjunct professors in residence." These people have been with _____ for a long time. The
appointment is continuous. It is for people who come

here after distinguished careers in the federal government. We only employ about three people in this category who teach three to four courses a year. All three are members of the National Academy of ———— .

This dean then talked about his use of part-time faculty to teach the undergraduate curriculum:

You must know why you are hiring them and be honest and set expectations based on this. Every teaching unit needs a *philosophy of part-time faculty utilization* [italics added]. [You have] to be clear about why they are here and reach agreement with the faculty in the school. Then adjuncts have more than a job. They have distinction and integration. They diversify our curriculum . . . [and] we remain current in the practice we teach about. It is very easy for us to articulate a mission for the part-time faculty. If you don't have a sense of why you hire them, you will devalue them, and if you do this, you'll get what you ask for in the classroom. We treat them well. Our expectations are clear; our students are good. Our literature makes it plain that we are *proud* of the adjunct faculty. You get in trouble when part-time faculty are the only way you can offer a program. Then they understand that they are just labor. We are explicit about what we want them to provide, and if they don't, we'll find others to do it. We have first-rate people.

One of this dean's department chairs compared the teaching performance of the part-time faculty in his department to that of the tenure-track faculty as part of his academic program review. Stressing the importance of continuous monitoring and assessment of teaching quality, he praised the university's policy of annual reviews:

In June we review all our adjuncts. Do we want to retain them? If so, do we want to promote them? Do

we want to give merit raises? . . . We do a thorough
review of every one of them. The idea of a review is
good.

Conclusion

Our examples of planned use of part-time faculty have certain key
components regardless of the size of the institution or whether it is
public or private. Planned use derives from a clear statement of
mission and from a common view of why and how part-time faculty can contribute to the mission. This common view permeates
the institution from the central administration to each department
within the college or university. Most planned use also derives from
a philosophy that part-time faculty can and do contribute to academic quality and enhance the instructional mission of the institution. When planned use is accompanied by central administrative
review, policies or practices for employment of part-timers are
clearly articulated and followed. Planned use has led institutions to
reach internal agreement on the acceptable numbers and assignments of part-time faculty, and it has led to the adoption of policies,
practices, and quality-control mechanisms to ensure that the common understanding is being adhered to.

Planning for the use of part-time faculty is critical to their
ultimate success. Academic quality is not related to the numbers of
part-time faculty employed. It is, instead, a product of institutional
agreement about the proper use of part-timers and the adoption of
policies, practices, and monitoring systems to ensure that part-time
faculty are indeed employed for the reasons the institution espouses.
Because the number of part-timers has been increasing steadily, and
part-timers appear to be here to stay as a permanent part of the faculty, it is critical that institutions acknowledge part-timers' increasingly important role in teaching and adopt models of planned use
appropriate for their particular circumstances.

Seven

Employment Policies and Practices

A simple statement by a provost at one of our site institutions captures institutional attitudes and values about employment policies and practices:

> Part-time faculty offer us "fine wine at discount prices." They are often very fine teachers, and our money goes much farther than when we put it all into full-time faculty. Furthermore, we can "pour it down the drain" if they have any flaws at all. We have made no big investment in part-time faculty.

When institutions believe part-time faculty value derives from the quality of what they do, employment policies and practices tend to translate this belief into practice. When institutions believe part-time faculty value derives from the dollars they "save," or the "buffer" and "benefits" they create for tenured faculty, employment policies and practices are markedly different. No institution in our study exemplified either of the two extremes. However, their approaches to employment policies and practices are based on strong institutional beliefs about the value and appropriate use of part-time faculty. These beliefs have their roots in the history, traditions, culture, and mission of the individual institutions.

141

Despite the enormous variety in backgrounds, motivations, and work patterns of part-timers, we did not find much flexibility for them in current employment policies and practices. Part-timers are generally treated as a homogeneous mass and afforded few options or alternatives.

Variation in employment practices among and within institutions arises instead from factors unrelated to the part-timers themselves. In part, variation arises from the uniqueness of institutions—their individual missions, funding circumstances, market niches, staffing patterns, and educational philosophies. Variation in employment policies and practices also arises from external forces that are often beyond the institution's control, such as state laws, system-wide policies, and accreditation agency requirements, as we have seen in earlier chapters.

In this chapter, we examine the range of policies and practices for hiring, assigning, compensating, supporting, and evaluating part-timers that we found at our site institutions. Even the most casual analysis shows how different these policies and practices are when contrasted with those covering full-time faculty. Deep and obvious inequities can be found, and the disparity sets up a potential triadic conflict of interest.

Using their experience from nearly two decades of occasionally contentious collective bargaining negotiations at York University in Canada, Rajagopal and Farr (n.d.) (b) point out that "the real objective of the part-time faculty union is (and has been) to get what the full-time faculty have" (p. 7). Recognizing that literal parity is not possible because the use of part-time faculty is "a critical cost-saving expedient," the authors conclude that the role of "management" in negotiations has become one of mediating between the interests of the two separate and competing faculty sectors. The university, for example, could not remain fiscally viable if part-timers achieved parity with full-time faculty. Nor could full-time faculty be supported without a large part-time work force. Thus, a triangle of interests forces management to consider a far more complicated set of issues than would simple bilateral negotiations with one union.

It is worth adding that the part-time faculty unit at York has engaged in two highly disruptive strikes, reinforcing the importance of recognizing their interests. While this experience is far more extreme than that of most U.S. institutions, it nevertheless presents in sharp relief the need to confront the way in which part-timers', full-timers', and institutions' interests are reflected in employment policies.

This chapter is based on interviews with chief academic officers, deans, department chairs, senior faculty, and part-timers. We also reviewed NSOPF '88 data, policy documents, faculty handbooks, and collective bargaining agreements. We cover employment policies and practices in perhaps more detail than some readers will wish to pursue. These readers may want to skim the chapter to decide which sections are of greatest interest to them.

Responsibility for Part-Time Faculty Employment

Responsibility for part-time faculty employment tends to be hierarchical and reasonably well defined within institutions. Responsibility for resource allocations, including faculty positions, remains solidly in the hands of vice presidents or deans of instruction. Some institutions (more frequently those with collective bargaining contracts) also monitor all part-time faculty appointments for contract compliance and/or budgetary control at the level of the vice president.

In the large institutions in our study, deans of schools or colleges exert authority and responsibility similar to that of the vice president, provost, or dean of instruction in smaller institutions. Once resources have been allocated by the academic vice president, deans assume the responsibility for control of dollars and faculty positions within their schools, colleges, or divisions.

However, almost universally, deans and vice presidents delegate to department chairs responsibility for the implementation of employment policies and practices, and the choice of whom to hire. It is the *department chair* who, with or without the participation of the tenured faculty, makes decisions that affect the lives and, occasionally, the careers of part-time faculty. As one chairperson put it:

> The chancellor allocates the permanent positions to the deans. The deans allocate the resources to the

chairs. The department chairs and faculty establish
the teaching needs and make the decisions regarding
individuals.

From the chairs' perspective, they are responsible:

The chair controls everything. Who comes and goes,
who is hired, what they are paid.

Some chairs use departmental committees of tenured faculty to
make decisions about hiring, evaluation, and rehiring part-time faculty, and some do not.

Our site institutions tend to follow one of three patterns
when delegating responsibility to department chairs: little or no
policy, policy that is promulgated but not enforced, or policy that
is established and implemented consistently. Where colleges and
universities have institutional policies for the employment of part-
time faculty and monitor adherence to these policies, part-time faculty experience more consistency of treatment. Where there is little
or no institutionally promulgated policy, department chairs are left
to supervise and manage part-time faculty according to their own
beliefs about their value. In these institutions, we found experienced, sympathetic, and understanding chairs who devote much
time and attention to supervising their part-time faculty. One part-
timer said,

The department supports me—more than other institutions support the full-time faculty. I have been hard-
nosed in class, and the department chair has been
supportive.

Alongside these chairs, however, we encountered chairs who,
because of lack of knowledge, training, interest, or experience, are
not as skillful or concerned in their management of part-time faculty employment matters. Said one part-timer:

Our employment is dependent upon the chair. New
chairs have a very different attitude about part-timers.

> I am an asset. I teach five classes. They weed and weed
> and weed part-timers. [Their] attitudes changed from
> "We're lucky to have the part-timers" to "They are
> lucky to be hired."

Department chair training and central administration commitment to certain basic principles in part-time faculty employment are inexpensive and relatively simple ways to improve the
working conditions of part-timers. Yet we saw little recognition of
the need to invest in chairs' ability to deal with part-timers during
our site visits, despite their pivotal role in the management of part-
time faculty.

Laissez-faire approaches to the use of part-time faculty risk
inconsistency among departments, especially when the chairs receive no training or guidance. Inconsistency in employment practices makes the institution vulnerable to charges of capriciousness,
discrimination, and inequity. We do not believe that "no policy"
is an adequate response to the substantial level at which most institutions now rely on part-time faculty.

Recruiting and Hiring Part-Time Faculty

Recruitment and hiring set the tone for employment relations with
part-time faculty because they are frequently the first contacts between the institution and the part-timer.

Criteria for Appointment

All our site institutions have formal or informal criteria for the
appointment of part-time faculty. Several have formal, written policies regarding qualifications that are published in handbooks or
policy statements. One such policy lists the required terminal degree for part-time faculty appointments within every discipline in
every department. Institutions with written policies on qualifications for appointment usually monitor individual appointments
centrally.

Community colleges tend to have standardized qualifications
or criteria for appointment. The most common requirement is a

master's degree and a specified number of graduate credit hours or a certain amount of experience in the particular discipline. Occasionally, the criteria are enforced by accrediting agencies, as in the Florida community colleges.

> At _____ the minimum qualifications are a master's degree and eighteen credits in the field. Noncollege credit courses and vocational courses don't have this requirement. We can't always hold to the minimums. SACS [accrediting agency] requires reporting individual qualifications when anyone is hired with less than a master's plus eighteen hours. Limits are also imposed by other accrediting bodies—dental hygiene and nursing, for example.

At the other end of the continuum, several of our site institutions have no formal policy or criteria for appointing part-time faculty, and judgments are left up to department chairs. Still, at institutions without formal written policy, there are solid institutional understandings about the minimum qualifications for appointment to part-time faculty positions. These minimum acceptable qualifications may be met by a composite of an unusual array of experience.

At every institution we visited, we found that part-time faculty were generally well qualified to teach. For example, one part-timer we interviewed has a bachelor's and a master's degree and had worked in management for a major corporation for forty-five years at a variety of international locations. Upon retirement, he decided to take a course at the local community college and found he was better prepared in the subject than the instructor. He wound up teaching the course and has been teaching it ever since. As he said,

> I had to find some constructive way to occupy time in retirement. Community college teaching was not in my plan until I discovered I was qualified to do it. I love the students and the courses I teach. It has turned into one of two real highlights of my life and career.

Recruitment

Recruitment for part-time faculty is usually informal and left up to department chairs to handle as they see fit. Regardless of location or discipline, finding qualified part-time faculty is not a major issue for the department chairs we interviewed except when they are confronted with the need to find someone at the last minute. Those in urban areas are typically flooded with applications.

> We are the only game in town. We don't have to do anything for the part-time faculty, and we don't. We have a very rich market. Everyone wants to come to [this city] from across the country. And there is a captive audience living [here] because the other colleges and universities in the area are not competitive. This rich pool makes it possible for [the university] to behave the way it does.

Though some departments and institutions advertise their vacancies regionally or locally, most of the actual recruiting is by word-of-mouth. Departments consider their current part-timers as members of the pool, along with individuals who send unsolicited applications and others who are recommended by part-timers or tenure-track faculty. Some department chairs and deans actively solicit "stars" or experts to teach a course or two. Ph.D. students from local universities are popular candidates for part-time assignments at many colleges and universities.

One private institution, located in a rural area, reported considerable difficulty finding applicants:

> There are a lot of ABDs in the area, but we can have trouble recruiting people. We might have to scramble. We call the chairs at [all the regional universities with graduate programs within a hundred miles]. We get people. Most part-time faculty commute. We pay additional money for commuters.

Some departments, for example, in schools of business, also reported difficulties in finding qualified part-timers.

Several of our site institutions, particularly small liberal arts colleges, use part-time faculty positions to attract dual-career academic couples. When confronted with tough recruiting situations for tenure-track faculty, these colleges and universities occasionally make offers of a tenure-track position for one spouse and a part-time position for the other.

We did find more formal approaches to recruiting part-timers at some of our site institutions. For example, at Saint Mary's College, the School of Extended Education has a rigorous screening procedure for its part-time faculty who teach nontraditional adult students at off-campus sites. This recruitment and screening process is described in depth in Chapter Eight.

At one university, there was an elaborate "posting" requirement in the collective bargaining contract for courses that will not be taught by full-time faculty: "Except as otherwise provided, all positions in [the part-time faculty] unit shall be posted as they arise, clearly identified as Unit 2, and shall identify to the extent possible the course, the classification and reasonable qualifications of the position, the salary, the projected class enrollment [where relevant], and the application deadline. The qualifications for a position shall be stated as 'required,' 'preferred,' and 'desirable'" (*Unit 2 Collective Agreement, 1989–91*, 1989, Article 12.01.1, p. 34).

About three thousand part-time positions or courses are "posted" at this institution each year, usually in May for September employment. At the time of our site visit, decisions regarding who would be hired to teach courses were almost entirely based on the seniority of the part-time faculty members who applied: "The candidate with the most experience gained in applicable teaching, demonstrating, tutoring, and marking within the University . . . shall be appointed and, where applicable prior experience is equal, the candidate with the desirable qualifications shall be appointed" (*Unit 2 Collective Agreement, 1989–91*, 1989, Article 11.02.1, p. 24). "Applicable prior experience" is defined in the contract as experience in the same discipline or in a discipline that is not "academically remote." Thus, at this institution, part-timers with seniority in one department could take their seniority with them to another department where a position was posted.

The "posting" system was uniformly disliked by department chairs:

> The academic labor union is an oxymoron—paradoxical. The chair of mathematics says someone is not qualified to teach. The union says the person is qualified. There is an increasing tendency in the union to think they are qualified to assess the qualifications rather than the academic experts in the departments. This is the union's position.

At the time of our site visit, department chairs reported that there were numerous outstanding grievances over the "posting" requirement. To circumvent the requirement, they told us, they could "jump ovei" the seniority provisions to hire a "hotshot." However, when a department hired someone outside the seniority system, it had to pay the union an additional sum of money.

Affirmative Action

We found little evidence of attention to affirmative action in the recruitment and appointment of part-time faculty who are members of underrepresented groups. Community colleges in urban areas tended to have the best representation of racial and ethnic minorities. One of our community colleges capitalizes on the affirmative action efforts of local businesses, many of which are Fortune 500 firms. Since these corporations emphasize affirmative action, the community college profits by recruiting its part-timers from among their employees. One of our urban universities is attempting to increase the representation of minorities among its part-time faculty through established goals and active recruitment. Progress toward reaching affirmative action goals for part-time faculty is monitored annually.

At the time of our site visits, other institutions showed little or no commitment to affirmative action or interest in the possibility that part-time faculty could contribute to the racial and ethnic diversification of their teaching faculty. We interviewed fewer part-time minority faculty members than we would have anticipated and encountered some examples of insensitivity to the valuable perspectives racial and ethnic minorities can bring to campuses and classrooms.

A perceptive African American with a part-time position in social work at an urban university assessed the absence of affirmative action this way:

> The institution needs part-time faculty with clinical experience; they are vital in some fields. [But] part-time faculty jobs are not generally advertised. Most hiring is done through closed networks. Broader recruiting and affirmative action are needed if minorities are to break in. Broader nets need to be cast to attract [the] best people in some fields and the previously excluded as well. The business world and the professions would be good sources; minorities from these areas could be recruited and attracted to part-time positions. Part-time positions can be "elevators" for minorities, entrée to academic careers. I am less concerned about "ghettoization" [of minorities in part-time positions] than about the current lack of minorities in higher education overall.

Attracting qualified members of underrepresented groups to part-time teaching is not always easy, however. At one institution in a major metropolitan area with a mix of ethnic and racial groups, we were told by an administrator that,

> [This institution] badly needs more minority instructors to serve as role models for minority students. It is hard to compete for the best minority instructors in this market. They can get more money at [a competitor institution]. There are few blacks and no Hispanics [available] in math and science.

Administrators at this institution noted that the faculty at one campus with a heavy minority student population was hired early in the institution's history and is almost all white. These faculty members are now approaching retirement, and assuring diversity among new hires is increasingly difficult. Fiscal difficulty has prevented the filling of vacated lines with new full-time people, and it has been difficult to locate minority faculty to teach part-time. Ironically, displaced white males tend to be more available for part-time work because the trend in this particular city to hire individuals from underrepresented groups in all kinds of jobs has reduced their availability. (We did not observe this trend elsewhere, however.)

Affirmative action is certainly more than a matter of quotas or of putting people from racial or ethnic minorities in visible positions. At many institutions, minority faculty can make a substantive difference in whether young people succeed in getting an education or become alienated and drop out. As one part-timer put it:

> Predominantly white institutions don't have enough minority faculty or enough role models for minority kids.

Notification of Appointment

With very rare exceptions, all our site institutions notify part-time faculty in writing about their appointments. Notification is usually in the form of a contract, though occasionally it is given in a letter from the vice president.

A common complaint among part-timers is the lateness of notification. Many receive it within days or weeks of the beginning of a semester. When part-timers are notified about their teaching assignments only days before classes begin, they obviously have very little time to prepare. New faculty members also have no time to be oriented to the college or department. Thus, late notification can have an important, deleterious effect on the quality of part-timers' teaching performance.

For part-timers with other income, the late notification is only a personal inconvenience. For part-timers dependent upon the income they receive from teaching, failure to notify them early can have a seriously disrupting effect on their lives. Late notification regarding appointments was a source of frustration for the part-time faculty we interviewed at almost all our institutions.

We found an exception to the common practice of late no-tification at DePauw University, which prides itself on notifying its part-time faculty in the spring semester regarding the next academic year's teaching assignments. Other exceptions were found in collective bargaining agreements such as York University's, where the timing of notification was specified in the collective bargaining contract. At York, this time frame was "at least six weeks in advance of the beginning of classes for the term in which the course will be offered in order to allow adequate preparation time" (*Unit 2 Collective Agreement, 1989–91*, 1989, Article 12.02, p. 35).

Terms, Conditions, and Limits of Appointments

Part-timers generally work under terms and conditions that offer little security, continuity, or incentive to remain at an institution.

Length of Appointment

Eighty-five percent of part-time faculty members are appointed for one year or less. Sixty-four percent are appointed for only one term at a time, and 20 percent receive an academic year appointment. An additional 11.3 percent of the part-timers in the NSOPF '88 survey responded that the length of their appointment was not specified. Only 1.7 percent of those surveyed responded that their appointments were for two or more years' duration (NSOPF '88).

These data reflect the practices we found at our site institutions. In keeping with the belief that part-time faculty are a temporary, expendable work force, available to meet shifting enrollment demands and budgetary situations, institutions are reluctant to make commitments for more than minimal time periods. Some institutions specify that appointments are for no more than a term at a time; others simply make term-by-term or year-by-year appointments a matter of informal practice. Generally speaking, chairs are reluctant to give up their flexibility and offer longer-term appointments even though they offer term-by-term appointments over and over again and even though some collective bargaining agreements stipulate the availability of multiple-year appointments for part-time faculty: "Temporary appointments may be for periods of a semester, a quarter, parts of a year, or one [1] or more years" (*Agreement, July 1, 1987–June 30, 1991*, 1987, Article 12.3).

Some institutions also have formal policies or informal practices that encourage breaks in part-timers' continuous employment after a certain number of appointments:

> The average is about six semesters of continuous employment. Some have been here long term but not continuously. The longest-term people are in small fields where we can't get full-time faculty. If growth continues as it has recently, we are going to find it harder to break continuity no matter what we want as policy.

While some institutions strive to break continuity to avoid any appearance of de facto tenure, others "reward" continuous service. For example, several of our site institutions offer professional development opportunities after a certain number of years of teaching. Other institutions occasionally negotiate benefits coverage for long-term and highly valued individuals. Because this practice leads to inconsistent treatment, it tends to breed discontent among part-timers as a whole.

Time Base of Appointment

Limiting the time base of an appointment is a very common practice. According to the NSOPF '88 survey, part-time faculty work an average of 13.4 hours a week at their institutions and teach an average of 1.5 courses per term. This does not vary significantly by type of institution except for public research institutions, where part-timers average 20 hours per week.

Almost all our site institutions have formal or informal limits on time base whether or not they adhere to them in practice. Occasionally, the limit is around half-time employment; more often the limit is two courses when three courses would constitute a full-time teaching load.

*Impact of Time Base and Continuity
on Eligibility for Benefits*

A frequent reason for limiting the time base of an appointment is
to avoid providing benefits. At some institutions where there are no
uniform policies or practices limiting work load, work load limits
are nevertheless invoked to avoid paying statutorily required benefits. (See Chapter Four.) Occasionally, part-time faculty are employed in several appointments in different departments. Separately
each of these appointments constitutes part-time work, but together
they constitute a full-time load or more. At some institutions, some
part-timers with multiple appointments have successfully negotiated benefits for themselves. However, most part-timers with multiple appointments do not receive benefits no matter what the
cumulative time base is.

      The use of restrictive practices such as limits on time base,
term-by-term appointments, or breaks in continuity to avoid benefits eligibility causes considerable frustration among part-timers:

> I am in class twelve hours a week for two courses and
> one studio class. I get $3,200 per course and no ben-
> efits. On paper my teaching load is .67. I also direct
> a play, but this is paid from the department's endow-
> ment. I don't get [work load] credit for this, but a full-
> time person would. So I am .03 below the benefits line.
> I don't get benefits. The chair said, "Don't push me
> on this or I'll be told to hire another person and lower
> your time base."

Work Load and Assignment

Work load for part-time faculty is defined in terms of teaching load.
With very few exceptions, part-timers who participate in departmental committees, take on special assignments, or otherwise make
themselves available for nonteaching service are not compensated
for these activities. The chairs, deans, and chief personnel officers
we interviewed routinely responded that part-timers volunteer for
these activities.

One exception to this practice occurs within the University of California system, where the collective bargaining contract for part-timers stipulates compensation for all components of work load: "In determining the relative workload value of instructional offerings and course equivalencies, the University shall consider the instructional and evaluation methods employed, the nature of the courses assigned, the preparations required, the number of students expected to enroll, [and] the availability of support employees. In addition, the University may consider other factors. . . . *In determining workload, the University shall consider other duties that have been assigned* [italics added] " (*Memorandum of Understanding, July 1, 1991–June 30, 1993,* 1991, Article 25.A.5–6, p. 28).

The actual teaching assignments of part-time faculty are decided by senior faculty serving as course coordinators or by department chairs. We found practices regarding course assignments and work loads as varied as the number of academic departments whose chairs we interviewed. Part-time faculty are at the whim of their departments with regard to assignments.

> This is my first year here. I got my Ph.D. this past summer. I am full-time this quarter. I have two classes of basic chemistry with 450 students in each class. I have 900 students total. This is a real service course. Twenty TAs assist me. I oversee the twenty TAs. . . . I have secretarial support and a general chemistry account. I have my own office and telephone. Faculty tease me about seeing students. My biggest disappointment is that teaching is not valued, is of secondary importance. I had to search out the chair and give him a progress report on how I was doing. I got no orientation. There is another lecturer in the department, and I picked his brains [when I arrived.]

Many of our part-timers talked appreciatively about the opportunities they had had to try new courses, build new curricula, and open up broader teaching assignments for themselves. Others wistfully expressed great interest in having these opportunities, or bitterness about their second-class status when it comes to teaching assignments. In any event, part-timers rarely have the opportunity to teach at all levels of the curriculum and therefore do not see the program "whole." This condition is perceived by full- and part-timers alike as a threat to program continuity and integrity, and it has led us to a more extensive exploration of "integration" in Chapter Eight.

Full-Time Temporary Appointments

The use of part-time faculty in disciplines such as English and mathematics at some of our institutions has become so extensive that a new genre of faculty position has emerged: the full-time temporary position, frequently with a limited-term appointment of three to five years. Through such full-time appointments, these institutions hope to obtain more service from "temporary faculty," provide more instructional continuity, and cut down on the number of part-time faculty employed. For example, in 1984, the English Department at Loyola University had thirty-four tenure lines and used sixty-five part-time faculty members, who taught 58 percent of the curriculum. At the time of our site visit, the university had converted thirty part-time faculty positions to ten full-time temporary positions for the writing program. These instructors teach four courses a semester (the normal course load is three) and receive benefits. Loyola's appointments are for up to five years and are renewable.

American University is using full-time temporary appointments at the rank of instructor. These appointments are limited to five years. Faculty teach six courses a year, are required to perform service functions, and receive benefits as part of a reasonably attractive compensation package. However, at the end of the five years, an appointment cannot be renewed. One chair commented:

> We have had a dramatic increase in the number of positions in the _____ program. We have thirteen full-time temporaries. We have tried to say, "This appointment is only for five years. What can we do to help you move to another position?" Five years is, by policy, the limit for a temporary appointment. Per-

sonally, I'd rather be able to hire them, keep them, and
promote them. . . . But we try to define their service
requirement to help them get a job later. We consider
it career development. Most of the people are in transition anyhow in their careers. . . . Out of thirteen,
eight were new, [and] only two had teaching problems. The rest were top notch. Two of them were the
best in the department. I would staff the entire _____
program with full-time temps and lift the five-year
cap. In terms of quality, I'd put them on tenure track.

Within the California State University system, for the most
part, full-time temporary faculty are treated the same as part-timers
by terms of the collective bargaining agreement. Faculty staffing is
viewed from the perspective of "temporary" versus tenure track regardless of time base. The California State University collective
bargaining contract covers *all* faculty—tenured, tenure-track, and
temporary—regardless of time base. A temporary faculty member's
time base can range from .07 to 1.00. At one typical university in
the system, 546 full-time-equivalent faculty positions are temporary. Of these, 120 positions are filled with full-time temporary faculty members.

Full-time, temporary, fixed-term appointees generally teach
multiple sections of basic courses in the undergraduate curriculum,
such as composition, speech, and mathematics. Occupants of these
positions receive better compensation packages than do part-time
faculty, have more clearly defined work loads, and are usually eligible to participate more actively in governance. However, full-
time temporary appointments are not viewed positively by all
members of the academic profession. Some senior faculty regard
full-time temporary appointments as an erosion of the tenure system and as setting an undesirable if not dangerous precedent. In our
view, they offer an attractive alternative to part-time employment.

In sum, at our site institutions, we found that the terms and
conditions of part-timers' appointments put limits on how much
they could work. Part-timers are not usually able to negotiate more
flexible terms and quickly conclude that institutions carefully control the situation to avoid any commitment at all. This, of course,

is an essentially accurate view. But we question whether there is perhaps too rigid control over terms and conditions for individual part-timers, some of whom would be far more valuable if they were given more employment options and more opportunities.

Salary

At our site institutions, salary policies vary, depending upon institutional cultures, ability to pay, and reasons for employing part-time faculty. Policy alternatives range from setting salaries on a case-by-case basis to having one salary schedule for all faculty, part-timers and tenured alike, with departmental discretion as to where to place part-time faculty on the schedule. The vast majority of our site institutions, however, use one of two alternative salary policies: either a flat rate of compensation for all part-timers or an established range, frequently defined on the basis of qualifications or seniority. Occasionally, salary ranges are defined within a system of ranks. All institutions using a predetermined range pay part-timers a fixed rate per course for each course they teach. We encountered only one institution in our sample where part-timers are paid on a pro rata basis of a full-time salary, and this policy applies only to those part-timers who have a time base higher than .70.

At the time of our site visits, the salaries of part-timers started as low as $800 per course and went as high as $5,000 per course. Community colleges tended to pay at the lower end of this range, for example, from $1,000 to $1,500. Among the four-year institutions, salary variation was not based upon type of institution or geographical location. Instead, salaries varied among institutions because of market factors, institutional philosophies about compensation, or collective bargaining agreements. For example, at the time of our visit York University paid "those individuals assigned sole or principal responsibility for the design and/or presentation of a course" a flat rate of $9,828 per twenty-six-week course (*Unit 2 Collective Agreement, 1989–91,* 1991, Article 10.04.1, p. 20). At the opposite end of the continuum in terms of salary flexibility, the collective bargaining contract in the University of California system in effect at the time of our visit provided for the placement of part-time faculty at any place on the "Academic Standard Table of Pay

Rates" at the discretion of the department chair. If individuals were appointed in more than one department, they could have several different salaries.

Within these general guidelines we found some unusual salary practices. One institution with a flat rate of pay per course paid $2,000 per course when taught by the day faculty and $1,500 per course when taught by the night faculty. When part-timers were both day and night above a certain time base, they received the $2,000 flat rate. Another institution distinguished between graduate and undergraduate courses in establishing its salary rates per course.

Whatever the salary policy, the NSOPF '88 survey data indicate that in 1988 the average part-time faculty member was paid $6,212 in basic salary, which represented 18 percent of his or her total mean income of $34,173. Other income from within the institution was minimal, about 2 percent of the total. Consulting income was almost the same as base salary, at $5,702 or 17 percent of the total, and income earned from employment outside the institution was $21,612 or 63 percent of the total. While part-timers' total income varied by type of institution, the percentage of this total deriving from part-time faculty employment did not vary significantly from the average of 18 percent.

Salary Adjustments

Once hired, part-timers do not necessarily receive automatic cost-of-living increases or merit adjustments. We almost always found that cost-of-living adjustments for part-timers were lower than those for full-time faculty. At several institutions we visited, anticipated increases had been cancelled or lowered because of budget exigencies.

> [Part-time] faculty are not happy about resource allo-
> cation decisions. . . . The full-time faculty are getting
> a 6 percent raise, while part-time faculty are getting a
> 20 percent cut in total positions and no raise.

Most of our site institutions did not have merit salary provisions for part-time faculty. Instead, movement on the salary schedule tended to be on the basis of seniority. In some instances, the lack of merit salary increases held true for all faculty and was a matter of institutional tradition; at other institutions, tenure-track faculty increases were made on the basis of merit, while part-time faculty salary policy did not allow for merit.

A few institutions, however, did have merit salary adjustments for part-timers. At American University, for example, all part-time faculty are reviewed annually by their department chairs for merit salary adjustments or promotions.

Within the California State University System, part-time faculty are paid according to the same salary schedule as the tenure-track faculty. A 1990 arbitration decision awards "automatic step increases" (merit salary adjustments) after a part-timer has taught the equivalent of one year of full-time employment and if the part-timer requests a step increase (California Faculty Association and California State University, 1990). The potential effect of this arbitration decision, which came in the midst of a statewide fiscal crisis, was unclear at the time of our site visit. As a department chairperson at one of the California State University campuses commented:

> They don't get step increases unless they are superlative. We have such a rich pool that if they wanted a raise, we'd hire someone else. It's not nice, but the budget controls us. We have a limited amount of money. We haven't given any raises for several years because of budget cuts. We used to think it was automatic, but we found out it wasn't and we stopped giving them. University policy is that it is up to chairs and deans.

Satisfaction and Dissatisfaction with Salary Policy

Inevitably, every salary policy in place at the site institutions during our visits was perceived as causing some problems for institutions and individuals. Some institutions complained that they were not competitive with surrounding colleges and universities. This was particularly true of community colleges in urban areas with comprehensive regional or research universities nearby. Some institutions (particularly small colleges) that used salaries to attract part-timers had eroded their established salary policies by allowing individual negotiation directly with vice presidents. One part-timer told us:

> A year ago I complained to the chair regarding pay. I talked to the provost. He said he would give me $1,000 more per semester. That was the most he could do.

This part-timer was not satisfied with this individual adjustment:

> Because of my personal integrity and professionalism, I will continue to do well. I feel genuinely appreciated by the department. The chair wrote me a thank-you note. My husband and I laugh about taking thank-you notes to the grocery store.

Opinions about salary policies and about actual salaries paid vary a great deal, depending on discipline and circumstances. Comments from deans and chairs at one urban university reflect the diversity of viewpoints held by those responsible for making salary decisions. One chair commented:

> The people who are adjuncts are earning six-digit salaries [elsewhere]. The fact that we are paying them $1,500 or $3,000 makes no difference for most of the people we deal with.

Another chair found the salary policy totally unacceptable:

> We should pay double the salary. I don't feel bad about the benefits. We get pretty competent people, but we could get better people if we paid more. I am almost embarrassed to mention the numbers.

Part-timers themselves have different views about their salaries. On the one hand, some part-timers who are employed full-time elsewhere are not particularly concerned. On the other hand, some part-timers depend upon their salaries as an important part of their income. For them, a fair wage and merit salary adjustments, as well as recognition of their service contributions and early notification of employment, are very important:

> If you really want a strong faculty, you do it with the paycheck. That the secretaries get paid more is a hell of a statement.

A few part-timers who carry extraordinarily heavy teaching loads can earn a good income:

> You can earn $100,000 a year if you work twelve months.

By far, however, the majority are very dissatisfied with their salaries:

> We get the low-level, nonglamorous courses and take low pay to teach them. I can't afford to teach part-time much longer. I'm netting the same amount of money teaching part-time that I made typesetting full-time. I can't rely on getting any summer support either.

And from another part-timer at the same institution:

> We are basically in the same position as migrant workers. There is a lot of wasted energy and unnecessary expense involved in trying to stay alive with part-time teaching.

Benefits

Very few institutions provide benefits for part-time faculty, and when they do, it is usually the result of collective bargaining. According to the NSOPF '88 survey, overall only 16.6 percent of the part-time faculty receive subsidized medical insurance compared with 97.4 percent of their full-time counterparts. Only 20 percent receive subsidized retirement plans compared with 93 percent of their full-time counterparts. And only 8.5 percent receive tuition grants for children compared with 47.7 percent of the full-time faculty.

Generally speaking, institutions formulate benefits policies according to the time base of the individual's appointment rather than continuous service. Part-time faculty with ten to fifteen years of teaching experience are usually treated the same as part-timers hired to replace someone in the classroom for only one semester.

Some institutions, while not providing benefits across the board to all part-time faculty, do provide them when the time base is sufficiently high. Eastern Kentucky University and Saint Mary's College provide benefits when the time base is .70 or higher. The California State University system provides medical, dental, and vision benefits to those with a time base of .40 or more. By contrast, most institutions do provide benefits for all full-time faculty even if they are "temporary."

Health Coverage

By far the most important and controversial benefit for institutions and part-time faculty alike is health coverage. At every institution we visited where health benefits were not provided, this was a hot issue. For some part-time faculty who are dependent upon their teaching for income, it was more important than salary.

> I don't have health insurance here. I panicked. I started working at a financial planning service to get the benefits. I work there one-half time. I work one-third time at [an art gallery]. I work two-thirds time at [this institution]. That is my schedule for this fall. My daughter just turned two. I got laid off from my arts curator job. I don't know what the future is for me.

Institutions are also concerned about the lack of health coverage. Some allow individuals to buy into the group plan on their own; others are exploring this alternative. However, some insurance companies will not allow this option. One dean's comment is illustrative of administrators' frustration over health benefits coverage:

> We don't provide health coverage [to part-timers]. We
> are looking into it. We just had a faculty member die
> of AIDS. His medical bills were $300,000 in the last
> year of his life. There is a major crisis in health ben-
> efits for everyone.

Retirement Coverage

Part-timers are less concerned about retirement benefits. While only
20 percent of part-time faculty are in retirement plans to which the
institution makes a contribution (NSOPF '88), some states require
part-time faculty to contribute, and other states are considering this
option. In California, for example, retirement system membership
is ordinarily mandatory for those employed full-time for more than
six months or half-time for three consecutive semesters.

Tuition Remission

An important benefit to some part-time faculty is tuition benefits
for dependents. Cuyahoga Community College, for example, provides tuition remission for part-timers and their families. At other
institutions where tuition remission is not available to them, part-
timers are outspoken about perceived inequities:

> Benefits are a problem. The staff can be here two years
> full-time, and the third year they get the tuition remis-
> sion benefit. Their child only pays 10 percent of tui-
> tion. As a part-time faculty [member], I've been here
> eleven years and taught up to five courses a year.
> There is no tuition program for me. I will argue this
> with the provost. I can't get a penny for it. This is an
> unfair disparity.

A union leader at another campus commented:

> We've tried to get prorated or buy-in benefits for part-
> timers, but the college won't agree. One of the things
> we'd like to get, and it is essentially cost-free, is tuition

remission for part-time faculty dependents and spouses on a space-available basis.

Inconsistencies in Benefits Administration

While nonavailability of benefits remains the greatest source of frustration for part-timers, they are also unhappy about institutions' failure to communicate their policies regarding benefits clearly. At several of our site institutions, we found that policies or practices concerning benefits were not clearly communicated or were confusing or inconsistent. For example, from a part-time faculty perspective, when the combination of part-time appointments in multiple departments is full-time or greater, part-timers should receive benefits. From an institutional perspective, part-timers remain part-time even when their multiple appointments reach or exceed a full-time equivalent. In rare cases, we found personnel offices informing part-timers about one set of requirements for benefits eligibility at the same time that department chairs were referring to another set of requirements. Finally, at a few institutions, individual part-timers told us about their ability to negotiate benefits packages that were not available to others.

With benefits, as with most other aspects of employment, the attitudes of department chairs and senior faculty have an enormous effect on part-timers' sense of status and acceptance. One chair at one of our site institutions is a strong advocate of benefits for his part-timers:

> English has gone on record as supporting benefits for part-time faculty after a certain number of years of service. We also gave part-time faculty the right to vote.

Another chair at the same institution stated a very different viewpoint:

> It [health insurance] has never been discussed in our department. [Part-timers who are faculty] spouses are

covered anyway. ABDs get it as graduate students. It's never come up, and I haven't given it much thought.

Pay and benefits for part-timers are neither adequate nor consistent when compared with compensation for full-time faculty. While we do not believe a direct prorating of compensation is necessary or even practical, we do think most institutions can develop more thoughtfully designed and more equitable approaches to salary and benefits.

Support and Services

Campuses furnish part-timers with office space, supplies and equipment, and access to secretarial services as best they can. Usually, it is left up to department chairs to decide what kinds of and how much support to provide. During our site visits, we found all faculty, full- and part-time, working with very low levels of support and frequently in very cramped space.

Space for part-time faculty offices was a major problem at many of our site institutions. Horror stories about space were abundant in our interviews.

> Off the theater there is a dressing room. It was the star's dressing room. It has a toilet and a sink. The office is as wide as the toilet and the sink. (It was really convenient when I brought the baby to work!) My desk is the makeup table and mirror. The windows are all frosted. When a student comes to talk to me, one of us has to sit on the toilet! There is a chair and a toilet seat. It was a joke at first; within the department it was funny. I had an office-warming party. Then a Japanese student came to see me, and I was humiliated. I had to invite him into my "office." Then it wasn't a joke anymore. I have been there for two years. Now I am going to the basement to a redone janitor's room. There are no windows, but it is more presentable.

When we found part-timers housed in "bull pen" offices, it usually was because that was the best institutions could do.

Crowded conditions for everyone were very evident, for example, at Loyola University in Chicago, where space was at a premium. Even so, the Water Tower campus had managed to create a faculty lounge from a former faculty dining room. This important facility was used by part-timers for work and social contact.

Most institutions try, and some try very hard, to support part-time faculty. For example, at Cuyahoga Community College, each campus has an assistant dean for the evening/weekend division. The assistant dean provides a general office for part-time faculty, with mail boxes, telephones, secretarial services, and photocopying, test-scoring, and other equipment and supplies. However, part-timers must turn in their requests for the materials and services a week in advance. Nevertheless, these offices are staffed from 7 A.M. to 11 P.M. We found Cuyahoga's lengthy service hours unusual; more frequently, part-timers teaching in the evening arrive at their campuses after all offices are closed.

Some institutions, generally those with fewer part-time faculty, are able to provide a reasonable level of support services. Part-timers at DePauw University, for example, praised the support services they receive. DePauw University provides support services to part-time faculty on an equal basis with the full-time faculty. By university policy, everyone who teaches is entitled to an office, desk, chair, phone, and filing cabinets. All departments give part-timers access to a faculty computer room or personal computers in their offices, clerical support, and shared office space.

However, resources for support are scarce and part-timers are usually at the bottom of the pecking order. As part of the University of California (UC) system, UC Davis receives support funding on a formula basis. The formula is based on tenure-track faculty at a fixed rate per faculty member. Support for part-timers must come from the funds allocated by the system to the institution for its tenure-track faculty. As a result, at the time of our visit, departments with large numbers of part-timers had more difficulty providing adequate space and services to full- and part-time faculty alike. One union leader commented that the contract provision of "reasonable access" to support services would be a high-priority issue in the next round of negotiations.

Evaluation of Part-Time Faculty

Evaluation policies and practices regarding part-time faculty range from giving department chairs full discretion to well-established institutional requirements for evaluation. While evaluation methodologies may vary widely within and between institutions, the bottom line for part-time faculty is that poor teachers are not rehired. The department chairs we interviewed were clear and unequivocal in agreeing that they know, regardless of evaluation methodologies, when part-time faculty members do not teach well. Decisions to reappoint—or not reappoint—depend heavily upon the individual department chairs.

Formal Versus Informal Methods

When teaching is not evaluated or monitored systematically, the institution does not develop an adequate base of information about its part-time faculty. Those institutions most interested in the quality of instruction not only require standardized student evaluation forms of all faculty on a regular basis but also arrange for classroom visitation and direct observation by senior faculty. Feedback is systematically gathered by department chairs and/or deans and is made available to each part-timer. Where weaknesses are identified, part-timers are counseled and offered resources to help improve their teaching. In the best cases, some kind of mentoring relationship with an experienced faculty member is provided. In addition, several of our site institutions have evaluation systems that are integrated with orientation and development programs. This is a tight method of gathering feedback on teaching quality, and it contrasts sharply with practices at institutions that do not require regular evaluation.

Several of our site institutions have college- or university-wide evaluation procedures that serve as examples of the variety of evaluation techniques in use. At Cuyahoga Community College, each part-time faculty member is visited in the classroom and evaluated by students in his or her first quarter of employment and once a year thereafter. At Hamline University, student evaluations and an annual report from department chairs to the dean of the college are required, but an informal system of student feedback also operates. Chairs told us, "We hear about it." In the School of Extended Education at Saint Mary's College, the chairs visit classes at off-campus locations and prepare narrative evaluations in addition to relying on the regular student evaluations. A student representative elected by each class serves as a liaison between the class and the chair and is quick to let the chairperson know about problems in the class. As discussed earlier, American University requires an annual review and evaluation of its part-time faculty, which is used as the basis for decisions about merit salary adjustments and promotions.

In contrast to the more uniform college- or universitywide practices described above, some site institutions have strictly informal evaluation procedures based on longstanding beliefs about collegiality. At one liberal arts college, the probationary and part-time faculty must administer student evaluations every semester, but they are not required to show them to anyone. According to policy, department chairs do not see the results of a review unless the faculty member gives it to them. Chairs have learned to get information by conducting peer evaluations and maintaining an open door to students. We think that part-time faculty, who frequently begin college-level teaching with no prior experience, need and benefit from more formal and comprehensive approaches to evaluating their teaching performance.

Impact of Collective Bargaining

At one of our site institutions, the collective bargaining contract stipulates that informal evaluations will occur solely for the purposes of professional development or to trigger a recommendation for a formal evaluation. The contract states that evaluations cannot be used in making a reappointment decision; instead, the institution must have evidence of negligence or incompetence. This negotiated system has its roots in a failure to perform evaluations before the contract and in the union's belief that evaluations are punitive.

My experience is that evaluations are used punitively.
[They are] used when they feel they have a problem.

> In this atmosphere, our people want no part of them.
>
> The union's position is to protect our members.

At this institution reappointment is automatic if the course is available, prior performance of the part-time faculty member notwithstanding.

In contrast, evaluations at several of our site institutions have become more regularized because of collective bargaining contracts. For example, the California State University system contract requires that previous evaluations of part-time faculty receive "careful consideration" in decisions regarding reappointment (Article 12.7). It also specifies what constitutes an evaluation of part-time faculty. For part-timers appointed for two or more semesters, the evaluation shall include "student evaluations of teaching performance for those with teaching duties, evaluations by appropriate administrators and/or department chair, and an opportunity for peer input from the department or equivalent unit" (*Agreement, July 1, 1987–June 30, 1991,* 1987, Article 15.21, p. 34; *Agreement, July 1, 1991–June 30, 1993,* 1991, Article 15.21, p. 39).

The phrase "careful consideration" and other contractual provisions have received close scrutiny by arbitrators. Arbitration decisions have led to certain entitlements for part-timers in reappointments. These arbitration awards based on contract provisions may appear on the surface to benefit part-time faculty, but they can have very negative effects. For example, within the California State University system, an important entitlement arising from an arbitration decision is the requirement that part-timers who have had an annual appointment in the previous year and are now being reappointed, be reappointed at the same or a greater time base. The arbitration award discussed in the section on salary (California Faculty Association and California State University, 1990) provides for automatic merit salary adjustments after the equivalent of one year of full-time teaching and if the part-timer requests it. These two arbitration awards taken together have resulted in far closer scrutiny of teaching performance and evaluation data prior to making decisions about reappointment. As one dean commented:

> All courses are evaluated, and all evaluations go to the
> chair. We have an annual review of part-time faculty.

> People will be less gentle now. . . . [Part-time faculty]
> will be priced right out of the market. I told my chairs
> to produce a written evaluation record with reasons
> for step increases.

San Jose State University, a member of the California State
University system, has required formal evaluations for many years
because of concern over teaching quality. This established policy
now serves it well in making decisions within the framework of
the union contract and recent arbitration awards. As one chair described it:

> We look very seriously at the evaluations. If the eval-
> uations are not *above* the department means, we don't
> hire back. . . . The evaluation of teaching is the *same*
> for temporary faculty and for tenure-track and tenured
> faculty. Criteria and expectations are the same.

Another chair commented:

> As for evaluation, we use the university's required
> form. The department also has its own evaluation
> during the fourth week of the semester. We type all the
> comments students make. Then the undergraduate
> and graduate coordinators for the subspecialty area
> discuss *each* comment with the part-timers. Then we
> give [students] the questionnaire again at the end of
> the semester. We do this for the new part-timers in the
> first semester of teaching and for part-timers teaching
> new courses. It adds up to three [student] evaluations
> and a peer review. We do the same thing for proba-
> tionary faculty.

Impact of Capricious, Informal Evaluation Practices

Part-time faculty benefit when evaluation procedures are clearly
defined and consistently administered. Evaluations are particularly
effective when they are linked to instructional development pro-

grams and provide direct feedback to the faculty member. On the other hand, when evaluation procedures are informal and left to individual chairs, inconsistency of practice can result. One of our site institutions had no college policy for the evaluation of continuing part-timers at the time of our visit. With no policy in place, some chairs used the same form developed for tenure-track faculty to document the performance of part-timers as a justification for merit salary increases. As one chair described his use of the form:

> I review these people [continuing part-timers] the same way I review the full-timers. I use the same form. [They are] reviewed in all categories. The administration only sends out the form for the tenured or tenure-track [faculty]. I copy it and use it for the part-time faculty.

Other chairs took a different view:

> We are a small department, and we communicate a lot. Formal evaluation is *not* required. I did one when we had a department review, but I now do it informally. [I have] regular contact on a daily basis. We know what goes on in everyone's classes from the students. . . . Evaluation is not part of the merit salary process for part-time faculty. [We] do this for the tenure-track people. The process of salary increases and reappoint[ment]s of part-time faculty is something I am not familiar with. They get an across-the-board increase. It makes it a lot easier for the chair.

The end result of this informal and inconsistently administered evaluation practice could be seen in the salaries of the continuing part-timers. We found several cases of salary differentials among part-timers with similar employment histories and teaching performance that appeared to be explainable only in terms of who each person's department chair was and what he or she knew about the "politics" of evaluation. In group interviews, part-timers were startled and angry as they discovered their differences in salary.

In sum, we believe that evaluation should be based on well-articulated criteria that part-timers understand. Capricious evaluation effectively denies part-timers fair opportunities to improve and develop. Part-timers should be informed about the criteria upon which they will be evaluated before they begin to teach.

Job Security and Seniority

Job security for part-time faculty is a major concern of part-timers and of institutions. In our site visits, part-time faculty vulnerability was highlighted over and over again. While we encountered many part-time faculty who had enjoyed long and mutually productive associations with their institutions, we are painfully aware that these stable situations arose from institutional goodwill, not from part-time faculty rights to job security. We discuss both aspects of part-time status here: the vulnerability and the stability.

Vulnerability

Part-timers' vulnerability was illustrated recently within the California State University system. During the 1990–91 academic year, the CSU system employed a total of 21,290 faculty, of whom 8,834 were part-time. During the 1991–92 academic year, the numbers shrank to a total of 17,732 faculty, of whom 5,912 were part-timers. While some of the loss of part-timers was attributable to the removal of 1,099 graduate assistants from the faculty bargaining unit, most of the shrinkage was due to budget reductions (Office of the Chancellor, California State University, 1990, 1991).

At one of the institutions we visited, a retrenchment of part-time faculty was occurring. Facing the need to cut faculty after tightening all other areas, the institution was letting part-timers go. Interviews with department chairs focused on how they had made the cuts within their departments and told their part-timers. One chair stood out for his sensitivity and consistency in handling a very difficult situation:

> We are being cut eleven sections next year because we
> are anticipating a smaller freshman class, and we lost

several more sections because of the budget. . . . I sent
a note last fall to alert the part-time faculty *early*. I
said, "Things look bad for next year. Start planning."
Then I went in person. I said, "It looks right now like
we can't use you or we can only give you one course."
I did it in terms of seniority. I kept those who had been
here the longest. I said, "If things change, I will let
you know." At the administrative level, my impression is there is less sensitivity. Part-time faculty are
viewed as a commodity, not as people. I see them as
younger versions of myself. They are trying to survive
while getting a degree.

Stability

Institutions believe that part-timers are a temporary and flexible
work force. They also believe that they have a responsibility to long-
term and valued part-timers. We call this latter phenomenon the
"all but tenured." One individual told us:

I was a senior at _____ . They told me, "If you go get
your master's (this was 1949), we'll hire you." So I did.
I taught for three years and got pregnant. I had four
children in five years. I didn't teach for thirteen years.
Then I went back and redid the master's and took all
the course work for the Ph.D. I was called back in
1966. I taught part-time and built up to full-time. I hit
the six-year maximum. Then they created the [name
of faculty member] position. If I don't teach during
the interim semester, I teach [a total of] five classes a
year, which is part-time. It is an arrangement between
the chair and the provost. I have nothing in writing.
I have the assurance of two dead people that _____
will always need me.

The chair verified her story:

When I came in 1965, she was already teaching here.
She was a _____ graduate who lived in the neighbor-

hood. She filled in. I called her and asked her if she could teach a course. Then she got a master's degree. It sort of perpetuated itself. No one knows why. I have been to at least three farewell parties for _____ . We were going to have all tenure-track people. Then there would be an emergency, and she would be called back. Then the department got embarrassed. [We] went all out to get her tenure. The college refused because of the lack of a Ph.D. We've given up trying on tenure. We now contrive her schedule to keep her part-time. She is the department's *most productive* classroom teacher.

The "all but tenured" concept is fairly pervasive among long-term part-timers at our site institutions.

Seniority Provisions

At our site institutions, we rarely found seniority provisions for part-time faculty, and those we did find were the result of collective bargaining. The three examples described here follow a continuum from vulnerability to increasing stability in the negotiated provisions.

According to the *Memorandum of Understanding* (1991), in the University of California system part-timers can be reappointed on a year-by-year basis for up to six consecutive years. During their sixth consecutive year at one campus, the department must determine whether or not there is a continuing need for the part-timer and then review his or her performance. After the sixth year, when part-timers are reappointed, they must be offered a three-year contract. The three-year contract is binding (*Memorandum of Understanding*, 1991, Article VII, pp. 6–8).

At the time of our UC Davis site visit, this contract provision was causing a "weeding out" by department chairs who were afraid to make a three-year commitment. As one chair stated:

We regret putting people into three-year contracts. The process whereby one gets rid of these people is complicated. [You] get entangled in legal hassles.

> Once the three-year people get into the cycle, it is very
> hard to get them out of it.

Part-timers whom we interviewed were well aware that they were
vulnerable and that they had no right to continuing employment
based on the quality of their work:

> I'm paid $40,000 a year to work twenty hours a week.
> The problem is that after eighteen quarters [six years]
> the $40,000 will go away.

The newest collective bargaining contract for the California
State University system, in contrast, stipulates that "temporary faculty unit employees employed during the 1990–91 academic year
and possessing six or more years of service on that campus since
July 1, 1983, *shall be* [italics added] offered a two-year, temporary
contract commencing with academic year 1991–1992" (*Agreement,
1991–1993*, 1991, Article 12.18, p. 29). The unconditional language
of this contract provides more stability for part-timers.

At the time of our site visit, the collective bargaining contract
at York University allowed for part-time faculty to carry their seniority from one department to another. As discussed earlier, the
concept of "applicable prior experience" and formulas for calculat-
ing seniority had, to a large degree, taken decisions regarding who
would teach what course out of the hands of department chairs. The
history of negotiations and the power of the union at this campus
had created a situation in which decisions regarding part-time faculty employment made in academic departments were sometimes
overturned or eroded at higher levels through the settlement of
grievances.

For the most part, department chairs, unhappy with the por-
table seniority concept at York University, were skilled at finding
ways around it. As one chair said:

> We need a balance of forces to be worked out between
> job security and academic decision making. Part-time
> faculty have a right to protection, but departments
> have rights too. There is a balance between avoiding

department abuse and protecting department prerogatives to render academic judgments. The union is attempting to control the curriculum through grievances.

While job security provisions in collective bargaining contracts provide some measure of stability, even these provisions have unintended and unexpected side effects and can work to the detriment of part-time faculty. Most institutions want to protect themselves against claims of seniority rights or de facto tenure and thus have formal or informal policies to limit part-timers' abilities to make such claims. These policies or practices control the time base of appointments, the number of consecutive appointments that are possible, or both.

Some balance needs to be struck between the institution's interest in flexibility and part-timers' need for security. Long service and high performance count for little at present, and part-timers think this is unfair. We agree, and we believe that far more can be done to help part-timers feel that they are investing their time, skill, and energy wisely. They should be able to achieve some measure of security if they perform well and demonstrate their loyalty and commitment over a sufficient period of time.

Conclusion

The policies under which part-time faculty work vary as much as the apparent sensitivity of institutions to part-timers' situations. But that is not the whole story. The institutions in our study were being buffeted externally and internally by rapid changes at the time of our site visits. Expanding or contracting enrollments, different levels of student preparation, changing student interests, diminishing financial resources, and policy constraints of many kinds were making it difficult to continue the informal, collegial practices with which most of the institutions were familiar. At one end of the continuum, some institutions were making no changes in their traditional approaches to employing "temporary" faculty and showed little interest in doing so. At the other end, some had developed comprehensive employment policies for part-timers either through collective bargaining agreements or because the central administration foresaw the consequences of failing to "do the right thing." Institutions that were unable to control enrollments, funding, and staffing in a strategic way were having the most difficulty establishing clear policies.

Whatever the institutional position, the key to effective implementation was the department chair. We found concerned chairs who were working quietly and effectively to improve the situation of part-timers in their departments. We also found unconcerned chairs who saw part-timers as temporary buffers against fiscal stringency. In the departments of the latter, part-time faculty were more vulnerable to exploitation. In those of the former, part-timers seemed more satisfied and fulfilled. In both situations, however, we saw tensions and frustrations among the part-timers and between part- and full-time faculty. This apparent tension led us to examine another variable: the integration of part-timers into the academic community, the subject of our next chapter.

In concluding this chapter, we want to reemphasize three key building blocks of fairness and equity in the treatment of part-time faculty. Institutions must assert control and develop sound policies and practices for employment, they must recognize the pivotal role of department chairs in implementing whatever policies are developed, and they must focus on treating part-timers as an integral part of their faculty rather than as peripheral and temporary workers.

Eight

Participation in
the Academic Community

One institution we visited has a strong culture that appears to value and support the contributions of part-time faculty in ways we did not see at most schools. The president of this institution began his career there twenty-seven years earlier as a part-timer. During our interview with him, he estimated that perhaps 40 percent of all full-time faculty at this institution had themselves begun as part-timers, and he noted that one member of the board of trustees taught occasionally as a part-timer.

As we began talking with him about our project, he interjected that he would prefer that we not identify people as "part-time" faculty, which he considers an unfortunate label. He argued, "They are simply members of our faculty, and we ought to treat them as such." He had several specific recommendations about how to treat them:

- Treat them like visible people. They are our faculty. The label "part-time" only tells how much they teach.
- Select them with the same degree of care used in selecting full-time faculty.
- Help them learn about our institution, our students, and how to teach.

179

- Don't be afraid to try new things. Focus on custo-
  mer satisfaction. Satisfied employees will result in
  satisfied customers.

Many of the same issues are at the heart of a Vermont State Colleges
(1990) task force report that argues for increasing the "connected-
ness" of part-time faculty to campus life.

Part-timers have very strong feelings about whether they are
or are not "connected" to or "integrated" into campus life. For the
most part, they feel powerless, alienated, invisible, and second class.
They view their work as principally serving to protect the interests
and security of the full-time faculty, and they are able to cite many
instances of neglect.

As Jackofsky, Salter, and Peters (1986) point out, however,
increasing portions of the work force are choosing to work part-
time. For everyone who chooses to leave, the institution loses its
investment in a potentially valuable employee and becomes less
competitive because it cannot hold good people. A department
chairperson at one research university noted,

> We are eating our seed corn by degrading this part of
> our profession.

Integration is our word for the effort institutions make to
ensure that their part-time faculty members are successful, valued,
and supported in what they do. In this chapter we look at the
integration of part-timers through orientation programs, relationships with tenure-track faculty, opportunities to participate in governance, and professional development programs. We also examine
the attitudes we found in departments because these attitudes color
the climate within which part-timers work and directly affect their
morale. We found some particularly successful efforts to integrate
part-time faculty and present several case reports of these efforts at
the end of this chapter.

Orientation

An important factor in integrating part-time faculty into the academic community is the way in which they are "socialized" to their

roles, their jobs, and the institution's culture. Campuses in our study differed greatly in their commitment to the socialization process and in the extensiveness of their orientation programs for part-time faculty. This variation was evident in the time and effort devoted to orienting part-time faculty to the campus and the emphasis each campus placed on important aspects of orientation: acculturation to the campus mission, learning about department curricula and pedagogy, and "how-to" handbooks describing services available and how to find and use them.

Approaches to the orientation of part-timers range from a sink-or-swim philosophy of benign neglect to elaborate programs that link orientation to instructional development and evaluation. Institutions that appoint relatively few new part-time faculty each year tend to have an informal approach to orientation, leaving it up to department chairs. Some have handbooks to assist with orientation, and some do not. Even those that have handbooks may not keep them current. At one institution we were told:

> We have a part-time faculty handbook, but it is badly
> in need of updating.

At the other extreme, some institutions publish annually updated handbooks and guidelines for part-time faculty. At some of our site institutions, part-time faculty are welcomed to the campus by the central administration, either through a university orientation program or by correspondence.

Usually, however, orientation is left up to department chairs, and some of them do it extremely well. One department chair, who has nine full-time faculty members teaching 60 percent of the department's sections and twenty-nine part-timers teaching 40 percent of them, is an excellent example of how chair leadership can make the best of a difficult situation.

> In math we are committed to working with adjuncts.
> All our faculty are involved in classroom observation.
> Our adjuncts are also involved in course and curriculum development. We have our first fall faculty
> meeting in the evening so the adjuncts can attend. We

> have a buddy system that pairs up full-time faculty
> with part-time faculty. We have meetings of course
> instructors to monitor student progress. We made
> space for adjuncts in the math lab. We have a full-time
> instructor serve as a course coordinator to keep every-
> one on the same schedule more or less. When I hire an
> adjunct, I make sure [he or she gets] oriented to the
> syllabus, the schedule for the semester, the tests we use,
> and so on. . ʃ . We coordinate the pace and sequence
> of instruction among sections. We involve adjuncts in
> curriculum change, invite them to workshops and fac-
> ulty meetings. I am here from 5 to 7 P.M. with the
> coffeepot on. I encourage the adjuncts to come in and
> talk.

This chair combines orientation with instructional development
and evaluation in a setting in which full- and part-time faculty
members work together to achieve common goals. Establishing
cooperative relations with full-time departmental colleagues is
widely viewed by part-timers as perhaps the most valuable aspect of
their orientation. (See also Williams, 1985, p. 107.)

Institutional Policies and Practices Regarding Orientation

Orientation is mandatory for part-time faculty at some institutions,
optional at others, and not available at still others. Its focus, content, and operational details vary greatly from institution to
institution.

One comprehensive university, for example, dictates that all
new part-time faculty attend an on-campus orientation session. It
provides dinner for those who attend and requires those who are
unable to attend to visit the campus at the university's expense on
a mutually agreeable date.

One of the community colleges we visited allows each of its
campuses to develop its own orientation policy. At two campuses,
all new part-time faculty are required to attend an orientation session, as are all part-time faculty who have not attended one for at
least three years. Everyone who attends is paid $15 per hour during

the session. A third campus makes orientation optional, allowing each department to handle its own.

At small private institutions, where many of the part-time faculty continue to teach over a period of years, there are only a few new people to orient in any given year. For these institutions, it makes more sense to simply let the department chairs handle whatever orientation may be needed on an individual basis; in general, there are no formal policies or programs at these institutions.

Common Orientation Practices Among Institutions

Although there is great individual variation in what institutions actually do to orient part-time faculty, several components are commonly included among the more developed programs. Four components in particular stand out:

1. A *social event* of some kind is held.
2. A *general introduction* to the institution is conducted, usually in the form of handbooks and other written information.
3. An *overview of effective teaching* is provided.
4. *Linkages to departmental faculty* are established, which sometimes means the assignment of a full-time faculty mentor.

Several institutions in our study host part-time faculty at a dinner event as part of their orientation program. This involves key administrators (to elevate the symbolic importance of the event) as well as full-time faculty who serve as liaisons, mentors, or helpful contacts when questions arise.

A number of institutions have prepared handbooks for part-time faculty. Although some of these go beyond basic information, most are very straightforward reference manuals detailing operational information (the institution's history, library hours, emergency procedures, personnel policies, grading policies, exam policies, and so forth) that any faculty member would need. Orientation sessions often include a general review of the handbook content—or at least a presentation that covers basic information about the institution and its policies. One community college has developed a videotape that it plays twice a day during the first week of every quarter so that part-timers can see it at their convenience.

The institutions in our study commonly want to provide part-timers with some orientation to effective teaching practices. Some institutions distribute a short, commercially published paperback on effective instruction entitled *A Handbook for Adjunct and Part-Time Faculty* (Greive, 1990). Others conduct more elaborate programs. Seminar or roundtable formats are sometimes used to stimulate discussions among part and full-time faculty, and outside speakers are occasionally brought in.

Several of our site institutions use senior faculty mentors as an integral part of orientation. Of at least equal importance to the obvious impact of orientation on part-time faculty members is the impact on full-time faculty. They, too, benefit by getting acquainted with their part-time colleagues. Several full-time faculty members who served as mentors for part-timers were enthusiastic about their contacts with new people:

> [This] is a good program, and the relationships between mentor and [part-timer] usually continue beyond the end of the program.

A full-time faculty mentor took special pleasure in the relationships with his protégés:

> We went for coffee after the classes in which visits took place. I got more out of this than the [part-timers] did, I think!

Involving full-time faculty with part-timers in a teaching-oriented professional relationship helps form bonds that both groups seem to enjoy and appreciate. It is clearly a step in the direction of effective integration of part-time faculty.

All the foregoing components of orientation are illustrated in the examples of professional development programs at the end of this chapter. Readers might also appreciate Boice's (1992, pp. 227–229) recommendations concerning orientation of new faculty.

Participation in Departments

Part-timers are members of departments first and institutions second. Within their departments there is normally a well-established tradition for how they are viewed and how much they will participate in the affairs of those departments. In our interviews with part-timers and chairs, both groups had much to say about this aspect of "integration."

Part-timers' participation in the activities of a department depends on an array of factors: the culture of the department, the attitudes of the tenured faculty, the leadership of the department chair, and the degree of participation sought by the part-timers. Some part-time faculty members enjoy and seek opportunities to be involved in departments; others prefer to limit their time on campus to teaching their assigned classes. Many have other jobs or responsibilities that preclude involvement.

Department Culture

Throughout our study we found part-time faculty who are more than satisfied with their situation: they are enthusiastic about their decision to teach part-time and about the way in which the institution treats them. We cannot find any particular correlation between this upbeat attitude and the kind of department or institution where it occurs. One private liberal arts institution seems to be particularly supportive of its part-timers. But we found similar support at universities, comprehensive colleges, and community colleges (just as we found strongly negative attitudes at all types of institutions). Perhaps the key variable is to be found in departmental culture. Departments that care deeply about education, about teaching and learning, seem to foster an atmosphere in which faculty members talk with each other about these issues. Such departments also appear to involve part-timers in their talk and seem open to what the part-timers have to say. People sense that they can have an effect on what happens—not just in their own isolated classroom but on the entire program of the department. For part-timers, this environment produces feelings of efficacy and of satisfaction. There is far less faculty bifurcation in these participatory departments and far more focus on how everyone contributes to achieving the academic outcomes department members consider important. Even where there is universal dissatisfaction with pay, benefits, and other tangible support, part-timers who feel as if they are part of a collaborative faculty seem to have more positive feelings about their work and about their involvement with the institution.

For example, performing and studio arts departments tend to integrate part-time faculty very smoothly. They bond within their subdisciplines, and tenure status seems not to be an impediment to good relations among all the faculty. At one college, for example, the chair reported:

> The arts faculty treat . . . adjuncts as full members of the departmental family. They do shows together, eat together, and so forth. Their schedules are arranged to bring them together more frequently. . . . We try to do a lot together and have a department party every semester.

The attitude of the department chair makes an enormous difference in the degree to which part-timers are integrated. The divergent perceptions of two chairs at the same institution illustrate this point. According to the first chair:

> The department gave them the right to vote, and they can come to meetings. . . . Most of the senior faculty respect the part-time faculty. One or two are insensitive. But there is the inevitable institutional humiliation in the lack of benefits and the attitudes of some faculty. I talk to the part-time faculty all the time, and they come to the meetings.

From the second chair's comments, one senses a far more passive and disengaged view, with the resulting obvious differences for the part-timers themselves:

> The part-time faculty haven't been integrated and haven't felt integrated. My predecessor never thought

of inviting them to meetings. Now they get invited to
meetings but can't vote. It's rare that they come. A lot
of our part-time faculty are commuters. . . . It's the
attitude of the faculty and the nature of the part-timers
themselves. They are not counting on [this institu-
tion] as their primary job. The part-time locals are
more integrated at the university level. They go to
university events but don't come to department events.

Another chair we interviewed takes considerable pains to establish a colleague relationship with part-timers. In his words:

I have people teaching part-time who make $80,000 on
the outside. They are important to me, and I need to
retain their interest. So I don't talk down to them or
play the authority with them. I treat them as peers.

This department chair was reported by part-timers in his department
to make considerable efforts to stay in touch, usually by telephone
and at least several times during the course of a semester.

Private liberal arts colleges tend to accept part-timers. Several
department chairs at these institutions reported that their departments are highly egalitarian and inclusive in their decision making.
Part-timers are considered full colleagues and act as such.

At one private liberal arts college, the issue of participation
in governance is generally seen as a matter of common sense with
respect to the institution's character, to its obligation to its students,
and ultimately to its survival:

We don't want anyone in the classroom who isn't a
part of [this institution]. Students pay a lot of money
to come here. They have a right to a committed faculty. . . . There are *no* second-class faculty. [Part-time
faculty] participate in department meetings. They are
fully integrated into the life of the department.

The part-time faculty at this institution obviously feel that they are
part of the system:

> Good things go on [here] in the departments. . . . I get
> to vote in the department. I fully participate.

For the most part, we found that department chairs and
deans expressed concern about integration throughout our interviews. We were more impressed with the little things some departments or colleges did than with any grand designs. For example,
one dean at a small liberal arts college with limited financial resources interviews all candidates for employment and tries to make
them feel welcome, includes part-timers in receptions honoring faculty achievements, and gives them small gifts such as school shoe-
laces. Occasionally he finds funds for a stipend for a special project
to show his appreciation.

Providing a time and place for informal contact and communication seems to be an important priority at several institutions
in our study. Two community colleges we visited have established
a central location where part-timers have access to office services,
telephones, mailboxes, and a coffeepot. Part-timers gravitate to
these social centers and find others with whom to talk and associate.

Many departments invite their part-timers to social events,
faculty meetings, retreats, workshops, and other formal and informal events. Often, they schedule these events to accommodate part-
timers, who may not always be available during normal working
hours. At one community college, part-timers are invited to attend
commencement and are reported to participate enthusiastically. At
another, part-timers are invited to a "teacher work day," when
classes are canceled and faculty meet to discuss teaching and learning issues.

Most of the institutions in our study are at least cognizant of
the need for symbolic recognition. Although not all individuals
were equally attentive to providing such recognition in tangible
ways, they nonetheless talked with us about ideas their institutions
were pursuing at the time of our interviews, as reflected in these
comments by a math department chairperson:

> We should make . . . gestures of appreciation. We
> should welcome them to the institution, write a per-
> sonal thank-you to each adjunct at the end of the term,

invite them to ceremonial and festive occasions like
awards convocations and commencement. I review all
the student evaluation forms, and put stick-on notes
beside especially complimentary comments with a
congratulatory note of my own.

In sum, we found many good-faith efforts to make part-
timers comfortable, to help integrate them into departmental affairs, and to provide them with some appropriate voice in decision
making. However, we must temper this generalization with a
healthy dose of caution. A survey by Williams (1985, p. 101) showed
that only about one-third of part-time faculty at innovative community colleges reported any level of involvement in departmental
affairs. At almost all our site institutions, most part-timers said they
did not feel that their role was sufficiently respected or that they
were provided with an adequate opportunity for involvement. In
some cases, they had good reason to feel excluded and relegated to
marginal status because administrators and full-time faculty seemed
disinclined to recognize the need for integration of part-timers.
Part-timers, as noted earlier, can be acutely sensitive to the informal
and symbolic aspects of their treatment and can readily tell when
they are being patronized or marginalized, as represented in this
vivid account from a part-timer at a comprehensive university:

Once when I was bored in a meeting, I started to write
a story about the English department as a plantation.
I am the nanny. They trust me with the silver, the
babies, and so on. The department chair is the massa
and the part-time faculty are the field hands.

Status in the Academic Community

Over and over again, whether they were aspiring academics or specialists teaching one night a week, part-timers we interviewed alluded to their status in a bifurcated academic career system. They
expressed anger and frustration about their perceived exclusion from
collegial activities and career opportunities and the lack of appreciation for their efforts. They often felt deep anger and anxiety about

the temporary and indefinite nature of their employment. Many expressed clear annoyance over the lack of consultation and involvement in decisions affecting them, an annoyance that was only exacerbated by their feeling that protesting or demanding a more substantive role would jeopardize their continued employment.

Part-timers were frequently bewildered by the apparently low regard in which they were held by their erstwhile colleagues who would say one thing—"Adjuncts are as good as the full-time faculty" or "You can't imagine a more talented and conscientious and able group of people than the adjuncts in the writing program"—and behave quite differently. In some cases, the contrast between an individual's earned status in another primary job or role and the same person's ascribed status as a part-timer produced jarring disparities:

> The nonexistence [as a part-timer] is insulting. I was
> a hotshot graduate student and went from that to being unknown.

The perception that one has been relegated to second-class status may stem from the initial contact with the institution, a point eloquently made by one part-timer:

> We need to be treated as respected colleagues. The
> medieval caste system that is now in place needs to be
> fixed. . . . We need . . . to feel as if we are part of the
> team. We want to be treated as equals. Don't ask us to
> teach the day before—as if we were the last choice and
> there is no one better to do it!

Perceptions of status acquired at the initial point of contact do not readily disappear. No matter how long some part-timers have taught and no matter how well they do it, they continue to sense that they can only earn limited visibility and recognition.

> Very little communication exists with full-time faculty, so [they] don't really know what [we] do. . . .

> Part-timers have to earn their reputation and status
> inch by inch.

Earning status, even "inch by inch," can be difficult or impossible
when one is fighting deeply rooted bias. Part-timers sense that their
status does not entitle them to full participation. According to one
part-timer,

> There is a lot of territorial protection and jealousy on
> the part of full-time faculty. I proposed two new phi-
> losophy courses that are badly needed and got shot
> down on the basis of things other than merit, as I see
> it. There is a heavy sense that you don't threaten some-
> one's territory.

Symbols are extremely important signals of status. Part-
timers are very sensitive to symbolic segregation:

> Part-time faculty mail slots in the humanities depart-
> ment were set up as a separate class, positioned below
> those for the full-time faculty. After we protested, they
> are now alphabetically integrated. It is little things
> like this and like having our names left out of depart-
> ment or university publications [that] make us aware
> of status inferiority.

Reiterating this sense of perceived status discrimination, part-timers
we interviewed at almost all institutions mentioned, usually with
a wry comment, that the courses they taught always had "Staff"
listed as the instructor—even when the same part-timer had been
teaching the same course for several years. Kekke (1983) also recognized part-timers' widespread concern about the practice of listing
anonymous instructors in her paper "Who's Mr. Staff: Cheap Labor
or Valued Resource?"

The focus of greatest concern is the department chair, who
may be guilty of sins of commission:

> The chair makes incredibly condescending remarks.

Just as easily, however, the chair may be guilty of sins of omission:

> I do quality work and feel it is appreciated. I get good
> feedback via informal channels, but I do not get any
> at all from the department chair or the dean.

Tucker (1984, p. 372) emphasizes how important the chair's
role is in "enhancing the prestige of part-time faculty" through
"shepherding and introducing" them at official events. He further
recommends that full-time faculty assume this role, too.

In reality, however, some full-time faculty are perceived as
unsympathetic, at best:

> I feel that full-time faculty would rather have more
> full-time faculty than adjuncts. . . . I don't have any
> way to get my ideas for change into the full-time fac-
> ulty decision stream.

In sum, a lack of integration and participation in a department produces feelings of being a second-class citizen, of being
outside the mainstream and isolated or invisible:

> In [my department] they have a reception for . . . new
> teachers. I'm teaching for the first time and I was in-
> vited. But [as a part-timer], I was not mentioned. No
> one thought of introducing me as a new person. I'm
> a nonperson. I'm teaching the course better than it's
> ever been taught, but I'm a nonperson.

The part-timers we interviewed expressed the same feelings over and
over again:

> We are treated as second-class citizens by the [full-
> time] faculty. It's the manner in which you are dealt
> with. You are not asked to go to lunch or seminars.
> No one says hi. The department is research-oriented.
> The faculty are not interested in teaching; [they] have
> nothing in common with the lecturers who like teach-

ing. . . . Their attitude is that the senior faculty are it. They see status as fitting a rigid hierarchy. All they . . . have is their status. [There is a] sheer pomposity about it.

Actions of senior faculty reinforce these feelings:

The Xerox machine is right by my office. I've seen faculty outside the department for two years who don't even talk to me. I don't go to faculty meetings or parties. There is no reason for me to go. I did go. I talked to people. But you feel like two left feet. You feel you are taking their time. You don't have connections, don't know the gossip. No one spends time with you. You are a face that comes and goes. "Oh, you are *only* part-time." I worked my butt off last year and was here as much as the full-time [faculty].

The Devaluation of Teaching

Bifurcation along full- and part-time faculty lines appears to be symptomatic of a fundamental and insidious trend that has major consequences for the academic profession. The profession seems to be increasingly split into teaching and research tracks. At research and comprehensive universities, the emphasis on research leads full-time faculty to withdraw from undergraduate teaching to the extent that they can. The remaining vacuum must be filled, and it is filled substantially with part-time or temporary faculty or graduate teaching assistants. At the institutions we visited, use of part-timers is heaviest in lower-division courses, while the tenure-track faculty concentrate on upper-division and graduate courses with release time for research.

Part-time faculty who are aspiring academics are excruciatingly conscious of the devaluation of teaching. They feel that they are treated as if they are "less educated and don't publish" and understand that "if you are going to be serious about [advancing in] your profession, you've got to move on." The full-time faculty, they reported, see part-timers as "worker bees," "housekeepers," or "migrant workers" and relegate them to a servile status. Some point out that they know teaching part-time is hurting their chances to find full-time positions.

The devaluation of teaching was particularly troubling to part-time faculty at one of our site institutions. They felt strongly that a major shift in the institution's value system from teaching to research had affected the way they were viewed and treated. Essentially, the new signals from the top levels of the administration to the departments were that research should be encouraged and rewarded. Effective teaching, long a part of the institution's value system, seemed no longer to be honored. This shift was seen as having devalued the role part-time faculty play. Acutely sensitive to the nuances of this perceived change, the part-timers we interviewed showed flashes of anger and resentment. One said,

> The university is for research and not for teaching. Teaching is of secondary importance. Therefore, part-time faculty [who carry a heavy load of undergraduate teaching] are seen as second-class citizens.

The part-timers also reported that it was "hard to convince the administration that part-timers are a resource, not a liability."

Part-timers at this institution echoed the perception that they were excluded rather than included. The theme of invisibility arose in comments by several of them during our interviews:

> You are anonymous and your status is ambiguous. This produces an identity crisis for most part-time faculty. We are perceived as itinerant teachers.

If symbolic gestures are important in setting the tone of an institution and in making its values explicit, then it is easy to see why part-timers at this institution felt that their teaching was not viewed as important work:

> I've been nominated for a teaching award, but it [is] not available to part-time faculty.

At best, these comments indicate a lack of appreciation for the talents and contributions of part-time faculty, as well as a lack of courtesy to people who ought to be seen as colleagues. At worst, if it is true that institutions and their faculties have so lost touch with (and so devalue) the obligation to teach well and to honor good teaching, then perhaps the perceptions of the part-timers should serve as an early warning that critics of the academy have a point.

Several part-timers who taught writing at another site institution echoed the view that teaching was becoming less valued within the academic profession. They discussed in some detail the general decline in level of preparation of entering undergraduate students and noted that the education of these progressively less qualified students was being increasingly entrusted to part-timers, particularly in areas of such fundamental importance as writing and math. Yet just as part-time faculty were taking on increasing teaching loads, the institution seemed (to these part-timers) to be placing increased emphasis on the research credentials required for full-time positions. Ironically, the more skilled and effective the part-timers became at educating undergraduates, the less likely they were to meet the criteria for entry to the tenure-track faculty. "We are," said one, "where the college gets the biggest bang for its buck; they are getting a lot more mileage out of us" than out of the full-timers who are more interested in teaching literature than in teaching freshman composition.

For several in the group, it was clear that teaching remedial and introductory writing was an attractive professional opportunity, one that they would have liked to consider a career. But the rules of the game obviously favored the creation of full-time positions exclusively for people with research interests and training. The part-timers lamented,

> We have written novels, published poetry, run theaters
> and performing arts centers. . . . We've done creative
> work of high quality.

They also noted their records of effective teaching, some for a considerable number of years. Still, they realized that their institution would not provide them with any opportunity to fulfill their aspirations for a tenure-track position because they lacked a research background.

Intelligent, dedicated teachers who are committed to doing a job that badly needs doing become disillusioned and alienated by the almost total absence of rewards and security. They see rather clearly that their work is dishonored in the eyes of those with higher status, and the consequences for their morale and self-respect are serious.

Participation in Governance

Part-time faculty have no role in institutional governance at most institutions. Although part-timers are sometimes allowed to attend department meetings, committee meetings, or meetings of campus-wide faculty governance bodies, their voting rights are typically restricted. Within departments, voting rights vary considerably, from full to pro rata to restricted to none. In some cases, senior faculty are well aware that part-time faculty could outvote them in key department decisions. Where part-time faculty do participate, it is voluntary, and the time they spend is not compensated except under very unusual circumstances.

Perceived lack of status is exacerbated by part-timers' inability to participate in discussions affecting their lives. Even at institutions where there are large numbers of part-time faculty, they typically have no formal avenues through which they can present their collective concerns, no matter how serious the situation. At one institution, for example, the stark prospect of a substantial reduction in force without consultation caused fear and uncertainty for part-timers, who anticipated a very direct impact of this on their lives.

There is obvious frustration among part-timers who feel deprived of a voice. For some, there is a sense that each part-timer is an individual and not part of a larger group:

> I would like to [have meetings] to discuss the conditions under which we are working so we could press for our group needs. Keeping us apart doesn't let us

> know what is going on. I'm not adversarial, just cur-
> ious. For example, [why are appointment] contracts
> with part-timers arranged in different ways in differ-
> ent departments?

Some part-timers have strong motives to be more engaged in the life
of the institution, and they have ideas about how to strengthen their
role as constructive participants:

> We could improve things if we could be more in-
> volved. Why not, for example, have a departmental
> seminar in which . . . each [part-time and full-time
> faculty member] would talk about [his or her] creative
> and research interests? We could also talk about how
> to deal with beginning students, learning-disabled
> students, and so on.

For others, there is no clear sense of their status or right to participate in decisions:

> Part-timers don't have a vote in faculty meetings. How
> we fit in the university is ambiguous. But the depart-
> ment doesn't know my place either. Am I a member
> of the faculty or not? Where do we fit in? What is our
> role?

Disenfranchisement of a large portion of the profession—or
even perceived disenfranchisement—allows potential conflict to
build because people do not have a viable way of dealing with their
concerns.

When senior faculty are involved in governance, a schism
sometimes develops in their reactions to part-time faculty. On the
one hand, in the department, they support long-term part-timers
with whom they have had lengthy associations and whose work
they know. On the other hand, in governance bodies, senior faculty
may view part-timers as second-class citizens who represent a covert
attack on the tenure system, and these seniors may take positions
antithetical to the interests of part-time faculty. At one campus we

visited, the tenured faculty supported the long-term part-timers in their departments but stated in the faculty personnel committee that they did not approve of part-time faculty appointments in general and did not want part-timers' employment rights expanded. Institutional governance bodies almost always exclusively represent the perspectives and interests of the tenure-track faculty.

Where part-timers are denied meaningful participation in their departments and institutions, feelings about integration can run high. At several institutions, we found an undercurrent of views not unlike that in rebellious states or territories of confederated nations. Part-timers in some departments have a great deal of potential power and could, if motivated, take control through sheer numbers. As one chair put it:

> As a group they could outvote the full-time faculty,
> but they have no voting rights.

Sometimes perceptive and radicalized part-timers are almost viscerally aware of their potential:

> They fear us. We vote for the department chairs. We swing the election. We control the vote. We're underpaid, yet we pay the bills. Everyone knows this and it frightens them.

In contrast to the normal practice of limiting involvement, two of our site institutions had taken important steps to provide for and encourage part-time faculty participation in governance at the time of our site visits. At Loyola University of Chicago, the vice president for academic affairs had appointed a part-time faculty committee to advise him directly on matters of concern to them. This committee has contributed to changes in the salary schedule, the creation of new part-time faculty ranks of senior lecturer and adjunct professor, a handbook for part-time faculty, and professional development opportunities for part-timers. The committee also functions as a peer review committee for part-time faculty promotions. Using procedures similar to those used for tenure-track faculty, the committee conducts substantive reviews of each candidate's qualifications and makes recommendations to the vice president. This committee is widely viewed as a forum where part-time faculty concerns get a hearing.

At the University of California at Davis, an independent governance organization known as the Academic Federation serves as an advisory group to the administration. The Academic Federation has been instrumental in obtaining teaching awards, professional development leaves, and nonvoting membership or representation on senate committees. It is composed of lecturers, extension specialists, librarians, professional researchers, and others. Its membership closely parallels that of Unit 18, which represents the part-timers in collective bargaining. The leadership of the Academic Federation and the local chapter of Unit 18 is highly motivated and has a strong commitment to improving conditions for part-time faculty. Exposure to the class system in which part-timers find themselves, and experience in trying to change attitudes and policies of the institution, sometimes generate powerful feelings. "Working here has radically politicized me," reported one leader of the federation.

Institutionwide committees have also been established elsewhere. However, they have had only one or two part-time representatives, or their charge goes well beyond issues specific to part-time faculty, or they have been, in effect, ad hoc committees, without a standing mandate.

Professional Development Opportunities

We use the term *professional development* to refer to a wide array of efforts to invest in the expansion of people's capabilities. Although considerable literature exists on faculty development for full-time faculty, very little has been published on how to help part-time faculty become more productive. Studies by Craig (1988), the ERIC Clearinghouse for Junior Colleges (1986), and Williams (1985) provide useful overviews of common practice. Hoerner (1987), Leitzel (1990), and Pedras (1985) offer conceptual schemes that might prove helpful in designing professional development opportunities for part-time faculty. Boice (1992) provides an especially helpful overview of practices that work well in the development of new faculty members.

Professional development represents an investment in people's future capabilities. Making such an investment in part-time faculty is a measure of how integral they are to the institution's programs and an incentive for both the institution and the individual to continue their relationship. For these reasons, we think professional development of part-timers is one aspect of integration that needs to be more fully considered. We have found a far more positive climate for professional development than is implied in Biles and Tuckman's (1986) brief treatment of this issue.

Some of our site institutions have a clear sense that part-timers are often long-term employees who can return, many times over, a small investment in expanding their capabilities. These institutions tend to have well-established policies and programs for professional development. Other site institutions had no formal policy for part-time faculty development at the time of our visits, and whatever opportunities were provided existed at the department level. Still other institutions routinely provide part-timers with access to services and opportunities without making such access a formal requirement or establishing any definite policy regarding it. Available programs are purely optional and voluntary. Finally, some institutions provide financial incentives to promote involvement.

A few of the institutions we visited have mandatory faculty development activities. At several community colleges, professional development activities are required either through collective bargaining contract provisions or through state funding formulas. Some institutions have voluntarily initiated their own faculty development policies. For example, at Cuyahoga Community College, every part-time faculty member is required to attend one faculty development exercise per quarter of employment. The requirement is specified in the appointment contract each part-timer receives when he or she is offered employment. The operative language in this contract reads: "The . . . assignment include(s) responsibility for participating in at least one College-sponsored development activity during the quarter."

Funding for Professional Development Programs

During our site visits, we found that both internal and external sources of funding were being used for part-time faculty development. In some cases, department chairs or faculty development directors had discretionary control over travel funds and other perquisites that could be used to facilitate various activities such as attending conferences and undertaking research or course development. Paid professional development leaves were available to part-time faculty at one of the research universities in our study. As one chief academic officer said, "I would like to have a modest competitive reward program—not an entitlement" to give part-timers incentives to develop themselves.

The private liberal arts colleges almost uniformly reported that part-timers qualified for small travel and research grants from a professional development fund. Sometimes these funds were competitive, and sometimes they were available in fixed amounts. Usually these funds did not distinguish between full-time and part-time status. (From $1,000 for every three years of employment to $550 in any given year was the range of support available at two institutions with specific policies at the time of our site visits.)

Most planned development programs at our site institutions did not have financial incentives for participation. For example, some of the programs promised nothing more than a free meal and a day or an evening of camaraderie, along with whatever intrinsic value might be gained from attending. (We should point out that even these modest programs were well-attended and appreciated by the part-timers.)

In several cases, faculty development programs were being externally funded. Loyola University, for example, had a Sears Foundation grant to help develop better teaching among part-timers. Although the program was strictly voluntary, those who were selected to attend received stipends of $250 for a total of three sessions. The Fund for the Improvement of Postsecondary Education provided a grant for Cuyahoga Community College to pilot its "EPIC" program, described below. The New Jersey Institute for Collegiate Teaching and Learning seeded the orientation and development programs at Raritan Valley Community College in that state. All external funding was temporary; each of the grants was clearly of the "seed money" variety, and the institutions were all grappling with how to continue these programs after expiration of the temporary external funding.

In the case of Florida community colleges, state law had required that each institution set aside 3 percent of its annual budget for facility and staff development—some of which was spent on part-timers at the institutions we visited. Although budget constraints led to the suspension of the set-aside requirement in 1991, some institutions in Florida continue to fund faculty development activities nevertheless (Rosenberger-Webb, 1991).

The Role of the Department Chair in Professional Development

Many of our site institutions had no formal faculty development program for part-timers; and as with so many aspects of employment, it was left up to departments to provide whatever orientation and development they felt appropriate. Vice presidents and other campus leaders told us repeatedly that the key player in the orientation, development, integration, and evaluation of part-time faculty is the department chairperson. They saw the professional development of part-time faculty as linked directly to the attitudes and training of department chairs. Training of chairs, we found, is conducted systematically at some institutions, erratically at others, and not at all in too many cases. At one unionized institution, central administration staff members pointed out that confrontations with part-time faculty and grievances occur because department chairs are not trained and do not understand or like the constraints of the collective bargaining contract. At this institution, education of chairs is viewed as critical to avoiding problems.

Several other institutions we visited were planning to extend their usual department chair training to include more material and discussion about part-time faculty. At one comprehensive public college, the goal of the central administration is to create a "safety net for adjuncts" by building an infrastructure of concerned and trained department chairs. Although department chairs at this institution currently get release time and a contractually mandated stipend to work with adjuncts, they are reported to be unevenly interested and involved.

Where department chairs are committed to the integration

and development of their part-time faculty, the immediate payoff in terms of morale is clear:

> The department is great. [It holds] useful meetings throughout the year. Meetings are planned to give us content. This is real professional development. There is a coordinator here who really helps. This university is different from others. . . . It is sensitive about use of adjuncts. . . . The department has an adjunct newsletter. Kudos are given out to those who publish. . . . We have freedom to teach the course the way we want and get to choose textbooks for the second semester. We aren't regulated.

A well-arranged faculty development program at one of the community colleges has also helped one individual who teaches part-time at the college in his full-time job:

> I feel I'm a part of the department. I'm listened to, and we talk a lot about how to be better teachers. It has been a good experience professionally and personally, and it has helped me in my work as a full-time English teacher in high school.

Types of Professional Development

We found three major types of professional development activities for part-timers at our site institutions: special development programs for doctoral candidates; grants for travel, research, or other professional development activities; and planned programs for developing and improving teaching effectiveness.

Although many ABD doctoral students are now teaching part-time in a variety of institutions, supporting activities and the mentoring of a senior faculty member are rarely available to them. Several of our site institutions offer part-time faculty positions (as opposed to traditional teaching assistantships) to doctoral students at the dissertation stage. They help these students develop teaching skills and gain experience before entering a teaching career. At Loyola University, a teaching fellows program operates on a competitive basis. Doctoral students at Loyola or other institutions in the area who are currently working on a dissertation are eligible to apply for a fellowship. They design courses in their area of expertise and may teach two courses a semester, for which they receive a stipend. The teaching fellows work together in seminars to develop teaching skills and strategies. Some departments support the teaching fellows program with well-developed mentor programs involving senior faculty. Macalester College has a similar program that funds minority doctoral candidates from nearby universities.

Occasionally, institutions provide support for part-timers to engage in research and other professional activities, such as travel to conferences. Several of our site institutions made some funds available to all part-timers for these purposes; others had competitive grant programs. At UC Davis, the Academic Federation described earlier has been instrumental in making paid professional development leaves available to part-time faculty on a competitive basis. During 1990 five full-time, quarter-long leaves with pay were awarded to part-timers. These leaves sometimes also included equipment and travel funds.

Professional development activities often focus on improving teaching. The best programs, in our view, involve continuing efforts to help part-time faculty shape their teaching to the needs and goals of the institution and focus on achieving the learning outcomes considered important. By "continuing" we mean efforts that usually begin during the part-timers' orientation and extend well into their first year of teaching or beyond. On occasion (as at Cuyahoga), these programs provide some kind of ongoing exposure to and reinforcement of good teaching practice. The underlying assumption of such programs is that part-time faculty know the subject matter of what they are teaching but need assistance with pedagogy and the interrelationships between their courses and the rest of the department's curriculum. At Loyola, for example, videotapes about teaching in the multicultural classroom and about how to make effective class assignments form the basis for workshops offered to part-timers.

A dean at a private university reported that he had encouraged co-teaching arrangements in which a part-timer shares a course with a full-time faculty member. With the right "chemistry" between them, this experiment has proved highly successful and is an effective way of bringing a part-timer into much closer contact with a senior faculty member and the substance of the department's courses. A successful mentoring program that we think can be adapted for part-timers is described in Boice (1992, pp. 107–192).

Examples of Comprehensive
Professional Development Programs

During our site visits, we encountered several orientation and professional development programs aimed at promoting excellence in teaching. Those described in this section are illustrative examples of the many excellent programs we found within departments, schools, and institutions.

The Orientation Program at Eastern Kentucky

Eastern Kentucky University conducts one of the more comprehensive orientations to effective teaching that we encountered. Considerable attention is paid to symbolism. The orientation is held at the university conference center to ensure that it has the feel of "a first-class affair with all the amenities." This helps the part-time faculty feel welcome and important. Moreover, to short-circuit any potentially bruising encounters with the bureaucracy, campus parking stickers are distributed to those in attendance.

In addition to providing part-timers with handout material and general information, the orientation program includes a workshop session on the institution's expectations regarding the overall conduct of courses, standards for students (including grade distribution), the kinds of work students are required to do, and procedures for evaluating and grading student work. One of the goals of the orientation is to establish a climate of expectations that is reasonably consistent across courses. The discussion on evaluation of student performance stresses the "formative" side: how feedback can be used to help students learn and develop. The orientation program attempts to broaden the frame of reference well beyond the conventional summative, grade-giving process.

After the formal presentations, a discussion is arranged on the characteristics of good teaching. Participants reflect on the "best" teachers to whom they have been exposed, and the group discusses what these teachers did that gave their teaching more impact than that of others. The participants usually find that certain common characteristics are repeated over and over—for example, the best teachers are sensitive to student interests and backgrounds, they encourage discussion and critical thinking, they are open and supportive in class. In addition to discussing good teaching as a general topic, participants are provided with a copy of the faculty evaluation form. They review what the university is looking for and what kinds of evidence students will be providing when they evaluate each part-time faculty member at the end of each term.

After a break for dinner, each part-time faculty participant is paired with a full-time faculty mentor who teaches the same course (or one very closely related.) The mentor and part-timer talk about course-related issues, review the syllabus and text, and share views on what works with students. The mentor then remains in contact with the part-timer throughout the semester through consultation, mutual classroom visitation, and any other mutually agreeable kind of association.

The Eastern Kentucky University approach to orientation is very favorably perceived by administrators and part-time faculty alike:

> The orientation really pays off. We get our standards and expectations across to them . . . especially to those teaching off-campus, who would otherwise have difficulty understanding our grade distribution expectations, and so forth.

One of the part-timers we interviewed reported spontaneously:

> I went through the university orientation for part-time faculty. It was a good session. We talked with full-time faculty about what they do in their classes. We discussed being an effective teacher from the point of view of experience.

The Adjunct Faculty Institute at Burlington County College

Burlington County College is located in Pemberton, New Jersey, in a rural area between the suburbs of Philadelphia and two major military bases, McGuire Air Force Base and Fort Dix. For roughly twenty years, the college has hired its part-time faculty ("adjuncts") with the stipulation that they attend the Adjunct Faculty Institute. The institute was originally established to train part-timers in the college's approach to teaching and learning, but the program has changed over the years to accommodate shifting needs of the college.

At the time of our site visit, adjuncts were paid $20 per institute session, or a total of $100, to attend. In addition to direct compensation, adjuncts were eligible for status as "senior adjunct faculty" if they attended the institute and satisfactorily completed two semesters of teaching. (Senior adjunct faculty members were paid an additional $34 per semester hour.) About thirty adjuncts attend the institute sessions each semester.

The five institute sessions are held on three successive Saturdays every semester. The five sessions are structured to combine orientation to the campus with programs about effective teaching.

The first session focuses on the college catalogue. The history and philosophy of the college are reviewed, and an overview of the curriculum is provided. Grading and attendance policies are outlined and grade sheets and forms are reviewed. Faculty are given copies of the student evaluation form, and items are reviewed so that they will be aware of the criteria being used to evaluate them. Discussion is encouraged.

The topic of the second session is the adjunct faculty handbook and the operational aspects of the college. A tour of the facilities is conducted, including visits to the library, recreation facilities, testing center, video communications center, and security office (where faculty are issued parking decals and receive a briefing on emergency procedures). The third session focuses on the student body and its characteristics. Part-timers are oriented to the availability of services on campus to which they might refer students who need help.

The fourth session is devoted to Joseph Katz's "master teaching" model, disseminated by the New Jersey Institute for Collegiate Teaching and Learning (NJICTL). At the beginning of the session, adjunct faculty members are asked to write what they remember about the "best" teacher they ever had. These qualities are then shared in discussion. A videotape on master teaching prepared by the NJICTL is shown, followed by a presentation on Burlington County College's own master teacher program. Research on good teaching is reviewed.

The final (fifth) session deals with sensitivity to underrepresented students. A minority faculty member is the presenter for this session. A video is used to show examples of how comments by faculty may call attention to a student's race, ethnicity, or other qualities in ways that distract or cause offense. Adjunct faculty have given this session especially positive reviews. (Among other things, it is a good session for demonstrating the use of videotapes in instruction. Other methods and different styles of presentation are arranged during the earlier sessions to expose adjunct faculty to a variety of approaches to teaching.)

Participants in the program are invited to a dinner on the Friday following the last session. During a predinner discussion period, full-time faculty selected from the same disciplines as those of the participants relate the themes from the Adjunct Faculty Institute sessions to curricular and teaching issues in their respective fields. An outside speaker is often part of the dinner program.

The total direct cost of the institute program to Burlington County College is between $10,000 and $12,000 a year. Administrators at the college report very positive feedback from part-timers who attend. This feedback has led the administration to conclude that the return on this investment can be found in better teaching, morale, and continuity among the adjunct faculty.

EPIC at Cuyahoga Community College

Perhaps the most thoroughly "packaged" orientation and development program for part-time faculty among all the institutions we visited is the Educators Peer Instructional Consulting (EPIC) program at Cuyahoga Community College. EPIC originated as the result of a series of concerns and complaints about the reality of teaching at off-campus sites. Deans were receiving complaints that some part-timers did not know how to teach, sometimes did not appear for class, seemed uninformed about college rules, and were unavailable for consultation with students.

The initial response to these concerns about quality was a small-scale pilot experiment that paired part-timers with full-time faculty mentors. In its present, more comprehensive form, EPIC was first funded by the Fund for the Improvement of Postsecondary Education in 1987. The program, as funded by FIPSE, matches new part-time faculty with full-time faculty mentors. Overall, Cuyahoga Community College hires about 150 new part-time faculty members each year and averages 137 part-time faculty in EPIC mentoring relationships a year. About 65 full-time faculty members serve as mentors each term. Each full-time faculty mentor receives the equivalent of one-half credit hour release time from teaching to work with his or her protégé. Mentors are allowed to "bank" their release time credit until they obtain a sufficient amount, such as a one-course equivalent, to use for their own professional development purposes.

The mentor meets with the part-time faculty member three times in the first quarter. Both keep a journal record of their meetings. They go through the part-time faculty handbook together, review the syllabus for the course(s) the part-timer will teach, review teaching strategies, identify the resources available at the college, and discuss the kinds of students likely to enroll in the course(s). The mentor also visits classes to observe the protégé, and the protégé visits the mentor's classes. The relationship often continues beyond the obligatory three meetings, and some pairs continue to visit each other's classes after the formal relationship is ended. The mentor's classroom observations are never used in formal evaluation. (Classroom visits for purposes of performance evaluation are carried out by a division head or assigned to a full-time faculty member not serving as a mentor.)

Data from the journals kept by the participants indicate "enormous" success, according to the program's director. In addition, division heads see very positive outcomes from the program. For example, they now report receiving virtually no complaints about part-time faculty teaching off-campus, previously a major problem for division heads. The full-time faculty apparently find their relationships with the part-timers rewarding, although it is occasionally difficult to ensure that they complete the classroom visits and the journal entries.

One of the participants in Cuyahoga's EPIC program summarized her feelings this way:

> I don't feel second class here. The full-time faculty and evening deans are doing it right. I was in the EPIC mentor program. This was a very good experience. The mentor helped me fit into the college. I was invited to dinners, to workshops, and to Saturday morning [faculty development] programs. We are made to feel like we are a part of the college and that we are welcome here.

The School of Extended Education at Saint Mary's College

The School of Extended Education at Saint Mary's emphasizes the development of good teachers as early as the initial screening of applicants. This private college just outside San Francisco offers a broad array of degree programs to adults at many off-campus sites spanning the greater Bay Area. Its degree programs are highly innovative, serving a commuting, nontraditional student population. To teach these programs, the School of Extended Education intentionally uses part-time faculty almost exclusively. According to the school's *Data Book* (Saint Mary's College, 1989), there were 127 part-timers teaching all over the Bay Area in the fall of 1989, 6 of whom were "core faculty" (see below). (There were only fifteen tenure-track faculty in the School.)

Because of the nontraditional nature of the student population and the degree programs, the preponderance of the School's part-time faculty is viewed as the strength underlying the academic programs offered. Since the quality of these off-campus degree programs is critical to the success of the School of Extended Education, it has developed an elaborate protocol for ensuring that its part-time faculty meet standards of qualification and performance at every stage. Quality control is maintained through an extensive screening and orientation process and careful monitoring of part-timers' teaching performance.

Part-time faculty positions are advertised through a central personnel office. An initial screening of candidates is conducted by department chairs, who narrow the pool to those who seem best qualified. Ten to twelve of those in the pool are invited to participate in a standardized assessment process conducted by faculty members. The process, which takes three to four hours, is designed to identify each candidate's strengths and weaknesses as a potential teacher. The student body is principally composed of adults preparing in professional fields, and the school emphasizes Socratic teaching methods, so it is able to define in fairly explicit terms what kinds of skills and performance are required of faculty members.

In the first stage of the assessment, candidates are interviewed and given sample student work to critique. The way in which they communicate during the critique is observed. They are also put through a "fishbowl" experience, in which their group interaction skills are observed. The team of faculty evaluators then cuts the pool to six or seven candidates and continues with a more detailed assessment of the survivors. These candidates are invited to submit further data on their academic backgrounds and prior experience.

Candidates who remain in the pool at this stage are invited to an orientation for new faculty. They are assigned to teach one class and are observed by the department chair. If they perform satisfactorily, they are retained in the pool of those eligible for part-time teaching assignments. The names and qualifications of those in the pool are recorded in a computer data base from which instructors for extended education courses are drawn.

At this point, candidates for part-time positions are considered "probationary." If they are invited to teach, they are observed by another faculty member at their first class session and go through a formative evaluation with their department chair. Expectations for the course and for teaching performance are discussed during this evaluation session.

Multiple sources of data are used to evaluate teaching performance during a part-time faculty member's first course. Other faculty members and the department chair visit classes to observe. Some of the faculty who perform the observations are "core faculty"—part-timers chosen for their content expertise, teaching experience, and practical experience. They provide expertise on curricular matters and assist other faculty members in their development. Students provide evaluations on standard forms, and data are gathered on student performance. Each class elects a student representative, who assists in evaluation and serves as a direct communication link between the department chair and the students in the class. Student representatives receive a small stipend to attend meetings to discuss teaching performance. A postcourse conference is held with the chair of the department to review results.

After this intensive evaluation of the part-timers' first course, those receiving satisfactory evaluations are no longer considered "probationary". Although they are subject to further evaluation, they no longer receive intensive, course-long attention. Class observations, for example, are conducted less frequently.

Department chairs and part-time faculty at Saint Mary's are uniformly enthusiastic about this selection and evaluation process. Part-time faculty have a sense of confidence that they were chosen as a result of a rigorous screening process:

> The preemployment training program is superb. I was introduced to a philosophy, mission, vision. It was extraordinary. I was very supported.

Department chairs exercise their own discretion in following up after the first teaching experience. Some capitalize on their intensive work with the part-timers by holding dinners. Others appoint faculty mentors to assist part-timers. Funds are made available for travel and other developmental activities. Part-timers are also appointed to committees and some standing governance bodies. In sum, the School of Extended Education recognizes the extent to which it depends on part-timers to uphold its reputation, and it invests substantially in selecting, developing, and supporting part-timers who can perform effectively as part of an instructional team.

Conclusion

Why is integration of part-time faculty taken seriously at some institutions and not at others? We readily noticed the difference and found a culture of inclusion to be quite apparent at some schools. Just as obviously, integration did not seem to be a priority everywhere. We were able to recognize four differences that determined whether institutions in our study had or had not made significant progress in integrating part-time faculty.

First, attitudes of central administrators and department chairs help to establish a climate in which part-timers feel that their efforts are appreciated and that they have access to decision makers. Second, conducting a formal orientation for part-timers is both a symbolic and a practical gesture that helps them find their way into and around the institution with a sense that they are welcomed. Third, inviting part-timers to participate in department and institution decision making gives them a feeling that they have a stake in both program and personal development. Finally, encouraging and supporting professional development activities expands part-timers' capacities and improves their morale and commitment.

Comprehensive professional development programs have now been established at a number of institutions, and we have highlighted four successful ones in this chapter. We think they represent the best examples of long-term integration of part-time faculty because they do more than simply orient part-timers to the physical and bureaucratic map of the institution. Such programs focus on teaching, and they involve part-timers with key faculty members and administrators over a period of time. In our experience, the relationships established during mentoring and similar collaborative activities have a noticeable effect on both full- and part-time faculty at our site institutions and help focus attention on how instruction can be effective. This outcome goes beyond the mere inclusion of part-timers and helps establish a stronger teaching culture among all faculty. It shows how institutions can become stronger and more effective *because* they integrate part-time faculty in the core activities of teaching and learning.

Part Two

Enhancing Education Through the Use of Part-Time Faculty

In Part One, we discussed current institutional practices with regard to part-time faculty in three basic areas: the use of part-time faculty, the policies and practices under which they are employed, and the degree to which they are integrated into and valued by their institutions. We begin Part Two with a discussion of trends that are now affecting the academic profession. These trends were identified repeatedly in various contexts during the course of our interviews. In Chapter Nine, we explain how the trends will affect the use of part-timers and outline the challenges that must be faced. In Chapters Ten, Eleven, and Twelve, we recommend specific changes to meet the challenges, based on what we learned at the colleges and universities in our study.

We believe that our forty-three recommended practices will promote better performance and more satisfied part-time faculty who are integral members of the faculty as a whole. We have made these recommended practices simple, straightforward, and practical in the hope that every reader will find them useful. All our recommendations derive from a single underlying theme: it is time to recognize how important part-time faculty members have become and to develop constructive policies and practices to help them be effective in the jobs they have been and will be hired to do. These policies and practices should have as their focus the acceptance and integration of part-timers as members of the faculty and the elimination of their status as second-class citizens.

First, we recommend that institutions plan and manage their use of part-time faculty in pursuit of their educational goals instead of allowing fiscal conditions to dictate staffing decisions (Chapter Ten). Second, we recommend that institutions be fair to part-timers. Institutions need to be clear about their policies, provide information to part-timers and department administrators, and reduce exploitation and arbitrary treatment (Chapter Eleven). Finally, we make recommendations that will help part-timers grow and develop professionally (Chapter Twelve).

In Chapter Thirteen, the concluding chapter, we point out that institutions can strengthen themselves through use of part-time faculty. Although we acknowledge that there are powerful barriers to change, we also identify pressures that will force institutions to strengthen their curricula and find new faculty. Part-timers offer institutions ways to achieve these objectives because they provide a flexible human resource *and* because they add talent, skill, and breadth to the faculty. Investment in part-time faculty is a way to strengthen institutions, and the experiences of people at the institutions we visited demonstrate how to do it.

Nine

Recognizing
the Changing Context
of Academic Employment

Burton Clark (1987), in his close examination of academic life, identifies "conditions that . . . deprofessionalize the professoriate" (p. 273). Shifting clienteles, bureaucratization of colleges and universities, and the demise of strong professional cultures are the chief threats Clark sees.

The stresses and pressures for change in the academic profession were also evident in our study. Our look at the profession was from a different angle than that of Clark. He examined perspectives of faculty in the tenure stream; we examined the perspectives of part-time faculty, who operate from outside the inner—and privileged—strata of the profession. Either perspective, it seems, leads the observer to serious doubts about the vitality of assumptions, standards, and customs that have largely governed academic employment since the widespread adoption of the American Association of University Professors' Statement on Academic Freedom and Tenure in 1940. Very simply, we question whether academic employment still functions well under the single model of tenure-track appointments.

The academic world, just like the worlds of business and government, faces profoundly shifting forces requiring major changes and adaptations. Adaptation, to us, means broadened academic career options. The traditional tenure system, having enjoyed fifty

217

years of wide acceptance, may be putting a stranglehold on institutions' ability to accommodate pressure for change. It may also be responsible for the emergence of a faculty that is divided into two sectors.

This stranglehold has been somewhat alleviated by the use of part-time (and other nontenure-track) faculty, who are now responsible for a substantial amount of instruction at most institutions, particularly at the lower-division undergraduate level. Yet part-timers are treated as if they were marginal temporary employees, hired to meet contingencies of enrollment and exigencies of finance. They have few rights and are often denied the elemental support they need to do their jobs effectively. The use of an increasing number of part-time and other nontenure-track appointments now appears to be symptomatic of overriding pressures to provide more options for academic careers so that individuals and institutions may be freer to negotiate mutually satisfactory terms of employment.

In this chapter, we identify the conditions that we believe prompt consideration of new career options and more flexible employment alternatives within the academic profession. We first examine changes in the academic profession as foreseen by administrators and faculty at our site institutions. Second, we look at external factors that administrators at these institutions told us were putting increased pressure on them to use part-time faculty. Third, we outline changes in the balance of personal and professional lives that have increasingly strained the ability of individual faculty to commit to a lockstep tenure-track career. Fourth, we describe changes in the clientele of higher education, what they are being educated for, and how outcomes are being measured. These changes have, in turn, pressed institutions to broaden their definitions of what kinds of faculty they need. Fifth, we explore the balance between teaching and research, clearly a matter of concern and tension. Specifically, there is great concern about whether research-oriented faculty are teaching enough or teaching well. All of these changes lead us to question the viability of the existing tenure system.

Part-time faculty are now an integral part of the academic profession, and their importance is growing. How institutions choose to deal with them and how institutions support their work will have a major impact on the quality of education in the years ahead. In the chapters that follow, we recommend certain practices that we think will help make part-time employment a more acceptable and more productive career alternative—for institutions as well as for individuals—and thereby set the conditions in which all faculty can work together to improve education.

Trends in the Academic Profession

We asked administrators at all of our site institutions what changes they foresaw in the academic profession and why. We were particularly interested in how they saw those trends influencing future employment of part-time faculty. Almost all trends, they responded, point toward increased use of nontenure-track faculty, especially part-time faculty. The administrators based this conclusion on the following major trends: anticipated changes in retirement patterns, shortages of faculty in selected fields, and surpluses of aspiring academics in certain fields.

Anticipated Changes in Retirement Patterns

By whatever means one calculates, a very large proportion of faculty members currently working will retire within the next two decades. To paraphrase Keynes, in the long run, everyone retires. Conflicting factors may serve to moderate the rates at which some faculty will elect to retire, but there is no doubt that most academic institutions will have very large gaps to fill in the coming twenty years. Bowen and Sosa (1989) graphically project that the declining availability of qualified people, sharply increasing retirement rates, and increases in the college-age population will jointly create serious shortages in certain arts and sciences disciplines.

Projecting retirement rates is generally problematic because some factors encourage earlier retirement, while others encourage longer careers. For example, early retirement incentive programs were originally introduced to control projected salary and benefit costs and to help create new opportunities for younger faculty. It now appears that accelerated retirement rates could jeopardize the availability of enough full-time faculty in certain fields.

On the other hand, uncapping the mandatory retirement age for faculty may encourage those who choose to continue to teach to do so for as long as they wish. Two recent national surveys of faculty by the Carnegie Foundation for the Advancement of Teaching (1989) and the National Center for Education Statistics (1989, 1990) suggest that more faculty (17 to 20 percent) plan to continue working after age seventy than plan to retire before age sixty (8 to 14 percent).

Shortages of Faculty in Selected Fields

High-technology fields, among others, are caught in a double bind. On the one hand, there is a relative scarcity of people qualified for faculty positions, and the competition for this scarce talent comes chiefly from business, industry, and government. On the other hand, very well qualified people who work in such fields as engineering and management are sometimes attracted to part-time teaching without regard to pay. They have intrinsic motives to teach, and they bring with them knowledge of state-of-the-art practices in their fields.

In other words, the very people who choose not to take full-time academic positions may be prime candidates for part-time teaching in precisely those fields experiencing the worst shortages. Some of the best potential academics undoubtedly choose the richer financial rewards offered to them in other lines of work, and academic institutions may be able to tap their talents only by hiring them to teach part-time.

Surpluses of Aspiring Academics in Certain Fields

At virtually every one of our site institutions, we were told that a surplus of people with advanced degrees in the humanities made it easier to staff lower-level courses (especially in English) with part-time faculty. These surpluses are not uniform across all fields, but the availability of many people to teach at the college level is clear.

There is no doubt that "professing" is a strongly appealing and highly satisfying job. Data from the national surveys of faculty confirm this (CFAT, 1989; NCES, 1989, 1990). Part-time faculty "by choice or desire" may constitute a far larger potential pool than has previously been recognized. Even if one applies stringent standards of qualification to such a pool, it is a work force that institutions can and will tap to a greater extent in the future. It is a source of talent that needs to be more thoroughly investigated.

Changing External Conditions

Conditions that favor the use of nontenure-track positions seem to be intensifying and spreading. In our interviews administrators mentioned their concern about tenure ratios and their belief that, with no mandatory retirement, there will be too many tenured faculty in the fields that are overstaffed and underenrolled. Second, administrators are uncertain about how new patterns of student interest will evolve. The experience of the last twenty years has shown that enrollment has moved in cycles. When education and the social sciences were strong in the late 1960s, business and engineering were unpopular; more recently, business and engineering have experienced surges of enrollment that continue to strain existing resources. Enrollments in education, meanwhile, have begun to recover from low points in the 1980s. Third, administrators at our site institutions are concerned about fiscal constraints. The 1990–91 recession resulted in serious fiscal problems in a very large number of states, among them the so-called megastates of California, Florida, Texas, and New York. These pressures have forced institutions to economize—in some cases by substituting part-time or temporary faculty for full-time appointments. In this economic environment, the "market" for new students went flat or turned negative in at least some states. The widely observed "baby bust," although certainly a temporary phenomenon, hit institutions in some states at a very bad economic time.

College and university administrators at our site institutions indicated to us that these factors, as well as related manifestations peculiar to their own context, have caused them to become more conservative in their planning about the use of tenure-track appointments. Their planning horizons have shortened, in some cases to a semester-by-semester crisis orientation. This was especially visible at institutions we visited shortly before the beginning of the spring semester; in some cases, the state's fiscal condition was precarious enough to prevent any firm decisions about how many sections of some courses could be offered pending guidance on how much of the budget would be held back.

Under these circumstances, institutions frequently do not choose to place all of their faculty in tenure-track positions. Instead, the more fiscally conservative course is to rely on temporary or part-time positions. Tuckman and Pickerill (1988, p. 111) refer to this practice as "price-induced substitution" and observe that it is practiced without sufficient understanding of or preparation for its consequences. We project more use of both temporary and part-time appointments because institutions will continue to see part-time positions as the more conservative hedge they need against overcommitment of their scarce dollars.

Changing Life-Styles

Women and men who participated in our interviews expressed the need for more options than the traditional full-time, seven-year up-or-out ritual in their pursuit of academic careers. Changing marital (or domestic) patterns, changing family structures, and changing life-styles led many people we interviewed to recommend that institutions try to accommodate the pressures these changes have placed on individuals.

For example, we encountered a number of single parents (more often women than men) who had chosen nontenure-track positions to preserve the flexibility they needed to provide a stable family environment for their children. We encountered life-style dropouts who had chosen to leave the corporate fast track to pursue other interests, teaching among them. Some of those we interviewed simply needed more balance in their lives to recoup their enthusiasm and energy and were electing to work at a more controlled pace. Care-giving responsibilities—more often now shared by both men and women than in previous generations—and spousal commitments have led some individuals to reluctantly accept part-time positions that do not afford any more promise or security than semester-by-semester appointments. In sum, the lack of options in the academic profession has led to widespread alienation and despair among a talented generation of aspiring academics who struggle to combine marital and family roles with the demands of their careers.

As this redefinition of spousal, familial, and care-giving roles progresses—and it shows every sign of doing so among those we interviewed—there will be increasing pressure to provide career paths that accommodate personal as well as professional lives. Part-time positions with entrée to full career status are at the top of the list of changes many of those now teaching part-time want and need.

We believe that this interest in opportunities for part-time employment foreshadows major changes in the academic profession. The traditional segregation of academics into tenure and nontenure tracks and full- and part-time status probably cannot stand indefinitely against the social changes now under way. Many people with the qualifications, talent, and commitment to be outstanding college and university teachers would enter the profession if they did not have to meet the "all-or-nothing" commitment required of tenure-track faculty. There is room to experiment with new combinations of people and academic work that might yield incentives for talented individuals to spend part of their careers or part of their time teaching. In short, the academic career will need to accommodate increasingly legitimate life choices that involve less than full-time commitment to one work role to the exclusion of all else.

Changing Students, Changing Curricula

Pressures to improve the quality of undergraduate education and changes in the characteristics and preparation of students entering postsecondary education have generated incentives to hire faculty with more diverse skills. As institutions increasingly concentrate on teaching, learning, and the assessment of outcomes, they try to find ways to engage students individually and to provide an environment in which opportunities to learn are designed to accommodate widely varying styles and needs.

A substantial number of the part-time faculty members we interviewed have specifically elected to teach part-time because they do not wish to pursue the traditional faculty career, with its heavy emphasis on scholarship and publication. Because they take a primary interest in teaching undergraduates—even those who enter college with less than adequate preparation—part-timers often prove highly effective with adults returning to college, underprepared high school graduates, those from culturally different backgrounds, and students with learning problems.

Using Part-Timers for Student-Centered Teaching

At least two schools of thought exist among those we interviewed about whether part-time faculty are more effective than full-timers in working with students who need extra help and more individualized instruction. One school holds that part-timers are not available out of class and therefore cannot provide the degree of attention that these students require. The other school suggests that full-time faculty have little interest and little skill in working with such students, while part-timers with previous teaching experience are especially effective. It was noted more than once in our interviews that part-time faculty may put far more time and energy into a single course and into working with individual students than a full-time faculty member would. (Obviously, we must caution about overgeneralizing stereotyped behavior in any group, but impressions of people in decision-making roles shape the decisions they make, and it seems important to record what we heard and saw for that reason.)

There is far less ambiguity about the enthusiasm of part-time faculty for student-centered teaching. As a group, they profess to be far less discipline- or knowledge-centered than full-time faculty and far more interested in helping students learn, grow, and develop. In fact, many of the part-timers we interviewed expressed disappointment about the lack of a career path for teaching- and student-oriented faculty. They find working with students—in some cases, especially the less able and prepared—to be the most rewarding aspect of their work, and they acknowledge that the intrinsic satisfactions of close contact and involvement with students are what motivate them to teach. Almost universally, it was reported that part-time faculty with extensive backgrounds in business or professional practice are effective in working with adult students. These part-timers use their own practical experiences in illustrating points covered in class (with only rare overreliance on "war stories"), and they appear to be flexible and realistic in their relations with students in and out of class.

As the demand for quality in undergraduate instruction increases (as we think it will), as student preparation—or lack thereof—for college-level study makes it more challenging to produce results, and as characteristics of students continue to diversify, institutions will inevitably become more concerned with the teaching ability of their faculty. Where full-time faculty are either focused on research or overloaded with quasi-administrative duties, institutions will likely turn to part-time faculty (or other nontraditional appointees) who have a commitment to teaching.

We should caution that there is no reason to believe that research-oriented faculty members teach poorly or that faculty members committed to teaching do it well. That is another issue altogether. We merely wish to suggest that we foresee institutions providing desirable career options for faculty members who are committed to teaching and who devote their energies to teaching assignments.

Vocationalization of the Curriculum

Part-time faculty have certain obvious strengths in fields where professional practice and the development of skill are part of the curriculum. Part-timers often bring extensive and current experience to the courses they teach, and they can enrich their classes with their ability to be critical of conventional thought or practice and to encourage independent thinking. They can use real cases from their work to provide challenging material for students to analyze. We encountered some situations in which part-timers had developed sophisticated case studies and/or simulations based on actual problems encountered in professional practice.

Greater Focus on Learning Outcomes

The movement to assess outcomes of undergraduate education seems to presage a shift from an emphasis on presenting disciplinary knowledge to an emphasis on what students are learning. Instead of requiring mastery of a (sometimes) arbitrary body of facts and theories, there appears to be a growing consensus that teaching students how to think and how to construct ways of knowing is of paramount importance. Moreover, institutions have begun to assess the ability of students to examine and reconsider their own value systems.

This trend has an indeterminate effect on the use of part-time faculty. Clearly, it will require a far more intensive level of communication among faculty members and a far more participative method of developing curricula and assessing student learning (Study Group on the Conditions of Excellence in American Higher Education, 1984). On the other hand, the traditional focus of full-time faculty on disciplinary knowledge and on the competitive academic reward system seems to work against both collaborative curriculum development and the creation of more open, flexible, cooperative, risk-taking learning opportunities. Part-time faculty are not necessarily "better" at creating powerful alternatives to traditional learning modes. They are often vulnerable, inexperienced, and willing to adopt traditional—even stereotypical—teaching methods. However, at every institution we visited, some part-time faculty members showed remarkable creativity and independence in their approaches to teaching. Such individuals are typically those with extensive experience, either as teachers or as practicing professionals. They are not bound to the tenure system or the faculty reward structure. Instead, they bring a freshness and an unusual spirit of inquiry and experimentation to their teaching.

This dimension of part-timers' contributions is often not recognized or appreciated. It may not even be perceived. Part-timers, particularly those who have other professional commitments, are only segmentally involved at most institutions, either by choice or by process of exclusion. This means they do not typically participate with full-time faculty in the cooperative work of curriculum development or the creation of instructional strategies. Despite the enormous potential in the part-time teaching work force, it is not currently being fully utilized in ways that would almost certainly enrich the breadth and depth of students' exposure to a wider array of classroom experiences.

Balancing Teaching and Research

The profession seems to be increasingly split into teaching and research tracks. Ernest Boyer (1990, p. 29) documents the growing emphasis on research at the expense of teaching in terms of time faculty spend, what faculty are assigned to do, and how they are rewarded. Although there is considerable dissatisfaction with this shift in basic values, it continues inexorably and appeared to be very much alive at many of the institutions we visited (with the general exception of the community and liberal arts colleges).

At universities, the emphasis on research is often manifested in the withdrawal of full-time faculty from undergraduate teaching. The remaining vacuum must be filled, and it is filled substantially with part-timers, temporary faculty, or graduate teaching assistants. Although the aggregate level of part-time faculty may be lower at universities (perhaps 20 percent of all faculty versus 60 percent in a nearby community college), part-timers' assignments are likely to be almost entirely in the freshman- and sophomore-level courses, while the full-time tenure-track faculty concentrate on upper-division and graduate courses, with release time for research. Community colleges also assign a high proportion of lower-division courses to part-timers. It is not uncommon to find well over 50 percent of the instruction in a community college program in the hands of part-time faculty and not truly rare to find all of it done by part-timers. When classes taught by graduate teaching assistants are added, one can readily imagine how great a percentage of the undergraduate experience across the country is in the hands of nontenure-track faculty.

Four-year liberal arts colleges appear to be the exception. They tend to hire part-time faculty as specialists or as temporary replacements for full-time faculty on leave. Because the liberal arts sector places a high value on teaching, its full-time faculty commonly teach at all levels and typically do not have as much release time for research as one might find in the university sector.

Part-time faculty with academic career ambitions are excruciatingly conscious of the need to conduct research and publish results. Some point out that they know teaching part-time is hurting their chances to find full-time positions. When they must live by teaching heavy loads, sometimes commuting among institutions, most of them do not have time to do research or publish, and their curricula vitae begin to look skimpy or out-of-date.

Viability of Tenure

All of the foregoing pressures, repeatedly mentioned in our interviews, have already produced a two-tier faculty: tenure-track faculty and nontenure-track faculty. The former have considerable discretion in electing the kind of work they do while being paid comparatively well and enjoying the security of tenure. The latter are paid at much lower rates, are denied security, and must take the work that is available. This leads us to question whether the traditional system of academic employment remains viable.

Tenure-track faculty are essentially treated as "partners" in the academic enterprise, enjoying rights to participate in shared governance and to exercise academic freedom in their teaching and research. Nontenure-track faculty, of whom the largest portion are part-time, are denied even the most cursory privileges of shared governance and may be much more closely regulated and supervised in their assignments.

We can find very little substantive reason to so bifurcate the academic profession. There is a great deal of concern at our site institutions over the meaning of this bifurcation and its consequences for the academic career as well as for the preservation of academic freedom for those who are most vulnerable.

Bifurcation endangers the collegial nature of the profession and the integrity of academic programs at many institutions. Creating separate castes with opposed economic interests, as is often the case when full- and part-time faculty form separate units for the purpose of collective bargaining, sets up a classic Marxian competition for scarce resources and gives each "class" a rationale for economic conflict. This conflict makes it very difficult for an institution to pretend that it has a single, collegially motivated faculty.

The roots of this conflict are deep because the security, professional life-style, and economic well-being of the comparatively insulated full-time tenured and tenure-track faculty may depend directly upon the continued exploitation and disenfranchisement of part-time faculty. For example, we commonly found that institutions attempting upward mobility by encouraging their faculty to do research are displacing teaching assignments from the full-time faculty to more part-timers. In other words, more research time for tenure-track faculty means that more teaching has to be done by part-time faculty. Whether such a pattern is sustainable, given the apparent public impatience with high tuition and lack of sympathy for a secure professoriate doing esoteric research, is open to serious question.

Bifurcation threatens educational quality as well. Coherent and effective programs, in our view, require that faculty members agree on goals, collaborate on the design of programs, and cooperate in teaching courses that achieve intended outcomes. If some parts of the curriculum become the exclusive province of some (privileged) faculty members while other parts are in the hands of a disenfranchised group (as may be occurring when lower-division courses are substantially in the hands of part-time faculty), collaboration and cooperation may be difficult or impossible. Indeed, one common complaint we heard from part-time faculty was that they feel excluded from the collegial activities of their departments. Their voices are not heard because their status is ambiguous at best.

As we see it, the problem is for full-time faculty, the privileged members of the inner collegium, to resolve. Are they willing to preserve tenure and the associated privileges at the expense of exploited nontenure-track academic workers? Or are they willing to adopt a point of view that recognizes a single faculty with common professional and institutional interests working within a variety of career tracks?

Bifurcation of the kind now apparent in the academic profession does not have an attractive history. Unresolved, it can lead to conflict and to the degeneration of community. The more practical alternative lies in openness to change. Change is inevitable for the academic profession, and that change will almost certainly require more options than are found in the current bifurcated system.

Conclusion

Looking at the characteristics and use of part-time faculty has given us a somewhat unconventional perspective on the academic career.

The expanding use of part-time faculty is a very clear harbinger of change in the academic profession. Conditions in and around academic institutions are in flux, and the use of part-time faculty has become a way to adapt. These changes show every sign of continuing and intensifying. "New" students from all sectors of the socioeconomic and ethnic spectrum, changes in the faculty work force, shifting life-style priorities, and new programs that respond to market demand have all raised thorny issues about the academic profession.

Boyer (1990) has, it seems to us, captured the public mood when he suggests that institutions should put a higher priority on teaching. We are not sure that either full-time faculty or administrators who serve their interests have heard this message. One result is the emergence of an increasingly bifurcated faculty work force. One segment enjoys the security and economic protection of the tenure system, while the other segment carries a substantial share of the instructional load without commensurate compensation or enfranchisement.

Our analysis leads us to emphasize the need for (and inevitability of) substantial change in the options available in the academic profession. We question, for example, the viability of the existing tenure system because it requires that tenured faculty be subsidized with a work force that carries heavy loads at low pay. We also suggest that bifurcating faculty into classes hurts quality. This is emphatically *not* because part-timers are less qualified or less capable than full-timers of teaching well. It is, instead, a direct result of institutional practices that deny part-time faculty the basic conditions under which good teaching can take place. We agree with Feldman (1990) that performance in part-time work depends on the context and conditions under which part-timers do their jobs. Part-timers at many of our site institutions do not have the support they need. They have no security. They find it difficult to communicate with full-time faculty and administrators. Even the most talented and committed people find it difficult to do their best under such conditions.

Therefore, we believe that changes are required, and we believe that progressive institutions will initiate these changes before the present system topples under its own weight. We argue in the next three chapters that part-time faculty (and perhaps other varieties of nontenure-track appointees) can and will become increasingly important to colleges and universities in the coming years. They will carry an important part of the teaching load and add real capacity to the tenured faculty. They will help "new" students adapt to college instruction and provide them with a wider array of instructional approaches. They will bring the credibility of their experience to classes with a more clinical or vocational content. Part-time positions can become attractive career alternatives to help people of talent achieve balance between complicated personal and professional lives.

Ten

Using Part-Timers
to Achieve
Educational Objectives

Of all the issues that arose during our site visits and interviews, perhaps the most alarming was the sense in some departments and institutions that their use of part-time faculty had gotten out of control. Departments or institutions that felt that way exhibited some of the following characteristics: program decisions were made for fiscal reasons, planning horizons were short and often externally driven, faculty staffing was ad hoc and driven by noneducational factors, policies on the use of part-time faculty were informal and capriciously administered, little or no centralized record keeping or monitoring existed, integration of part-time faculty into the institution and/or department was minimal, and evaluation of performance was erratic or nonexistent. These departments and institutions risk serious deterioration of employee relations and productivity.

In this chapter, we recommend practices aimed at getting better control over the management of part-time faculty employment. Planning, controlling, and managing the use of part-time faculty begins with a sense of responsibility at the top levels of the institution. Specific policies, guidelines, and practices are developed and are known and followed by deans, department chairs, other responsible administrators, and faculty. Although no two institutions will follow the same policies, we have concluded that most institutions need to heighten their sense of responsibility for the people they put in the classroom and for the consequences of what those people do.

Establishing Goals Based on Educational Mission

Institutions must reach consensus internally on what kinds of faculty are needed to do what kinds of work. They should decide why and under what circumstances it is appropriate to use part-time faculty because the kind of faculty an institution chooses to hire directly reflects that institution's educational mission. An institution that has a clear sense of its mission can define the kind of faculty it wants and select the members of that faculty—regardless of full- or part-time status—because they have the qualifications, experience, and motivation to provide the education the institution wishes to provide for its students.

Some departments and institutions decide *reactively* what kinds of faculty they will hire. Reactive institutions view their use of part-time faculty as a temporary fix. They hire part-time faculty because they already have too many students and too few full-time faculty positions to handle all the courses and sections that need to be taught. Although there may be some concern about whether too many part-timers are being used, the principal goals of reactive institutions are accommodating uncontrolled enrollment, holding down costs, and minimizing long-term commitments.

Other departments and institutions have taken a more *proactive* stance. They have decided to use part-time faculty because they need teachers with special skills, knowledge, experience, and interests to enrich their academic programs in specific ways. The proactive institution sets academic program objectives first and then decides who should be teaching in order best to accomplish those objectives. The proactive institution can identify the varying needs for part-time faculty in departments throughout the institution and can identify the reasons why individual departments use them. This type of institution does not treat part-time faculty as if they were replaceable parts but puts paramount emphasis on hiring the right person for specific reasons. The proactive institution assumes responsibility for its own direction, and it attempts actively to create the conditions that best move it toward the accomplishment of its mission.

Recommended Practice 1: Develop goals for the use of part-time faculty that are based on the educational mission of the college or university. Planning begins with a consensus on the institution's mission. Why it is "in business," whom it serves, what its product is, and what kind of resources it will invest in its programs must be clear to everyone. To answer these questions for itself, an institution will also have to answer the fundamental question of what kind of faculty it takes to be a particular kind of institution, in other words, what kinds of skills that faculty must have to accomplish the educational goals the institution has chosen to pursue.

An institution might better understand itself by thinking about what its individual departments could *not* do without any part-time faculty. Do part-time faculty permit the institution to accomplish its mission with better quality and/or efficiency than some alternative? Do part-time faculty bring particular expertise to certain courses that is not otherwise available? Are they better teachers than the full-time faculty? If so, why? Does their experience provide a broader range of knowledge and insight into the subject matter for traditional and nontraditional students?

One could also pursue another line of questioning. Perhaps there are important things the institution should be doing that could be done better or more efficiently if it were to expand its use of part-time faculty. For example, an institution might consider whether it is making full use of a community's talent pool, or whether it could more effectively concentrate the efforts of full-time faculty if some teaching assignments were handled by part-time faculty.

Developing a Faculty Staffing Plan

Responsibility for establishing a faculty staffing plan based upon the educational mission ultimately resides at the top levels of the university or college. Such a plan matches the curriculum to be taught to the qualifications of individual faculty members, both full- and part-time. The central administration—the board of trustees, the president, and the chief academic officer—shares responsibility for developing the faculty staffing plan in consultation with faculty governance bodies, deans, and department chairs. The administration is also responsible for budget decisions that allocate resources to academic programs commensurate with the educational mission of the institution. These decisions essentially set the educational priorities and specify what is the appropriate mix of faculty to best staff each program.

Recommended Practice 2: Include the use of part-time faculty in the overall faculty staffing plan. An institution's faculty staffing plan should be an integral part of a road map for accomplishing the institution's educational mission. A principal question in developing the plan ought to be "How do our part-time faculty contribute to the achievement of our educational mission?" Analyzing who the part-time faculty are, what kinds of work they do, and how their assignments contribute to the achievement of the mission provides the necessary baseline information. Department chairs can supply detailed information on why and how they use part-time faculty and whether this is an appropriate way for the department to achieve what the institution expects.

Recommended Practice 3: Consult part-time faculty during the development of the faculty staffing plan. The appointment of a standing committee on part-time faculty affairs establishes the fact that part-timers have a stake in the institution and provides a vehicle for them to make contributions to the institution's planning. Part-timers can provide an important perspective in the development of the overall staffing plan. A standing committee, through its sustained attention to matters that affect the work, status, and terms of employment of part-time faculty, may be particularly well-situated to help review the contributions part-time faculty make (or do not make) in achieving the institution's mission.

Delegating Responsibility

Different levels of the institution have different responsibilities for faculty staffing, but these responsibilities have not always been made clear with respect to part-time faculty. Furthermore, although an institution may have an overall plan, policy, and organization for making faculty staffing decisions, we are concerned about whether they are actually followed. It is sometimes easy to let custom take over and formal policies and lines of authority atrophy under accumulated pressures. In the end, actual departmental practices may be quite different from what is specified in institutional policy, and central administrators may be unaware of changes in the common practices of some departments that have accumulated over time.

Recommended Practice 4: Assign responsibility, delegate authority, develop policies and guidelines, and review and monitor adherence to policy. Having a faculty staffing plan and continuously reviewing its appropriateness to the institution's mission will ensure a common vision. The next important task for central administrators is the delegation of responsibility to deans and department chairs. Each institution must assess what kinds of decisions are best made at what levels, because the extraordinary variability in use of part-time faculty simply does not allow a one-formula-fits-all approach. Many department chairs have few or no part-timers; others spend most of their time managing large numbers (as many as 126 in one department at one of our site institutions). In some cases, deans or provosts can be directly and personally involved in the selection and hiring of part-timers. In other cases, these decisions are made by department chairs or senior faculty who actually hold no formal administrative position. In-control institutions hold responsible administrators accountable. Out-of-control institutions operate in a decision-by-default mode; they have no sense of direction, no set of rules to follow, and no accountability. When there is no accountability for managing part-time faculty resources, lack of consistency and capricious treatment can lead to exploitation.

Gathering Accurate, Useful, and Timely Information About Part-Time Faculty

Planning, managing, and monitoring the use of part-time faculty depend on having accurate, useful, and timely information about them. One of the principal difficulties we and other investigators have had is gaining access to information about part-time faculty because the institutions themselves do not have it. At some of our site institutions, central administrators did not know how many part-time faculty were employed, what their assignments and work loads were, and what qualifications they had for their assignments. When institutions do not routinely gather and use the data they need for planning, policy is developed and decisions are made in a vacuum.

Recommended Practice 5: Systematically and routinely gather and use accurate and timely data on part-time faculty for decision-making purposes. Each institution will have different information needs based on its size and complexity, the number of part-time faculty it employs, and other variables, such as collective bargaining contract requirements. However the faculty data system is designed, every institution that employs part-time faculty needs certain basic data about these individuals. The following types of information are needed for every part-time faculty member if effective decision making is to occur.

Demographic and Personal Information

Age, race, sex, marital status, dependents, citizenship and visa status, highest degree earned, previous work experience, and home and business addresses and telephone numbers should be routinely collected and updated for all employees, including part-time faculty. This information is used for regular reporting to various external agencies and for maintaining mailing lists so that it is simple and convenient to communicate with part-timers.

Payroll Information

Payroll information is used for payroll purposes and analyses of faculty staffing patterns and work loads within departments. Data included here typically appear in the appointment contract: department(s) in which the part-timer is currently employed, the time base of the appointment (for example, .50 FTE, one-quarter time, or other fractional designation commonly used by the institution), salary rate and cumulative annual pay, length of appointment, and type of assignment. Some institutions might add to this type of information such items as the courses the part-timer is teaching, the source of funds for the part-timer's salary (hard or soft money), other assignments beyond teaching held by the part-timer, and the part-timer's eligibility for or participation in various benefits.

Employment History

Institutions will also want to maintain an employment history of each employee for purposes of analyzing various personnel actions and other information such as the employee's length of time at the institution. Employment histories are very useful, allowing institutions, for example, to calculate the total cumulative years of service of part-timers for purposes of their eligibility for various programs, leaves, or benefits and to monitor equity in salaries.

Part-Time Faculty Records

In small institutions with relatively few part-timers, information about part-time faculty can be maintained in a personnel file rather than in an automated system. Large, complex institutions with many part-time faculty, collective bargaining contracts, and the need for interactive analyses for budget planning will want to maintain part-time faculty records in data bases that are integrated into comprehensive faculty or personnel information systems that cover all faculty or all employees. Ideally, however the information is kept, it will be readily accessible for various analyses by those who need it. Information about all faculty, including the part-time faculty, is essential to building the academic schedule, engaging in fiscal planning and budget building, tracking academic appointments and teaching assignments, assessing patterns of use of part- and full-time faculty within departments, and monitoring employment practices for consistency in areas such as salary equity. It is critically important that information about faculty members be made available to schools and departments as needed. Departments may not have good records of their own, and they may also lack comparative information about how their use of part-time faculty fits the overall institutional picture. As information needs and reporting requirements become increasingly complex, we suggest that planning the part-time faculty data base carefully and making it part of the faculty or employee data base can save a great deal of time and effort in the long run.

Other Kinds of Information

To understand more fully the characteristics, attitudes, and satisfaction levels of their part-time faculty, institutions may want to supplement the personnel data they routinely gather with other information that helps draw a more complete picture of the factors that may influence part-timers' performance or institutional quality.

Recommended Practice 6: Periodically survey part-time faculty for additional information about their perceptions of the conditions under which they work, their satisfaction with their employment, and other concerns or interests. As part of the planning and evaluation of policy and practice, we think institutions should periodically examine the perceptions of part-timers about the institutional environment in general and specific policy or employment concerns. Although surveys can be conducted by administrators, surveys will probably be better formulated and receive a better response if they are designed in consultation with part-timers who are serving in a representative advisory body. Items of interest in periodic surveys would commonly include attitudes of part-timers about the institution, sources and levels of satisfaction and dissatisfaction with the terms and conditions of their employment, and information about their employment outside the institution. Giving part-timers the opportunity to provide open-ended responses and suggestions yields particularly valuable data on emergent concerns or potential problems.

As a largely invisible and silent group, part-timers rarely have channels through which they can make known their problems and frustrations. They also find it difficult to make suggestions for changes and improvements. Periodic surveys can keep administrators, chairs, and faculty leaders in touch with and well informed about the opinions of part-timers. If the results of surveys are widely disseminated and acted upon, part-timers will feel that their opinions and insights are valued. Surveys can also serve as a good source of feedback about existing programs or as the basis for an action agenda that takes the concerns of part-timers into account.

Assessing Fiscal Feasibility of the Faculty Staffing Plan

An institution's faculty staffing plan should specify a hierarchy of choices that puts education first and cash savings second.

Recommended Practice 7: Assess the benefits and short- and long-term costs of employing part-time faculty. Too often, the decision to employ part-time faculty focuses on cash savings instead of academic program needs because institutions have decided that in the face of fiscal stringency they must reverse their priorities. Focusing on immediate dollar savings to be gained by staffing with part-timers, while understandable given the fiscal situation at some of our site institutions, is shortsighted. Unfortunately, the hidden costs of employing part-time faculty are seldom factored in, as we have described in Chapter Five. Administrative overhead and diversion of full-time faculty away from teaching are two serious consequences of using uncontrolled numbers of part-time faculty. Segregation of the curriculum is another. Some parts of the curriculum, especially lower-division courses, may be taught almost exclusively by people who are not members of the tenured or tenure-track faculty and who are not in regular communication with the department about curriculum goals or outcomes.

Institutions often find that they can accommodate more students (paying more tuition) by staffing more sections with part-time faculty who are paid little. But "more" students can easily turn into overenrollment when the infrastructure of the institution does not expand to keep pace. Saving salary dollars under these circumstances merely results in overburdening people and facilities with students whose demands cannot be met and whose education is consequently far less than optimal.

In its own way, each institution should balance out the costs of employing part-time faculty against the benefits over time. Fundamentally, this balancing process will ask whether the dollars saved by using part-time faculty are worth the costs incurred. Because the use of part-time faculty and the consequences of varied practices will likely be different from one department to another, analysis of the staffing plan and its costs and benefits should be conducted for each department. What is reasonable for one department may not be acceptable in another.

Periodically Reviewing and Evaluating the Faculty Staffing Plan

Conditions change, so plans must change, too. Colleges and universities operate in a sometimes turbulent environment. The mission they choose to pursue at one point in history can be transmuted over time by changing environmental conditions. A staffing plan that "fit" in one era with one mission might not work so well in a different time. There are some obvious pressures working on institutions today that should force periodic reconsideration of staffing plans and patterns. As outlined in Chapter Nine, recession-induced funding problems, projected rates of faculty retirement, changes in the student population, pressures to broaden or shift curricular goals, increased attention to teaching and learning, the introduction of new assessment techniques, and concomitant trends toward greater accountability are among the most prominent issues with which colleges and universities must contend. Periodic review of the faculty staffing plan is almost forced by shifting conditions in this environment.

The faculty staffing plan should be reviewed to determine whether it is appropriate to the institution's mission and to the conditions in which it is currently operating. It should be evaluated to determine whether it is accomplishing what it was intended to accomplish. Reviewing the plan may lead to adjustments in the overall approach to faculty staffing. Evaluating the plan may lead to fine-tuning—or to restructuring if an institution decides that it is not getting what it wants from its present plan.

Recommended Practice 8: Review and evaluate the faculty staffing plan on a regular basis. Earlier in this chapter, we recommended developing a faculty staffing plan to achieve the right mix of part- and full-time faculty to accomplish the institution's educational mission. But periodically it is necessary to check to see if mission, policies, and actions still fit together. Is the plan working in the way it was intended to work?

Evaluation goes beyond the appropriateness and adequacy of the plan and focuses on whether desired outcomes are actually being achieved. Are part-time faculty providing the kinds of education the institution is trying to offer? A general assessment of the curriculum and of who is teaching what parts needs to be conducted. Knowing what is actually being taught and by what methods can help the institution identify strengths and weaknesses in the overall curriculum. Knowing whether students are learning what they are supposed to be learning from part- and full-time faculty alike or whether there are gaps in the system can help administrators and others document the relative contributions of part-time faculty.

It is our general impression that institutions have done little to plan, review, or evaluate their overall faculty staffing. Some do gather information conscientiously, if informally. They have a sound grasp of their purposes, of how their plans are proceeding, of who is doing what kinds of work to accomplish the overall mission, and of how the use of part-time faculty enables them to do what they are trying to do. Some department chairs and deans systematically review teaching evaluations and try to assess part-timers' performance in the classroom. (Several examples of planned use are described in Chapter Six.) Others operate with very little systematically drawn information about part-time faculty. Individuals at most of our site institutions were able to give us their impressions about the contributions they believed part-time faculty were making, but these impressions were, we think, usually based on anecdotal information.

Participation of faculty in reviewing and evaluating the faculty staffing plan is, of course, essential. We believe this is one of the functions of the standing committee on part-time faculty recommended earlier. A standing committee can be of help in determining whether the faculty staffing plan is achieving its objectives and in assessing the conditions under which part-timers work to determine whether the institution is providing adequate support for high-quality performance.

Conclusion

Use of part-time faculty is out of control at some institutions, especially those taking a reactive posture toward their faculty staffing needs. We suggest a much more proactive approach and believe that institutions can do a great deal more to plan and manage the use of part-time faculty to meet educational goals. Some institutions should plan and manage more assertively in order to avoid problems and abuses of part-time faculty. Others might plan to use part-time faculty to better advantage. For example, they might be able to realize savings while also achieving greater flexibility in programming and subject matter expertise.

We have been careful not to suggest that there is one best way to use part-time faculty or that there is a single best planning process. We have suggested, however, that every institution can clarify how part-timers contribute to its educational mission, develop a faculty staffing plan with the participation of part-timers, better assign responsibility and delegate authority for implementation of the plan, more systematically gather pertinent data on its part-time faculty, more effectively assess the costs and benefits of employing part-timers, and regularly review and evaluate whether the use of part-time faculty supports the mission. There is too much at stake to continue to forget part-time faculty when developing the institution's educational goals and staffing plan.

Eleven

Developing Fair Employment Policies and Practices

Part-time faculty employment has tended to be a casual affair based more on informal understandings and verbal commitments within departments than on institutional policies that provide fair and consistent treatment. Hired at the last moment to fill a vacant slot or pick up an extra course, part-timers within many institutions often find that their employment never moves beyond a "temporary arrangement." In the best circumstances, part-timers become valued and established colleagues despite the informality and insecurity of their employment. In the worst circumstances, part-timers remain marginal and invisible within their departments even though their teaching is excellent and their commitment longstanding.

This chapter makes recommendations about employment practices in regard to part-time faculty. These recommendations are based on our view that part-timers are members of the faculty and should be treated as such. They are hired to do faculty work; in many institutions, they carry a large part of the responsibility for academic quality in undergraduate courses and programs. Thus, institutions that are concerned about academic quality should consider their part-timers as important members of the faculty. They should develop and disseminate employment policies that ensure part-timers are treated fairly and consistently.

As a beginning step in developing new (or reviewing existing) policies for part-time faculty, institutions must answer these questions: What kind of employer are we? As an employer, what are our attitudes about part-time faculty? Are these attitudes a product of stereotypical thinking, or are they based solidly upon our knowledge of whom and how many part-timers we employ, why we employ them, and what assignments we give them? What policies do we already have for part-time employment, and do these policies reflect our basic beliefs about ourselves as employers? Are these policies up-to-date, were they developed with input from part-time faculty stakeholders, and have they been adequately disseminated to all who need to know about them?

These questions all relate to the central theme of this chapter: Are institutions' policies fair to part-timers? We begin by defining what we mean by "being fair."

Fairness Defined

First, "being fair" suggests that institutions that have not already done so must accept part-timers as important and valued members of the faculty. The current bifurcation of the faculty into haves and have-nots must be replaced by an inclusive concept of one faculty. This whole faculty includes a variety of people performing their assigned roles in teaching, research, and service.

Second, "being fair" means providing options within the part-time category of employment, options that allow for flexibility, that accommodate academic careers that must be balanced against personal commitments, and that provide career paths and rewards for demonstrated performance. Because institutions are dependent upon part-time faculty to teach undergraduate students and because there is an enormous variety of individuals and assignments among part-timers, fairness requires that options be available to accommodate individual and institutional needs.

Third, "being fair" means meeting the justified expectations of part-time faculty that they will receive decent and consistent treatment and will not be exploited. Currently, part-time faculty employment is often based on nothing more than a collection of practices adopted by individual departments. Institutions that do have policies sometimes allow frequent and random exceptions. The result, even within a single institution, can be a patchwork of practices without any particular logic or consistency. Some part-timers with more economic independence and leverage can get a better deal than others who are less skilled in negotiation or find themselves utterly at the mercy of the institution.

Fourth, "being fair" requires that part-timers be given the tools they need to do the job. They need advance notification regarding their teaching assignments to be able to prepare properly. They need sufficient knowledge about the institution, department, curriculum, and courses to be able to teach well. They need honest, objective feedback about how well they are doing. They also need the same opportunities to develop themselves as teachers and the same support services provided the tenure-track faculty in order to achieve comparable results.

Throughout this book, we have described situations and circumstances that vividly illustrate the marginal nature of part-time faculty employment despite the reality of their continuing presence as teaching faculty in all types of institutions of higher education. Treating a significant component of the work force as "temporary employees," no matter how long they have been employed, simply does not make sense, nor is it effective use of talented human resources. This practice also subjects part-time faculty to treatment that fails important tests of fairness if fairness is measured by respect for the commitments and contributions of all employees.

Developing and Implementing Policy

Our concept of fairness requires that the institution think in terms of the whole faculty. All faculty members, regardless of their status, make substantial contributions to educational and academic quality and to the achievement of the institution's goals. If some faculty members happen to work part-time, that does not mean that they are less important to the institution or that the institution should treat them with less care or respect. We argue that policies covering the employment of faculty—whatever their time base or status—should cover all the same *elements* or *topics* because the terms on which all faculty are employed make a statement about the institution-as-employer. If, for example, job security is an important value in faculty employment, then it is important for part- as well as full-time faculty. Although the policies themselves may differ substantially where the substance of the affected interests differ, the subject must nevertheless be thoughtfully and substantively addressed for each class or group.

One reason most colleges and universities are not fully implementing their employment policies is that there is a lack of communication about what these policies are. Some institutions simply do not have comprehensive, up-to-date, and published policies for the employment of part-time faculty. Nor do they have systems in place for routine monitoring of part-time faculty appointments for overall consistency and compliance with policy. Unfortunately, part-timers are not usually participants in the development of the policies that affect their employment. Instead, faculty employment policies, including those for part-timers, are recommended by faculty committees composed of tenured faculty members who, in our experience, show relatively little concern for or interest in the circumstances under which part-timers are employed.

Recommended Practice 9: Establish a campuswide representative body to give advice on part-time faculty employment policies. A standing forum ensures that issues that might otherwise be left unsaid and unheard will be brought into the open. Giving part-timers access to the decision-making process and a sense that their agenda will be heard is a critical component in the development of employment policies under which part-timers will work. (Our third recommended practice, in Chapter Ten, advocates creation of an advisory committee with specific functions related to planning and data gathering. Here we recommend a committee for employment policy development and revision. Campuses may prefer to use one committee for both functions instead of having two separate committees. The important factor is part-time faculty participation in decisions that affect them.)

Recommended Practice 10: Publish part-time faculty employment policies in the faculty manual and distribute them to all department chairs and faculty, especially the part-time faculty. During our site visits, we found wide variation in the ways campuses disseminated employment policies and publications. Communication of policies ranged from up-to-date, comprehensive handbooks to word-of-mouth transmission. We found that written employment policies for part-timers were distributed to department chairs or inserted within faculty manuals for tenure-track faculty, but they were not made available uniformly to part-timers. We recommend that policies underlying the employment of part-time faculty be published as such, be made a standard part of handbooks that contain "regular" faculty employment policies, and be included in orientation materials for part-timers. All part-timers should have access to and an understanding of the institution's policies regarding their employment.

Recommended Practice 11: Make department chairs responsible for implementing part-time faculty employment policies consistently. Throughout our site visits we were continually impressed with the critical role of the department chair in ensuring fairness in part-time faculty employment and in maintaining the consistency of practice with institutional policy. In the worst cases, we found part-timers hired "off the street," handed a course syllabus, and sent into the classroom with no further guidance. Although we know this laissez-faire approach is not universal, we are concerned that it may be more typical than it ought to be. However, we also talked with department chairs who showed great interest and concern about the performance of part-timers. They are careful in their hiring and conscientious in their supervision. Our recommended practice is aimed at making this latter approach universal and at according part-timers the same treatment afforded all other employees.

If department chairs are made responsible for part-time faculty employment on behalf of the institution, they need to be thoroughly knowledgeable about institutional policy. If they do not know what the institutional policies and practices are, they cannot be expected to be consistent in policy implementation. Variation in "common practice" among departments can be a major risk for the institution (see Chapter Four). It can also be a source of great unfairness because part-timers in one department may be treated very differently from part-timers in another. In Chapter Twelve, we make recommendations about how to assist department chairs in being responsible for knowing policy and supervising part-time faculty in order to ensure consistency of implementation and treatment across departments.

Providing Options

Employment policies and practices at many institutions seem to derive from the view that part-timers are strictly contingency workers, hired as temporary replacements for tenure-track faculty members. These policies and practices persist because of the desire of institutional leadership and department chairs to "have it both ways." For example, part-timers are frequently appointed over and over again and often become quasi-permanent members of the department faculty, but they are only offered term-by-term appointments as though their employment were truly based on a temporary contingency.

The contingency model of part-time employment is no longer valid. Half of the part-timers who responded to the NCES Survey of Postsecondary Faculty had been employed by the same institution for more than four years (NSOPF '88). A substantial fraction of the part-timers we interviewed had been employed by their institutions for extended periods of time. Many chose part-time employment because they sought options suited to their individual life circumstances, career goals, or qualifications.

Recommended Practice 12: Offer a range of employment options for part-time faculty. Although each institution must define the range of employment options that best meets its needs, we strongly recommend flexibility in the terms of part-time faculty employment. The possibilities extend from contingency appointments of very limited duration for short-term or emergency replacements of tenure-track faculty to tenure-track appointments for less than full-time commitments. Instead of putting all part-time faculty on contingency appointments, we recommend (1) that those with bona fide continuing relationships be given appointments that recognize the nature of their employment and (2) that only truly "contingent"—or short-term emergency—appointments be treated as such.

Recommended Practice 13: Provide for part-time tenure. We strongly recommend that institutions adopt policies providing for part-time tenure-track appointments under carefully defined circumstances. By "part-time tenure" we mean tenure in a position that is clearly understood to have a specified time base that is less than full-time.

We interviewed a number of part-timers who are fully qualified for tenure-track appointments but who are also dedicated to care-giving roles. These people are being forced to make extremely difficult and unnecessary choices between academic careers and their personal lives. We see no reason to require this choice when the only difference between their performance and that of already tenured faculty is amount of time worked. To the contrary, we see many benefits to part-time tenure-track appointments. For example, institutions are increasingly confronted with dual-career couples seeking employment for both members. As the faculty market changes and the supply of well-qualified potential faculty does not meet demand, institutions that accommodate individuals seeking less than full-time employment on tenure track will have the recruitment edge as well as a more satisfied faculty.

Recommended Practice 14: Provide security and due-process rights for part-timers with seniority and records of effective performance. Those who teach or perform other comparable professional duties beyond the usual equivalent of a probationary period for full-time faculty and who are not eligible for tenure should nevertheless be considered to have earned some measure of employment security. The part-time faculty member who has served effectively for a long period should enjoy security over those who have been appointed on a contingency basis. For example, the former should be afforded some combination of seniority rights or due process in layoff situations that is commensurate with the length and quality of their performance.

Although we recognize that these seniority rights can be overdrawn and this specific recommendation may not fit all situations, our general point should be clear. Those who earn some measure of security should have meaningful protection against summary personnel actions.

Recommended Practice 15: Appoint continuing part-time faculty for more extended periods. When institutions or departments continually reappoint part-time faculty term by term, an inordinate amount of time and energy goes into paperwork. We suggest that this time and energy should be redirected to the development and evaluation of continuing part-timers. In departments where part-timers are continually reappointed for the same or similar teaching assignments, we can see no reason to make these appointments on a term-by-term basis. Part-timers find that their lack of job security creates a very stressful sense of vulnerability even when they have been employed for years. A very important option to part-timers is one-, two-, or three-year appointments. Such appointments simultaneously simplify the administrative work load and provide a measure of job security to those who have earned it. Term-by-term appointments should be reserved for bona fide contingencies or replacements of tenure-track faculty on leaves.

Recommended Practice 16: Establish career tracks that provide rewards and incentives for long-term service and/or high achievement. Part-time faculty appointments are usually perceived by institutions and part-timers to be a short-term, dead-end, temporary arrangement. Some part-timers want to make a career out of academic work, but they are not given any opportunity or incentive to do so on less than a full-time basis. For at least some part-timers, institutions could provide real career options.

In addition to part-time tenure-track appointments, there are a number of other possible types of appointments to meet both the institution's and the individual's needs. These include full-time appointments for fixed periods of time, either renewable or not (a practice we encountered at several institutions); multiple-year appointments (three to five years) for part-time service; and appointments that allow for and compensate nonteaching assignments such as curriculum development and student advising. Whatever options an institution adopts, we recommend career tracks within part-time employment with added responsibilities, rewards, and incentives for length of service and excellent performance.

To be successful, options for nontenure-track or part-time faculty must be described and differentiated. Each option must specify the circumstances under which it is used, the qualifications required, and the nature of the assignments or responsibilities.

Having options may appear overly burdensome to some institutions long accustomed to term-by-term appointments, which provide great flexibility. However, we suggest that the hidden costs associated with treating all part-timers as members of a marginal work force are high. The needs of higher education for a variety of people performing a variety of tasks have become so great that flexible career paths within and outside the tenure track will serve much better than the current system, which offers security and incentives only to tenure-track faculty. Where innovative appointments are being adopted, they are for the most part being greeted enthusiastically by department chairs and part-timers alike.

Equity for Part-Time Faculty

Fairness requires equitable treatment. We do not define equitable treatment to mean *the same* treatment. We define equitable treatment to mean that part-timers are governed by a set of employment policies and practices that parallel or address the same general topics as policies for tenure-track faculty: recruitment, selection, terms of appointment, compensation, and evaluation.

In this section, we deal with the individual elements of faculty employment policy. However, lest our focus on the larger issue of equity be lost, we reiterate that our principal priority is to put the right people in the right jobs, to give them the support they need to do what is expected, and to provide them with rewards that are commensurate with their commitment and their performance.

Recommended Practice 17: Identify qualifications for part-time faculty that are legitimately related to the job requirements. In keeping with planned use of part-time faculty, we suggest that departments first decide what parts of the curriculum are best handled by part-time faculty and then delineate the essential qualifications for each type of teaching assignment. One of our site institutions had a formal policy on faculty qualifications that specified what academic degree was required for part-time faculty to teach in every discipline! While we are not suggesting that this is necessary or desirable for every campus, we do think that qualifications for appointments should be based on the skills and knowledge required for teaching or other assignments and adhered to. We return to the example of the mathematics department at one of our site institutions to illustrate this critical point. This department used its own graduate students in a carefully supervised program for teaching remedial math; it appointed people with master's degrees and teaching experience to teach required lower-division courses; and it hired individuals with doctoral degrees in mathematics to teach upper-division and graduate courses in their specialties.

Recommended Practice 18: Recruit, select, and hire part-time faculty proactively. At most of our site institutions recruitment of part-timers was ad hoc, primarily initiated by applicants themselves or by graduate students and faculty already in the department. We found a tendency to hire available and familiar people, certainly the path of least resistance for departments overburdened with excessive numbers of part-timers.

Yet part-time faculty should be recruited and selected for the particular qualities a department or program needs, not just because they happen to be available and cheap. Recruitment and hiring are the first steps in what may become a long-term employment relationship. We know from national data that the majority of part-time faculty do remain on the job for years and that they are not really casual, contingency, or temporary workers. If an institution knows that it will use part-time faculty for the long term, then it is dishonest with itself and with its employees if it fails to acknowledge this when it recruits, selects, and hires.

Institutions should define part-time positions in terms of the assignments to be filled, establish the qualifications they honestly feel are essential, and then seek well-qualified applicants. Creating a pool of potential part-timers through aggressive recruiting and rigorous screening procedures, as is done in the School of Extended Education at Saint Mary's College (see Chapter Eight), may be well worth the time and effort expended. Casting a wider net to obtain a larger pool of interested applicants may encourage departments to look beyond their current part-time faculty work force and not to continually reappoint individuals with whom they are comfortable but whose performance is marginal. While we found only limited evidence that part-time faculty were appointed for reasons other than quality of performance, larger pools of applicants, open hiring processes, and carefully delineated criteria and screening procedures should all contribute to enhancing the quality and diversity of the part-time faculty.

Recommended Practice 19: Diversify the part-time faculty pool through affirmative action. We suggest that higher education may be missing an important opportunity to diversify its teaching faculty through aggressive rather than passive recruitment of part-time faculty.

We are particularly concerned with one aspect of diversity—the employment of more part-time faculty members from underrepresented groups. We were surprised and dismayed to find their numbers so small among the part-timers we interviewed. In the interests of preparing students to live in a diverse, global society, we urge predominantly white institutions to recruit and hire more part-time faculty members from diverse ethnic and racial groups. Aggressive recruiting should include efforts to find and attract well-qualified members of all underrepresented groups. We think that affirmative recruiting has been less than energetic and less than effective in the part-time faculty arena and believe that there is considerable room for progress on this front.

We caution against several potential abuses in pursuit of diversity, however. Because minorities are underrepresented in the ranks of full-time faculty, an institution may be tempted to feel satisfied if it is successful in recruiting people from previously excluded populations to part-time positions. There remains both a legal and moral obligation to search affirmatively for full- *and* part-time faculty members from nonwhite populations.

We are also concerned that our strong recommendation for diversifying the part-time faculty work force could lead to part-timers' employment in an exploitive system. This is not our intent. In pursuit of diversity, we are recommending that campuses capitalize on the availability of members of underrepresented groups who are primarily professionals or specialists employed elsewhere or career enders. The recommendations in this chapter emphasize our point that all part-timers should view their employment as attractive, not exploitive.

Recommended Practice 20: Provide timely and early notification of appointments to part-time positions. As already noted, too much part-time faculty hiring is done at the last minute, just before the beginning of an academic term. This practice can gravely compromise any pretense of a fair search for well-qualified candidates, and it is grossly unfair to the part-timer who—perhaps for reasons of financial vulnerability—takes the job without adequate time to prepare properly.

At some institutions, part-timers are selected well in advance of the term in which they may be needed, and their names are placed in a pool of carefully screened potential part-timers. Selection to the pool is deliberate, with individuals' credentials and experience subject to substantive review.

However an institution recruits and selects its part-timers, individuals should not be put in the position of having to accept work without being able to prepare or without having been carefully assessed for their potential to do the job. Just as the institution does not want to put someone who is likely to do a bad job in the classroom, so the individual does not want to undertake a job at which failure is probable.

At many institutions, part-timers are reappointed year after year. Whatever the situation, either selection of new part-timers or reappointment of continuing part-timers, we think institutions can and should notify the great majority of part-time faculty members about their future employment much earlier than they do. Except for the most unusual and bona fide emergencies, we cannot condone the practice of last-minute hiring of part-time faculty. Failure to provide early notification of appointment was a major source of frustration expressed by part-timers in our interviews. All part-timers want sufficient time to prepare properly, and those who are dependent upon part-time employment for economic reasons find late notification particularly exasperating because it merely compounds their economic vulnerability.

Recommended Practice 21: Develop a salary scale for part-time faculty. Most institutions firmly believe that employing part-time faculty in substantial numbers and paying them at low rates allows institutions to save money. (See, however, our discussion of false economies in Chapter Five.) Yet in our interviews with department chairs, deans, and vice presidents, it was generally recognized that the pay for part-time teaching is well below any standard of equitable compensation. Institutions cannot afford to pay part-timers what they are worth, but they know that paying them less is exploitive.

A policy statement by the National Education Association (NEA) (1988) recommends paying part-time faculty *pro rata,* that is, at rates pegged to what the institution calculates it would be paying if a full-time faculty member were to teach the same course or assume the same assignment. Our study confirms that this practice would substantially increase the rates of pay for part-time faculty. The NEA argues that it would simultaneously decrease the use of part-time faculty, and we have no doubt that this assumption is correct.

We do not believe, however, that decreasing the use of part-time faculty is a desirable result of an institution's salary policy. Rather, we think the institution should focus its compensation policies on providing an equitable return for an individual's commitment and performance.

Whatever approach an institution takes to build a salary policy, it should be rational, clear, and based on the traditions and practices the institution has established for setting salary policy for other employees. In other words, the salary policy for part-timers should be consistent with the institution's overall faculty salary philosophy and practice rather than with a concept of part-timers as a transient and expendable work force. For example, if the tenure-track faculty are paid according to a salary schedule, we recommend that a salary schedule be developed and used for part-timers as well. If tenure-track faculty receive cost-of-living adjustments, then part-timers should receive them too. If tenure-track faculty receive merit pay, we recommend a merit pay system for part-timers. Whatever system is in place, "being fair" in salaries means equitable compensation for the work performed.

Recommended Practice 22: Ensure consistency of compensation practices for part-timers within departments and institutions.

Whatever salary system is put in place, it should be administered consistently. There should be "internal equity" in part-timers' salaries, and the reasons for any salary differentials among part-timers should be readily understandable to all parties. Individual negotiations of salary should be confined to addressing possible inequities.

Part-time faculty salaries have even more potential than those of full-time faculty to vary according to marketplace supply and demand, especially between individual fields. However, volatility in pay is aggravated by capricious decisions at the department level. Institutions should monitor compensation practices closely and correct inequities when they are found.

We are particularly concerned with the unfortunate practice of "bottom fishing." We found some institutions that offer a low wage and hire people who will teach for that low wage, a practice that ignores the potential availability of more appropriately qualified individuals. It is also a practice that demeans and degrades well-qualified people who may have little or no bargaining power for reasons beyond their immediate control. Again, we emphasize the importance of compensating part-time faculty commensurately with their qualifications and performance.

Recommended Practice 23: Set standards for progression through the salary scale. When part-timers are initially hired, their salaries should be based on their qualifications and assignments. Over time and in recognition of their contributions to the institution, we recommend automatic upward movement or merit pay as most closely fits institutional practices for all employees. Some institutions have incentive systems that involve "movement among ranks" or "promotions" for their employees; other institutions do not use merit pay. We think a system of advancement is an appropriate way to recognize the contributions and accomplishments of part-timers.

Recommended Practice 24: Provide benefits to continuing part-time faculty. Current benefits policies at most institutions are driven by the same motive as salary practices—saving money. But for part-timers who do not have benefits from any source, lack of benefits is the most critical factor in their employment and arouses their strongest feelings about being second-class citizens.

Institutions should provide basic benefits for continuing part-time faculty if they provide them for tenure-track faculty. Costs of health care and other benefits are soaring. Institutions can set limits on participation in the form of a minimum time base or length of service to be eligible; or institutions can explore the feasibility of allowing part-timers to buy into group plans at no or low cost to the institution.

Part-time faculty whose primary employment is elsewhere or who are covered by a spouse's health benefits plan are generally either ineligible for inclusion in the institution's programs or decline coverage if they have the option of participating. When so many part-timers are already covered by other means and neither want nor need additional coverage, an important question is raised about why institutions are so reluctant to provide health coverage to those who truly need it. Providing health benefits for their part-timers in need would not be an all-or-none proposition and would greatly improve the morale and commitment of those who received them.

It is often the "little things" that aggravate and frustrate part-timers. For example, they do not understand why tuition remission benefits are granted to full-time staff members who have been permanent employees for several years but not to part-timers with equivalent cumulative years of service. Part-timers are also sensitive about their exclusion from campus facilities or services, particularly from recreational facilities. Most important, part-timers are distressed by favoritism or the ability of a few individuals to negotiate benefits. They are confused by mixed or ambiguous messages about benefits eligibility that they receive from department chairs, vice presidents, deans, and personnel departments.

We recommend that basic benefits, particularly the ability to buy into health coverage, be provided to part-time faculty members (other than contingency replacements) who need them. We further recommend that the institution's policy regarding eligibility for benefits be clearly described in written materials and adhered to without exception.

Recommended Practice 25: Develop objective performance criteria and procedures for evaluating part-time faculty and use the results as the basis for decisions about reappointment. Part-time faculty sometimes operate with almost total independence from any responsible oversight on the part of the institution. They can be hired at the last minute, given nothing more to work with than an old course syllabus, left to teach without hearing from or seeing another faculty member or administrator during an entire semester, and receive no evaluation or constructive feedback on their performance. They may be renewed for another term or they may not, but they may never find out why. They may have no idea what they are doing right or wrong, or whether their work is valued in any way. Although we would not wish to imply that all full-time faculty benefit from good evaluation practices, we believe there is a great deal of room for improvement in how part-timers are evaluated. Part-timers typically are given only the most minimal performance feedback. They literally do not know whether they are doing their jobs as expected.

In Chapter Twelve, we discuss ways to invest in developing part-time faculty performance. Here, our concern is with being fair and equitable. Fairness requires that part-time faculty be made aware of the expectations and standards they will have to meet for reappointment. Every institution should have a standard evaluation process that is administered consistently within every department. Part-time faculty should be informed about how information will be gathered and interpreted. Chairs, too, should be fully informed about evaluation procedures and their responsibility to gather and use evaluative information in appropriate ways. Decisions regarding reappointment should be made on the basis of objective information that is carefully reviewed and shared with the part-timer.

It would, of course, be easy to forego any pretense of evaluation. Lacking solid information, a department chair would be free to make decisions on the basis of "informal" feedback—or hallway conversations—and could renew or not renew part-time faculty at whim. However, the unfairness of doing so should be obvious, notwithstanding how common this practice actually seems to be.

Fairness requires that part-timers have a chance to prove themselves against known standards. They should know that some objective and consistent process will be used to evaluate their performance, and they should have a reasonable opportunity to use feedback to improve.

Providing Support Services

If part-timers are to be evaluated by the same standards as full-time faculty, then it seems unfair to deny them the same tools to do their jobs effectively. Even though part-timers often teach at night, on weekends, or at off-campus sites where it is clearly more difficult to provide the full range of services, to deny them is to be patently unfair to part-timers.

Recommended Practice 26: Provide support services to part-time faculty. While space is at a premium on most campuses for all faculty, adequate space and access to equipment to prepare for classes and advise students is essential. We recommend "housing" part-timers in their departments to the extent that this is possible.

Part-timers also need clerical support and access to instructional materials no matter when or where their classes are taught. We recommend that institutions make support services available during the hours and at the locations where part-timers teach.

In sum, because part-timers are hired primarily to teach, we recommend that they receive the same instructional support services as the tenure-track faculty members receive. Since departments expect part-timers to teach as well as their tenure-track colleagues and, generally speaking, do not renew their appointments when they fail to do so, part-timers need the same tools to be successful in their assignments.

Conclusion

At the heart of this chapter is our conclusion that part-timers must be treated fairly and equitably. Policies that are important to the well-being and performance of full-time faculty are also important to part-time faculty. Therefore, part-timers should be employed under *parallel but different* employment policies that cover the same topics as those in place for full-time faculty. Part-timers should participate in the formation of these policies, and department chairs and faculty alike should be thoroughly informed in writing of current policy statements.

Part-timers form a population sufficiently varied so that no single model for employing them will work. Instead, we think that options, including appointments of varying duration and the possibility of earning tenure in part-time positions, should be considered. Because so many changes affect the commitment of contemporary academics to their careers, part-time appointments may become more attractive to some and may also be helpful to institutions faced with faculty shortages as a way to attract scarce talent.

Policies covering part-timers need to observe standards of equity. Pay, benefits, and support should be provided at levels that genuinely enable part-timers to do their jobs effectively and give them sufficient security and rewards to remain committed.

Finally, fairness requires that part-timers know what is expected of them on the job. Standards of performance should be established, objective evaluations should be conducted, feedback should be provided, and opportunities to improve performance with appropriate counsel and support should be offered.

Institutions *can* do a great deal more to ensure fairness for part-time faculty. They *must* do a great deal more to ensure quality. We have deliberately kept our recommended practices general, however, because we have seen variants of all our major themes working well. Although there is no one formula that we can recommend for all institutions, we can strongly urge that institutions consider whether they are in practice the kinds of employers they think they ought to be.

Twelve

Investing in
Human Resources

Most institutions invest in full-time faculty development by providing a variety of opportunities for conducting research, developing new courses or instructional methods, attending conferences, and taking leaves and sabbaticals. Full-time faculty also benefit from other institutional support programs, such as computer networks, libraries, support staff, research assistants, and equipment. Part-timers, as members of the faculty, constitute a no less important human resource. However, opportunities for professional development and growth for all faculty members are limited at many institutions. We are concerned that part-time faculty often fall to the bottom of the priority list when opportunities do become available. Finding good teachers, putting them in the classroom, helping them extend and improve their knowledge and skill, and sustaining their commitment to their work should be the main thrusts of faculty development programs for part-timers.

Part-timers generally receive far less support for their work than full-timers receive. In our view it is a terribly false economy to fail to invest in the development of part-timers. It is also unfair to part-timers because they are expected to perform at the same level as full-time faculty in the classroom.

At some of our site institutions, part-timers were receiving support and assistance in developing their teaching skills. These institutions have adopted a point of view that envisions part-time faculty as an important human resource on which they depend. We identified a number of situations in which part-timers were being supported in their professional development in affirmative ways. As a result, they felt their work was valued by the institution. In this chapter, we will focus on ways in which institutions can invest in their part-timers.

Valuing People

Institutions sometimes adopt a value system focused principally on money, prestige, and status. On more than one occasion, we have heard a department chair or dean lamenting that part-time faculty are undesirable because they "don't do research, and research is what builds prestige." Another refrain labels part-time faculty "cheap labor" and notes that saving money is the principal reason for hiring them. These messages reflect an institutional culture that devalues part-time faculty. In contrast, other institutions highly value the contributions of part-timers.

Recommended Practice 27: Communicate the message that part-time faculty are important to the institution. We suggest three ways to communicate the message that part-timers are valuable. First, negative messages about part-time faculty should be eliminated. Associating "quality" with the percentage of faculty members who are full-time is one example of a negative message. An institution should not imply, no matter how indirectly, that some of its faculty members are less than superbly prepared to do their jobs.

Second, positive messages about part-time faculty should be made explicit and public. Their qualifications, their accomplishments, their teaching performance, and their involvement in the institution and community are all important to emphasize. Presidents' speeches, annual reports, awards ceremonies, and press releases are all good vehicles for recognizing faculty accomplishments. What is missing in many, however, is recognition of individual part-time faculty members.

Third, part-time faculty, who often report feeling that they are "invisible people," should be included in visible roles. They should be participants in both the formal and informal cultures of institutions. They can be appointed to committees and governance bodies (if they are willing to serve), asked to speak about their specialties, and invited to social events. Their presence and their visibility are needed to establish that they occupy important roles and that they are valued people.

Symbolic recognition is important in establishing the perception that part-time faculty are valued, and such recognition helps build commitment and enthusiasm. It is, however, only a single ingredient in an institutionwide investment in developing the capacity of all faculty and staff. More substantive support, in addition to positive attitudes at all levels of the institution, is what pays off in real performance.

Role of the Department Chair

Department chairs are the principal contact people for part-time faculty members, who may have few or no other contacts among the faculty or the administration. Department chairs establish expectations for performance. They arrange for support services on which all faculty members rely, and they have a pivotal role in deciding how much support can be provided to part-timers. They supervise and evaluate faculty. How actively department chairs pursue their responsibilities to part-time faculty is crucial to part-timers' integration into the department and to their success in the classroom.

The skill and commitment of department chairs in dealing with part-time faculty varies. Some work hard to select part-timers with great care and to ensure that they feel supported and valued. Others do not include the welfare or performance of part-time faculty among departmental priorities. For the most part, department chairs are free to make their own decisions about how they treat part-timers. This may account for the great variability in the conditions under which part-timers work.

Recommended Practice 28: Give department chairs responsibility and incentives to supervise part-time faculty. Department chairs need to have a clear understanding of the institution's value system on important issues like the treatment of part-time faculty.

Department chairs should get a clear signal from the central administration that all faculty members—regardless of the fraction of time they are employed—carry a significant professional responsibility for achieving and maintaining excellence in the classroom. Department chairs must be held responsible for making sure that part-time faculty members are carefully selected and supported in achieving this end.

In some departments, chairs may be overwhelmed by the number of part-time faculty members. Some chairs do the best they can but have little time and only minimal awareness of how to supervise part-time faculty. On the other hand, we talked with department chairs who showed great interest in and concern about the performance of part-timers. They are careful about whom they hire, make sure that each new part-timer has some kind of orientation, and arrange for full-time faculty members to serve as mentors or resource people so that questions can be answered and problems worked out. Some visit classes (or have others do so) and actively try to help part-timers improve their teaching skills.

Usually, department chairs supervise part-timers as part of an already heavy administrative work load. Chairs need release time, administrative support, and incentive pay as compensation for their largely unrecognized efforts on behalf of part-timers.

Recommended Practice 29: Orient department chairs to good supervisory practice. Although many institutions hold training sessions, retreats, or institutes for department chairs, the subject of part-time faculty is often well submerged in the agenda if it is mentioned at all. We think it should be elevated periodically to become a focal point of the agenda because it is a subject on which there is so little knowledge and so much misinformation.

Recommended Practice 30: Invite part-time faculty to share their perceptions of effective supervisory practice at department chair training sessions. Typical orientation and training sessions for chairpersons emphasize policies, procedures, and resource allocations. Chairs might also benefit from hearing what part-time faculty have to say about their own experiences in their departments. Their views and their needs are seldom articulated via administrative channels. Having them speak directly with department chairs might help establish a climate in which part-timers' concerns and suggestions are given more legitimacy.

Newer department chairs might benefit from hearing a panel of seasoned peers with extensive experience in supervising part-time faculty report on "what works" and what practices are to be avoided. Chairs who have been especially attentive to the development of part-timers and whose departments have been strengthened by having a stable group of experienced, satisfied, and productive part-time faculty members can add a great deal to the perspectives of other chairs.

Involving Tenured Faculty

Unfortunately, tenured faculty members may not appreciate the extent to which their own security and work assignments depend on the availability and productivity of part-timers. It is very much in the interests of the former to assist in guaranteeing that part-time faculty members teach well, grow and develop as scholarly colleagues, and provide input into decisions about curriculum and program development. On the other hand, part-time faculty need access to tenured faculty, and they need role models and mentors if they are to develop as full participants in a collegial effort.

The entire faculty—both full-time and part-time—holds the responsibility for teaching and for ensuring that standards of excellence are met. However, because the faculty at many institutions is bifurcated along rigid status lines, full collegial participation is denied to those not in tenure-track positions. This serves neither the part-time faculty, the tenured faculty, nor the institution well. From the point of view of part-timers, it leaves them disconnected from policy and decision making. It reduces any stake they may have in the academic community to a very low level. In turn, they feel that they do not have to invest in or commit to the future of the institution.

The next five recommended practices encourage joint efforts and can help bring part- and full-time faculty members closer together. These five practices focus on ways to involve both groups in working toward stronger and better coordinated educational programs.

Recommended Practice 31: Use teams of experienced faculty (full- and part-time) to develop new faculty members' teaching skills. While part-time faculty members play a limited role in evaluations leading to faculty personnel decisions, experienced teachers—full- and part-time—can work together on the development of teaching skills. The "core faculty concept," which is the foundation for the assessment program in the School of Extended Education at Saint Mary's College (discussed in Chapter Eight), makes use of experienced part-timers to assist in the orientation and evaluation of new teachers. The program at Saint Mary's is an example of a broad commitment to human resource development, investing in people so that they can perform as expected. (For another example, see the "mutual benefit evaluation" idea discussed by Behrendt and Parsons, 1983.) Most important, bringing full- and part-time faculty members together in the assessment of teaching is a good way to encourage them to work together in developing a shared sense of what they jointly view as good teaching.

Recommended Practice 32: Provide faculty mentors to inexperienced part-time faculty. Perhaps the most cost effective way of helping inexperienced part-time faculty members develop their teaching skills and their familiarity with the department is to pair each one with a mentor from the full-time faculty. This is being done at several of our site institutions and has been generally productive for all involved. (See Chapter Eight for examples of several mentoring programs.)

In cases where mentoring is successful, part-timers feel they are supported by someone who has a great deal of experience and who cares about their development as good teachers. They get immediate feedback on what they are doing in the classroom, have someone to talk with when they have questions, and feel they have a safety net that will help correct things that may go wrong as a result of their inexperience. Full-timers who serve as mentors seem to be as enthusiastic about the process as the part-timers who experience it. Thus, mentoring appears to us to be a win-win proposition, with a major payoff being mutual involvement and rein-forcement. (Of course, there is no reason why part-timers could not mentor new full-timers, a practice that we did not find in our site visits but one that would signal the real value of part-time faculty to the institution.)

Recommended Practice 33: Engage full- and part-time fac-ulty in course coordination. Courses with multiple sections, some taught by part-time faculty, should have a course coordinator, either a full-time faculty member or a part-time faculty member with long experience. At several of our site institutions, course coordinators meet periodically with all faculty teaching the course to discuss progress and coordinate testing, to identify steps that might strengthen the course, and to delegate tasks to teams of faculty who do the necessary development work. Part-timers can both learn from this process and bring their own experience to the task.

Recommended Practice 34: Involve part-time faculty in the assessment of student learning. Assessment requires that faculty members reach agreement on common goals for programs and courses. It also requires that they agree on what they will use for measures of student outcomes, what standards of performance they will require, and how the assessments will be carried out. A great deal of collaborative work is needed to implement a valid assess-ment program, and this is fertile ground for cooperative efforts between full- and part-time faculty.

Recommended Practice 35: Appoint part-time faculty to committees. Part-time faculty members have a great deal to contrib-ute and to learn through service on committees. Some part-time fac-ulty members candidly suggested to us that they were uninterested in taking on extra "maintenance" work that committee service in-volves. However, many others are interested and want to be in-volved. Appointment to committees would seem to us to be a legitimate investment in the development of an integrated faculty culture. It would take very little for a department chairperson to ask part-timers about their interest in serving, to assign them to committees when such interest is expressed, and to compensate them appropriately for serving when this appears necessary.

Departmental Climate

In addition to setting up formal ways in which full-time faculty collaborate with part-time faculty, there are informal ways of fully involving all faculty members in their departments. The most poignant comments we heard from part-time faculty reflected their feelings about being left out of the social and professional interchanges that make departments the core of academic life (see Clark, 1987).

Recommended Practice 36: Involve part-time faculty in informal talk. As noted earlier, the part-timers we interviewed often reported feeling "invisible." They are present in departmental offices and classrooms, at social events and meetings, but they are treated as if they do not exist. No one speaks to them! As a result, they have an acute sense that they belong on the less privileged side of the status boundary. That boundary has been raised and is reinforced by many small acts of symbolic exclusion. Symbolic acts of *inclusion* are needed to tear down this wall and help part-timers feel that they are members of a unified faculty. The best way to start tearing down the barrier is through simple gestures, and talking to part-time faculty is something they almost universally told us they would appreciate.

Recommended Practice 37: Invite part-time faculty to social events. Part-timers would like to feel welcomed and invited to departmental events, both formal and informal. These social occasions are where bonding, camaraderie, and the trust necessary for cooperation are built. If a full-time faculty member routinely failed to attend such occasions, the department would be concerned. Yet some departments almost routinely exclude part-timers without a thought or the least regret. Others schedule social events at inconvenient times. Although some part-time faculty members may not be able (or want) to involve themselves because they have other commitments, the simple act of asking them to be part of the department makes a very large difference in their subjective feelings about whether they are part of the department.

Recommended Practice 38: Publicly recognize part-time faculty for their achievements and contributions. Beyond being welcomed and involved in the department's work, part-timers also appreciate gestures of respect, recognition, and thanks. The extrinsic rewards of part-time teaching—pay and benefits—are so small that most need at least some measurable intrinsic satisfaction from the work itself. Department chairs can help immeasurably by providing simple symbolic rewards. They can consult with part-time faculty about issues that are important to the department and demonstrate a regard for the opinions and ideas of people who have something significant to offer. They can also thank part-timers who complete an assignment. A brief note of appreciation or a kind word at the right time is always received warmly.

Tenured faculty and department chairs can offer small gestures of support to part-timers. They need help with things that veteran faculty might consider routine, but they may hesitate to ask. Other members of the department, including the chair, who take time to initiate conversations and help a part-timer solve a problem will be perceived as supportive and may make a part-timer's job easier. If it seems unnecessary to suggest these routine gestures, we assure the reader that many part-timers we spoke with were exasperated because they had never been thanked or offered gestures of support or made to feel appreciated—even after many years of teaching.

Developing Human Resources

Part-time faculty constitute an important human resource on which institutions depend to accomplish their goals. The resource can be maintained and developed, or it can be worn down and depleted. The analogy to other resources such as buildings and investments is not far-fetched. Each faculty member, part- or full-time, should be viewed as a capital asset in which the institution should invest intelligently throughout each member's career. Selecting the right people, working with them so that they understand their jobs and the expectations the institution has for their performance, helping them improve their skills and knowledge, providing them with the resources they need to do their jobs, and giving them adequate feedback on their performance are basic ingredients in a sound human resource development program.

Because we view all faculty as valuable resources, we believe part-time faculty should benefit from investment in them that is commensurate with their value to the institution and their contributions to its programs. We visited a number of institutions that were making very positive efforts—in some cases very sophisticated efforts—to help part-time faculty do their jobs at the highest level possible, and in Chapter Eight we have described several examples of what we found.

Recommended Practice 39: Orient part-time faculty to the institution and to the expectations the institution has for them. Orientation programs at institutions we visited were all variations on a theme. They provide part-time faculty with information, perspectives, and a philosophical frame of reference. They begin with some kind of welcoming ceremony. A formal setting in which a meal is shared with other part-timers and selected full-time faculty, department chairs, and central administrators elevates the symbolic importance of the event. A welcoming speech by the president or chief academic officer helps establish the idea that part-timers are valued by the institution's leaders.

Orientation programs are also an opportunity to present useful information about how the institution operates: where to turn with questions, what to do in emergencies, how to get supplies, how the library works, where to park, and so on. Handbooks for part-time faculty are useful references for most of this information. One of our site institutions had prepared a videotape presenting just such routine information, and the tape was available for viewing throughout the early weeks of each term.

Orientation programs should also help part-timers understand the relationship between the courses they will be teaching and the institution's goals (and curricular and instructional means for achieving those goals) for student outcomes. As accrediting agencies and a spreading "accountability" movement encourage institutions to develop overarching outcome goals for their undergraduate students, there will be greater need to focus faculty attention on understanding, achieving, and measuring common learning outcomes. These are important topics for orientation sessions. Part-time faculty who may not participate fully (or who may not have been included) in the development of common instructional goals probably need an intensive, "quick-start" orientation to the student outcomes the institution considers important. Although this is not the place to discuss outcomes in detail, some relevant examples might include the ability to use inductive and deductive logic appropriately, the ability to reason quantitatively, the ability to reason morally, and the ability to form aesthetic judgments. Without an orientation to desired student outcomes, part-timers may be more likely to focus on transmitting knowledge about their field and—without knowing that more is expected—fail to help students develop these other skills and abilities.

Some of the institutions we visited use their orientations as an entrée to the professional development of part-timers and to communicate the value placed on good teaching. In our view, orientation programs are most successful when they are linked to more comprehensive professional development opportunities for part-time faculty. The initial "induction" sessions are valuable only when the expectations they establish are followed and reinforced by more substantial development activities in the ensuing weeks and months.

Recommended Practice 40: Conduct frequent workshops on good teaching practices. Teaching well is, of course, part-timers' primary assignment. If they are not teaching for the pure intrinsic satisfaction (as many are), they at least know they have to be good at teaching to keep their jobs. Either way, part-time faculty know they are being judged as teachers.

Some of our site institutions have gone well beyond what they offer in orientation programs to support part-timers' teaching. (See Chapter Eight.) Full-time faculty are often involved in these efforts as mentors or consultants, and some find this involvement refreshing and supportive of their own efforts to revive and refine their own teaching skills.

One way to focus attention on teaching is to conduct workshops in which part-time and full-time faculty informally discuss their own experiences with outstanding teachers and then explore what these teachers may have had in common. Another approach to communicating good teaching practices is to use videotapes of real classroom performances to prompt critiques and discussion of various effective and ineffective teaching methods. Some institutions supplement the workshops with helpful printed materials, such as a handbook containing teaching tips for part-time faculty (for example, Greive, 1990).

Although the content of teaching workshops must meet the institution's needs, we think several themes may be especially important for inexperienced part-time faculty. At institutions with a diverse student population, it is important for part-timers to understand principles underlying adult education. They will often face classrooms substantially populated with adult learners from widely varying backgrounds who have needs, motivations, goals, preparation, and learning styles that are very different from each other's and from those of typical eighteen-to-twenty-year-old, middle-class, upwardly mobile undergraduates. Middle-aged adults preparing for a second career or trying to bootstrap themselves out of unemployment or divorce will want and expect learning opportunities that make use of their experiences and perspectives, and they will be far more self-directed and demanding of the faculty. Having some of these students talk with part-timers about how they view teachers and courses might help broaden faculty perspectives on how to approach their classes.

New part-timers (and full-timers) must also be prepared to teach classes with large numbers of minority students. New faculty may have had little recent contact with the changing undergraduate student population. Sensitizing them to the needs and perspectives of students from different ethnic and racial backgrounds can help teachers avoid basic errors in classroom or advising activities. The same sort of sensitization, of course, applies to gender relations, both in and out of class.

Recommended Practice 41: Provide in-service professional development opportunities for part-time faculty. Full-time faculty are usually eligible for a variety of professional development opportunities. They get sabbatical leaves, grants for research, release time to develop new courses or programs, graduate assistants to help them with courses or research, travel funds to attend professional meetings, and so on. These opportunities are expected to maintain and expand capabilities because full-time faculty are assumed to be long-lived capital assets on which the return is greater if appropriate investments are made.

Part-time faculty should be viewed the same way. Most part-timers actually continue in their assignments over a period of years. Although institutions sometimes do not see it this way, part-timers might well be viewed as assets whose value will appreciate if they have opportunities to learn new skills and expand their repertoires. In addition, some part-time faculty are looking for opportunities to be a continuing part of the academic profession. In fields where there will be shortages of qualified faculty in the foreseeable future, it may prove wise to invest in those who show potential and who have shown a commitment to the academic career.

It is simply good policy to invest in people's ability to do their jobs better. For this reason, part-time faculty ought to have at least commensurate access to the kinds of professional development opportunities and support that are made available to full-time faculty.

Recommended Practice 42: Provide incentives for good performance. Rewarding performance has become an axiom of sound management. Yet most institutions seem to let their part-time faculty work in a situation that offers virtually no incentives for outstanding performance or for improvement in performance. Low pay, intermittent or nonexistent pay increases, and ineligibility for various competitive rewards available to full-time faculty leave part-timers without the incentives that might motivate them to invest more energy and time in their work. It is simply unreasonable to expect part-timers (or any faculty members) to continue a high level of performance without at least some prospect of reward.

Eligibility for awards (either separate from or combined with those of full-time faculty), grants for projects, travel funds, and other appropriate incentives can be established. Assuming that outstanding performers ought to be rewarded regardless of their status, institutions can set up incentive programs to be sure that all part-time faculty, like full-time faculty, have a chance for rewards. Knowing that they are eligible for recognition and rewards can go a long way toward increasing the effort and the commitment that part-timers put into their assignments.

Recommended Practice 43: Use teaching evaluations to help part-time faculty improve. One aspect of faculty development involves building teaching skills. Yet one of the problems we encountered in the way institutions deal with part-time faculty is what we call the "weed 'em out" approach to evaluation. Over and over, we heard administrators say they were quick to judge the performance of part-timers and to invite back only those who earned good student evaluations. We think this strategy is a shortsighted way to deal with part-time faculty, especially in fields where there may be shortages in the years ahead.

A more progressive approach would help new part-timers focus on and develop good teaching skills. At the end of a course, new part-timers should have the benefit of a comprehensive assessment. They ought to see and discuss their student evaluations with the department chair or a neutral person who has responsibility for analyzing classroom performance and providing assistance to those who want it. They ought to have the benefit, too, of someone's analysis of the performance of their students on objective measures, such as exams or other course exercises. This may not be possible in all courses, but having a seasoned faculty member read over papers or exams might reveal certain gaps or difficulties that could be remedied. At the very least, department chairs should provide new part-time faculty members with useful feedback on their performance and help set up opportunities for them to develop further in areas where there is room for improvement. Except in the most extreme cases, part-timers should be given more than one opportunity to prove themselves as teachers. Once again, we think it is far sounder to invest in expanding the capacity of people than to discard more or less capriciously anyone who does not measure up from the very beginning.

Conclusion

In this chapter, we have advocated investing in conditions that support the efforts of all faculty members. Part-timers do a significant amount of the teaching at most institutions. Yet they are more often viewed as consumables than as capital investments. If appreciated, maintained, and developed, they can provide the institution with better performance, more continuity, greater commitment, and broader capabilities as they gain experience.

We believe that there are several important steps most institutions can take to get a better return on their investment in part-time faculty. These steps are described in our recommended practices in the areas of selection, orientation, professional development, the use of mentoring programs, assessment, and the provision of incentives to motivate part-timers.

Department chairpersons are the key leverage point in all of this, and they must have the awareness, knowledge, and desire to work closely with full- and part-time faculty alike to ensure that part-timers do have real opportunities to grow and develop into valuable employees. Chairs can create a departmental climate that supports and involves part-timers as colleagues and professionals. Among the most important factors in achieving this climate are sensitizing tenured faculty members to part-timers' needs, involving tenured faculty in helping part-timers develop their skills, and including part-timers in departmental affairs. The main point of this chapter, however, is a simple one. Part-time faculty are a valuable resource. Institutions should maintain and further invest in the capabilities of part-time faculty because that is the most effective way to improve the teaching and learning process.

Thirteen

From Invisible to Valued: Creating a New Reality for Part-Time Faculty

Finding the best faculty, supporting good teaching, and creating a campus environment in which people work together collegially and productively are the big challenges in putting together high-quality academic programs. Using part-time faculty has enabled some of our site institutions to draw on a pool of talented professionals, bring new ideas and fresh teaching strategies to academic programs, and take risks in curriculum innovation. In the best cases, part-time faculty help departments focus on their educational goals and develop a rich internal dialogue about their teaching, their students, and their curricula.

These institutions have improved their academic programs *because* they employ part-time faculty, not in spite of their part-time faculty. The institutions are models of academic *health* and academic *integrity* because they operate on the assumption that all their faculty are members of the academic profession. This assumption and the acknowledgment that major challenges were facing their institutions have led full-time faculty and administrators alike to integrate part-time faculty rather than to exclude them.

This is our concluding message: a college or university strengthens itself through the wise use of part-time faculty. Most institutions will have to rely on nontraditional faculty appointments in the future. They can learn from the successes of others that

277

have had the courage to experiment and to build a more inclusive academic community.

Barriers to Change

Delivering high-quality education to students should be a top priority of every department, college, and university. Individuals at most of the institutions we visited, however, expressed grave concern about the constraints that seem to stand in their way, making this goal seem merely a rhetorical mirage and an empty ideal.

These institutions face enormous challenges. They are challenged from the outside by changing student demographics, rapid progress in research and the rearrangement of intellectual frontiers, fiscal restraints, shifting market forces, and new expectations for accountability. They are challenged at the same time from the inside. Tenured faculty are aging and planning to retire. The marketplace for new faculty grows more competitive. Yet within these institutions there are barriers to making changes and meeting these escalating challenges.

Maintenance of the Status Quo

A serious lack of readiness for change pervades academia's internal culture. This culture, driven by tenured faculty's beliefs and prerogatives, has stratified the faculty into two separate classes. Accepting what has been a comfortable status quo, most institutions maintain employment policies and practices that support the hard-won privileges and perquisites of tenured faculty. These policies and practices encourage both directly and indirectly the widespread and unconscionable exploitation of part-time faculty and create an atmosphere of resentment and low morale among those in low-status, part-time positions. Rather than blaming the part-time faculty, who are the current system's victims, tenured faculty and administrators now need to recognize the inequities in this system as a threat to the quality of academic programs.

Exploitation of Part-Time Faculty

Up to now, part-time faculty have been treated as a casual and contingent work force. But their numbers have grown steadily, and we now know that they often become long-term members of the faculty. At many institutions, they are the "packhorses" of lower-division undergraduate teaching. They teach the least desirable courses at the least desirable times for the lowest pay. As a result, institutions can absorb more students and protect the security and preferred work assignments of the tenured faculty.

There is a fine line between using a resource wisely and using it up, however. Exploitive use of part-timers is dangerously short-sighted. It avoids the need for faculty to develop good lines of communication, a sense of shared purpose, and a high level of professional trust. It reinforces the illusion that part-time faculty are hired as a temporary bridge during hard times. It denies part-time faculty the basic elements of fair employment practices and sufficient instructional support services. It creates a false sense of fiscal stability. It fragments the institution and isolates people from any kind of coherent learning community. It breeds low morale and conflict.

Institutions damage themselves and hurt the quality of education they deliver when they exploit some members of their faculty. Part-time faculty often work under intolerable conditions at great personal sacrifice. Some deplore the treatment they receive and feel alienated from the institutions in which they teach.

Ironically, part-time faculty report that they are satisfied with the intrinsic rewards of teaching. While not choosing to be exploited, they will tolerate poor working conditions. In doing so, they simply cannot understand why a college or university—often viewed as the last outpost of purity and idealism in a world largely given over to rampant greed and cynicism—would use employment practices that some part-timers we interviewed characterized as medieval.

What Is at Stake?

We foresee profound pressures for change in the coming decade or two. *Change will come.* The real issue is whether it will be forced from the outside or whether institutions will choose to meet two major challenges: providing quality educational programs and finding a continuing supply of talented faculty.

Ensuring Quality of the Curriculum

An institution that values a coherent, purposeful curriculum and that chooses to be accountable for outcomes must be able to engage in rich internal discussion about what is going on. Faculty members who teach must be in a position to shape their own courses in concert with other faculty members. When part-time faculty are treated as a separate, inferior class with which it is not considered important to communicate, the creation of a separate, unaccountable teaching force will be an obvious and predictable consequence.

Part-timers carry substantial parts of the teaching load in many institutions; sometimes they provide the core of undergraduate education during the crucial freshman and sophomore years. An academic community that relegates to the margins of its institutional life those who teach important parts of the curriculum is sending a message about what it values and about what is important. It is also abdicating responsibility for the coherence and outcomes of undergraduate education.

Finding Faculty for the Future

The tenure system as historically and currently structured is far too rigid to accommodate the needs and interests of many prospective academics. In this system, most individuals must make an all-or-nothing choice about meeting the requirements for career advancement within an arbitrarily rigid and unreasonably brief probationary period. Many of the part-timers we interviewed, especially the women, wish to advance their academic careers but are frustrated by the system's inflexibility. They have elected to teach in temporary, nontenure-track, part-time positions because they cannot morally, emotionally, or financially sacrifice other roles they have chosen for themselves. Other part-timers do not want to make their principal work commitment to an academic career. For a variety of reasons, they want a different type of affiliation with a college or university. Some enjoy the competing roles and stimulation they receive from a variety of positions. Some want to phase into retirement by changing their assignments. Some have challenging primary jobs in another setting and teach only occasionally for the intrinsic rewards teaching brings.

Institutions can do a better job of recognizing that some of their best potential academics should be accommodated by a more flexible set of career opportunities. Instead of bifurcating the faculty into those with legitimate tenure-track positions and those who must depend on semester-by-semester contracts, institutions could provide a far broader array of options. Institutions must begin acting as more competitive "buyers" in what is becoming a "sellers'" market in some fields. Broadening employment options may be essential to attracting the next generation of faculty.

The bottom line is that colleges and universities are not going to be able to hire enough good teachers in tenure-track status to accommodate the next generation of students. The present generation of tenured faculty is aging and moving toward retirement in large numbers. The traditional academic career path looks increasingly unrewarding. Replacements in some fields may not be coming through the Ph.D. pipeline at sufficient rates. Those who will be available often will not have the teaching skills to address the needs of the shifting population of students. The big question, then, is who will teach?

In our view, it will be faculty members who are now being appointed in increasing numbers to nontraditional positions; most of these are our present part-timers. Investing in them now is necessary to ensure that there will be enough well-prepared faculty members for the future.

What Is to Be Gained?

How much more could institutions do if they treated part-time faculty as a valuable resource? What would happen if part-time faculty were viewed as a building block on which to base the institution's future?

We have found that there is much to be gained from the proactive use of part-time faculty. Employment of part-time faculty represents a very positive decision to expand the talent pool from which faculty are drawn. Almost half of all part-time faculty members are experienced veterans who have taught at their present institutions for four or more years. They often have a very broad background of experience, deep and productive career records, and highly specialized knowledge that is scarce in the overall faculty work force.

Many part-timers are skilled teachers. Their "real world" experience and connections bring an added dimension to the classes they teach. Many have great depth in the clinical aspects of their fields and can often help students locate and benefit from internships of various kinds. In some cases, part-time faculty have more current contact with the research and intellectual frontiers of their fields than do full-time faculty. Finally, part-timers, just like their full-time counterparts, have an intrinsic interest in the human development aspects of teaching. They want to help students realize their aspirations.

Moreover, part-time faculty help institutions make more effective and efficient use of scarce resources. For example, using part-time faculty often allows institutions to keep section size low in basic writing and mathematics classes. Part-timers may be available to teach off campus and at off-hours so that better use of space and schedules can be achieved. Using part-time faculty frees up full-time faculty for research or other assignments that may be in an institution's interest. Part-time faculty do not cost as much as full-time faculty. Part-timers constitute, instead, a flexible resource that allows an institution to adapt much more effectively to its market than it could if all its faculty lines were tied up in full-time, tenure-earning appointments.

Part-time faculty appointments also constitute a bona fide investment in future academics. As turnover among currently tenured faculty inevitably increases, as it must in an actuarial sense, it will pay to have a ready reserve of faculty members who are current in their fields, experienced and skillful in teaching, and familiar with the institution's goals and curriculum. Since many who chose part-time teaching are place-bound and apparently constitute a much more stable and committed work force than has been previously recognized, part-time faculty members may be particularly good risks for investment in long-term development.

In sum, by relying on part-time faculty, many of our site institutions have found themselves strengthening their academic programs. They are in no way compromising standards or lowering quality. They are instead adding energy and dimension to what their full-time faculty can provide within the constraints of existing resources.

The Action Agenda

Institutions should tackle the issues of part-time faculty employment from a foundation of self-interest. We cannot think of a better investment for a college or university than in its faculty. We think that relatively small investments in part-time faculty *now* will pay off over the next decade, when the faculty work force will experience turbulent times. Institutions that act with the foresight to hire talented and committed faculty members will have a big edge when the market tightens later.

We have identified forty-three "recommended practices" for institutions to adopt to strengthen themselves through the use of part-time faculty as a valued human resource. First, use part-time faculty for explicit educational purposes. *Plan and manage well.* Indiscriminate use of part-time faculty is just as irrational as using no part-time faculty at all. No institution can be as good as it wants to be without the kinds of expertise and talent certain part-time faculty members can bring to its programs. We were impressed by the institutions that have carefully defined their purposes, translated those purposes into a thoughtful faculty staffing plan, and sought a balanced mix of talents among their full- and part-time faculty. With mission, goals, and plans in place, they are able to forge constructive policies and hold administrators accountable for consistent implementation of those policies. These institutions understand the key role of involved department chairs in developing and implementing needed reforms. They are also conscious of the extent to which the use of part-timers for the purpose of saving cash represents a false economy.

Second, employ people under conditions that motivate the kind of performance that is expected. *Be fair.* Proactive institutions commit themselves to developing fair employment practices. They recognize the contributions of part-timers to the institution, help them do their jobs, evaluate their teaching objectively, and provide options for those interested in academic careers.

Third, help part-time faculty grow and develop. *Invest in human resources.* In our study we found that some institutions were investing in part-timers as valued members of the faculty. They worked with part-time faculty from the time of initial employment to develop their capacities as teachers and professional colleagues.

The future of colleges and universities is largely the future of its faculty, and part-time faculty will play at least as substantial a role in most institutions over the next decade as they do today. Institutions that employ part-time faculty strengthen themselves when they adopt a positive, fair, and investment-oriented stance toward their part-time faculty.

Conclusion

Our study has shed light on the academy's invisible underclass and the exploitive conditions under which its members work. Nevertheless, we also found considerable cause for hope in courageous attempts to put the system right.

There is a broad base of experience with part-time faculty. The directions in which we should be going and the ways in which we can reach our goals are greatly clarified by the trials and errors of those who have stepped forward and committed themselves to change. Part-time faculty themselves represent a source of energy, commitment, and creativity that colleges and universities can use to help make academic programs stronger. People at all levels of higher education are concerned and interested in doing the right thing. If we can draw the building blocks for change together and create an environment in which the need for change is acknowledged, then we will have succeeded in the task we set for ourselves when we began this project.

We applaud the institutions that have already taken important steps in the right direction, and we hope we have represented their wisdom and their experience fairly. To those institutions that are concerned and wish to change, we hope that the recommended practices in this book will offer a starting point and the encouragement to take simple, practical steps toward a better way of doing things.

To part-time faculty members themselves, we also offer hope. There is a great need for their talents and energy in higher education. There is also a growing consensus about the need to improve the conditions under which they work. Perhaps this book and the attention of academic leaders at all levels will galvanize a movement for change. Part-time faculty must help that movement by committing themselves to leadership and substantive participation.

It is time for cooperation and for making common cause. That common cause is academic excellence, which can only be ensured when the best faculty members, both full- and part-time, are working closely together.

Resource A

Site Institutions

American University
Washington, D.C.

Burlington County College
Pemberton, New Jersey

Cuyahoga Community College
Cleveland, Ohio
    East Campus
    Metro Campus
    Western Campus
    System Office
      (Downtown)

University of California at
  Davis
Davis, California

DePauw University
Greencastle, Indiana

Hamline University
St. Paul, Minnesota

Eastern Kentucky University
Richmond, Kentucky

Loyola University
Chicago, Illinois

Macalester College
St. Paul, Minnesota

Miami-Dade Community
  College
Miami, Florida
    North Campus
    South Campus
    Wolfson Campus
    System Office
      (Downtown)

Raritan Valley Community
  College
North Branch, New Jersey

Roger Williams University
Bristol, Rhode Island

Saint Mary's College of
  California
Moraga, California

San Diego State University
San Diego, California

San Jose State University
San Jose, California

Tallahassee Community
  College
Tallahassee, Florida

Vermont State Colleges
    System Office,
        Waterbury, Vermont
    Lyndon State College,
        Lyndonville, Vermont

York University
Toronto, Ontario, Canada

Questionnaires Used
in Campus Interviews

Exhibit R.1. Questionnaire for Part-Time Faculty.

1. Give a brief description of your academic background and professional experience.

2. How long have you been teaching here? Where else are you teaching?

3. What other jobs or roles do you hold at the present time? Which one is your primary job?

4. Why are you a part-time teacher here?

5. How satisfied are you with your current work/life situation?

    a. With your teaching at this institution?

    b. With your department (status, support, relationship to other part-timers and to tenured faculty)?

    c. With the relationship between your teaching here and other jobs/roles?

6. What are your career aspirations? Are you geographically mobile?

7. What are the most important issues our book ought to address?

Exhibit R.2. Questionnaire for Chief Faculty Personnel Officer.*

1. a. Does the institution have policies governing the employment of all part-time faculty? Are policies developed at the college/school or department level?

    b. What state laws or state-system policies affect employment of part-time faculty?

    c. Are any recent legal developments (court cases, grievances, arbitrations, etc.) affecting use of part-timers at your campus?

    d. Do part-timers belong to a collective bargaining unit? Is there a separate contract covering part-time faculty? Are part-time faculty included in a full-time faculty unit?

*Collect pertinent written materials (handbooks, work-force analyses, collective bargaining contracts) and look for exemplary practices.

2. Deciding when and how to use part-time faculty

   a. Who controls/monitors use of part-timers (centralized or decentralized; if decentralized, deans or chairs)?

   b. Is there written policy on their use (for example, ratio of full-time to part-time, limits on time base, etc.)?

3. a. How are part-timers recruited? How are they hired and rehired?

   b. What are the qualifications for hiring part-time faculty (terminal degree, teaching and professional experience)?

4. a. What are the terms of part-timers' employment?

    - Length

    - Continuity

    - Amount of work assigned (time base)

    b. How are the terms of employment communicated to the part-
        timers?‡

5. What kind of assignments are given to part-timers?

    a. Teaching
        - Undergraduate, basic subjects
        - Undergraduate, other
        - Graduate
        - Not-for-credit offerings (extension, etc.)
    b. Committee work
    c. Advising
    d. Research
    e. Other

    Are b, c, d, and e volunteer or compensated assignments?

‡Obtain samples of contracts.

6. What roles do part-timers have in institutional governance?

   a. Academic senate
      - Voting rights
      - Membership

   b. Schools/colleges
      - Voting rights

   c. Department
      - Committees
      - Social events
      - Voting rights

7. How much are part-timers paid, and how are the rates established?

   a. How much variability is there within the institution?

   b. Is there a written salary policy?

   c. How is salary information communicated to part-time faculty?

   d. How are salary increases handled? Are they routine? Are part-time faculty promoted? If so, what are the requirements for promotion?

8. a.   What kinds of institutional benefits are provided to part-time
         faculty?

         - Retirement plan, including 401-K
         - Health insurance
         - Dental insurance
         - Life insurance
         - Disability income
         - Sick leave
         - Vacation or other leaves
         - Child care

    b.   Are benefits available to part-time faculty based on the fraction
         of FTE they work (for example, benefits only for those employed
         at .75 FTE or greater)?

    c.   Can part-time faculty elect from among benefit options?

    d.   For what state-mandated benefits, if any, are part-time faculty
         eligible?

         - Worker's comp
         - Unemployment comp
         - Other

9. How are part-time faculty oriented to the campus?

   a. Handbook
   b. Separate orientation program
   c. Mentor program

10. How are part-time faculty supported?

   a. Office space
   b. Telephone
   c. Mail service
   d. Clerical support
   e. Photocopying service
   f. Library privileges
   g. Support services available during the hours they teach
   h. Parking privileges

11. What professional development opportunities are available for part-time faculty?

   a. Research support
   b. Travel funds
   c. Tuition remission for themselves
   d. Leaves with pay (sabbaticals)
   e. Leaves without pay
   f. Other

12. How are part-timers supervised and evaluated? Are decisions regarding reappointment based on evaluations?

13. Are part-time faculty eligible for any kind of job security (for example, tenure, multiple-year appointment, seniority system)?

14. What are the most important issues our book ought to address?

  a. Ideal ratio of part-time to full-time faculty

  b. Improving and assessing teaching performance (for example, providing mentors, resources on good teaching practices)

  c. Integrating part-time faculty into institutional life (for example, orientaton, participation in governance)

  d. Fair employment practices (for example, enhancing pay and benefits)

  e. Career development opportunities (for example, providing support for travel, research)

  f. Other

**Exhibit R.3. Questionnaire for All Administrators,
Including Chairpersons.***

Department Chairs to Be Interviewed

A.   Selected discipline (all site institutions)

    English
    Political sciences/government
    Mathematics
    Music or art
    Business (usually accounting and finance)
    Education (teacher preparation programs)
    Engineering/related technical fields
    Allied health professions/sciences

B.   Departments selected by site institutions for exemplary practices
    (These departments may overlap with A above.)

1.   a.   What portion of total instruction is provided by part-time fac-
        ulty? How many (head count) full-time and part-time faculty are
        there in your unit? How does this vary among colleges/
        departments?

     b.   Are there limits on how many part-time faculty can be used? On
        how many or what types of courses they can teach?

     c.   In your experience, is there some optimum ratio of part-time to
        full-time faculty that balances cost, program needs, and quality
        of instruction?

*Collect pertinent written materials (handbooks, work-force analyses, col-
lective bargaining contracts) and look for exemplary practices.

2. a. Who controls/monitors use of part-time faculty (centralized or decentralized)?

    b. Describe the pool from which you draw part-time faculty. Where do you find them, what kinds of qualifications (degrees, experience) do they have? Large pool? Much turnover versus many repeat hires?

    c. What motivates part-time faculty to teach at your institution?

3. What incentives do you use to attract and retain part-time faculty?

    a. Salary—what is the scale, if any?

    b. Benefits

    c. Support services
        • Office space
        • Telephone
        • Mail
        • Clerical support
        • Photocopying/duplicating
        • Computing/word-processing equipment
        • Parking
        • Library
        • Recreational facilities

        Are they available during hours part-time faculty teach?

    d. Professional development opportunities
        • Orientation to institution and department (handbook)
        • Orientation to teaching
        • Mentor teachers available to assist part-timers
        • Other support for instructional development and improvement
        • Research support
        • Travel funds
        • Tuition remission

4. What kinds of assignments are part-time faculty asked to assume?

    a. Teaching
        *   Lower-division undergraduate courses
        *   Upper-division undergraduate courses
        *   Graduate courses
        *   Not-for-credit courses
    b. Committee work
    c. Advising
    d. Curriculum development
    e. Course coordination
    f. Research
    g. Other

    Are any of these assignments (other than teaching) compensated?

5. How are part-time faculty supervised and evaluated? Are reappoint-
    ments based on evaluations of performance? How is part-time fac-
    ulty teaching performance monitored?

    a. Standard student evaluation form used throughout the
        institution
    b. Department evaluation form
    c. Peer visitation
    d. Videotaping/portfolio analysis
    e. Other

6. Do you have any evidence that the quality of teaching is better or worse when it is done by part-time rather than full-time faculty?

7. How are part-time faculty integrated into the department's life and work? Do part-time faculty participate in college or university activities/assignments?

8. What roles do part-timers have in governance?

    a. Committees
    b. Social events
    c. Voting rights

9. What does the institution *gain* by employing part-time faculty?

    a. Financial savings
    b. Access to scarce expertise
    c. Access to current knowledge and practice
    d. Links with employers and professions
    e. Visibility/credibility
    f. Flexibility in meeting student demand
    g. Extended use of retired faculty
    h. Other

10. What does use of part-time faculty *cost* the institution?

    a. High turnover
    b. More nonteaching responsibility for full-time faculty
    c. Supervisory problems (continuous need to search, recruit, orient, evaluate part-time faculty)
    d. Morale problems
    e. Problems with quality of instruction
    f. Problems with quality of faculty-student contact (advising, knowledge of university requirements, etc.)
    g. Other

11. What trends, pressures, deelopments will affect your future use of part-time faculty?

    a. Fiscal problems (including tenure ratio)
    b. Quality concerns
    c. Faculty work-force issues, such as retirement trends, and availability of faculty in high-demand fields
    d. Policy constraints (for example, budget formulas, state guidelines, worker's compensation, unemployment compensation, collective bargaining issues, and legal precedents)
    e. Other

12.   What are the most important issues our book ought to address?

   a.   Ideal ratio of part-time to full-time faculty
   b.   Improving and assessing teaching performance (for example, providing mentors, resources on good teaching practices)
   c.   Integrating part-time faculty into institutional life (for example, orientation, participating in governance)
   d.   Fair employment practices (for example, enhancing pay and benefits)
   e.   Career development opportunities (for example, providing support for travel, research)

References

Agreement between the Board of Trustees of the California State University and the California Faculty Association, Unit 3, Faculty, July 1, 1987–June 30, 1991 (1987). Long Beach: Chancellor's Office, California State University.

Agreement between the Board of Trustees of the California State University and the California Faculty Association, Unit 3, Faculty, July 1, 1991–June 30, 1993 (1991). Long Beach: Chancellor's Office, California State University.

American Assembly of Collegiate Schools of Business. (1991). *Standards for business and accounting accreditation.* St. Louis, MO: Author.

American Association of University Professors. (1984). *The status of part-time faculty.* Washington, DC: Author. (ERIC Document Reproduction Service No. ED 260 623)

American Association of University Professors. (1987). *Senior appointments with reduced loads.* Washington, DC: Author.

Association of Departments of Foreign Languages. (1987). *Policy statements on the administration of foreign language departments.* New York: Modern Language Association.

Astin, A. W., Korn, W. S., & Dey, E. L. (1991). *The American college teacher: National norms for the 1989–90 HERI Faculty Survey.* Los Angeles: University of California.

Behrendt, R. L., & Parsons, M. H. (1983). Evaluation of part-time faculty. In A. B. Smith (Ed.), *Evaluating faculty and staff* (New Directions for Community Colleges, no. 41). San Francisco: Jossey-Bass. (ERIC Document Reproduction Service No. ED 225 633)

Biles, G. E., & Tuckman, H. P. (1986). *Part-time faculty personnel management policies.* New York: American Education Council on Education/Macmillan.

Board of Regents, State University System of Florida. (1991). *Mathematics and statistics program review.* Tallahassee: Author.

Boice, R. (1992). *The new faculty member.* San Francisco: Jossey-Bass.

Bowen, H. R., & Schuster, J. H. (1986). *American professors: A national resource imperiled.* New York: Oxford University Press.

Bowen, W. G., and Sosa, J. A. (1989). *Prospects for faculty in the arts and sciences.* Princeton, NJ: Princeton University Press.

Boyer, E. (1990). *Scholarship reconsidered: Priorities of the professoriate.* Princeton, NJ: Carnegie Foundation for the Advancement of Teaching.

Cage, M. C. (1991, August 7). States questioning how much time professors spend working with undergraduate students. *Chronicle of Higher Education,* p. A–1.

California Faculty Association and California State University. (1990, June 7). *In re* grievances of Ann Robertson and Richard Kalkman. (CSU Nos. 3-87-77, 3-87-78)

Carnegie Foundation for the Advancement of Teaching. (1989). *1989 national survey of faculty: Technical report and detailed tabulations.* Princeton, NJ: Author.

Clark, B. R. (1987). *The academic life: Small worlds, different worlds.* Princeton, NJ: Carnegie Foundation for the Advancement of Teaching.

Commission on Higher Education, Middle States Association of Colleges and Schools. (1985). *Part-time and adjunct faculty: A position paper of the Commission on Higher Education.* Philadelphia: Author.

Commission on Higher Education, Middle States Association of Colleges and Schools. (1990). *Characteristics of excellence in higher education.* Philadelphia: Author.

Craig, F. M. (1988). *A study designed to identify organized faculty development programs for part-time faculty in technical-community colleges.* Unpublished Educational Administration paper, Kearney State College. (ERIC Document Reproduction Service No. ED 291 422)

Douglas, J. M., ed. (1988). *Collective bargaining for adjunct faculty.* New York: National Center for the Study of Collective Bargaining in Higher Education and the Professions, Bernard Baruch College. (ERIC Document Reproduction Service No. ED 298 820)

Dykstra, T. E. (1983, December). *Teaching underground: A study of cross-town, part-time teachers.* Paper presented at the annual meeting of the Modern Language Association, New York. (ERIC Document Reproduction Service No. ED 240 593)

ERIC Clearinghouse for Junior Colleges. (1986). *Approaches to staff development for part-time faculty.* Los Angeles: Author. (ERIC Document Reproduction Service No. ED 270 180)

Estate of Hagel v. Employees' Retirement System. 543 A.2d 1010 (N.J. Super. 1988).

Fairweather, J. S., & Hendrickson, R. M. (1990, April 15). *Part-time faculty* (Special Issue Report No. 5 from the 1988 National Survey of Postsecondary Faculty). University Park: Pennsylvania State University, Center for the Study of Higher Education.

Feldman, D. (1990). Reconceptualizing the nature and consequences of part-time work. *Academy of Management Review, 15*(1), 103–112.

Fund for the Improvement of Postsecondary Education. (1990). *Program book: Project descriptions and staff essays.* Washington, DC: Author.

Gappa, J. M. (1984). *Part-time faculty: Higher education at a crossroads* (ASHE-ERIC Higher Education Research Report No. 3). Washington, DC: Association for the Study of Higher Education.

Greive, D. (1990). *A handbook for adjunct and part-time faculty.* Cleveland, OH: INFO-TEC.

Hoerner, J. L. (1987). Innovative staff development strategies for adjunct faculty. *Community Services Catalyst, 17*(3), 8–12.

Howard University v. Best, 547 A.2d 144 (D. C. App. 1988).

Jackofsky, E. F., Salter, J., & Peters, L. H. (1986). Reducing turnover among part-time employees. *Personnel, 63*(5), 41–43.

Kekke, R. (1983, April). *Who's Mr. Staff: Cheap labor or valued resource?* Paper presented at the Conference of the Central States Speech Association, Lincoln, NE. (ERIC Document Reproduction Service No. ED 251 134)

Kethley v. Draughon Business College, 535 So.2d 502 (La. 2 Cir. 1988).

Leitzel, T. (1990). Implementing a team teaching approach for part-time faculty development. *Community Services Catalyst, 20*(1), 21–28.

Leslie, D. W., ed. (1978). *Employing Part-Time Faculty.* San Francisco: Jossey-Bass.

Leslie, D. W., Kellams, S., & Gunne, G. (1982). *Part-time faculty in American higher education.* New York: Praeger.

Lowther, M. A., Stark, J. S., Genthon, M. L., & Bentley, R. J. (1990). Comparing introductory course planning among full-time and part-time faculty. *Research in Higher Education, 31*(6), 495–517.

Lundy, K.L.P., & Warme, B. (1990). Gender and career trajectory: The case of part-time faculty. *Studies in Higher Education, 15*(2), 207–222.

Memorandum of Understanding. University of California and University Council–American Federation of Teachers, Non-Senate Instructional Unit, July 1, 1991–June 30, 1993 (1991). Los Angeles: University of California and American Federation of Teachers.

Modern Language Association. (1985). *Modern Language Association statement on the use of part-time faculty.* New York: Author. (ERIC Document Reproduction Service No. ED 267 670)

Mortimer, K. P., Bagshaw, M., & Masland, A. T. (1985). *Flexibility in academic staffing: Effective policies and practices* (ASHE-ERIC Higher Education Report No. 1). Washington, DC: Association for the Study of Higher Education.

Morton, R. D., & Rittenburg, T. L. (1986, April). *Motivations of part-time teachers in noncredit programs: A factor analytic approach.* Paper presented at the annual meeting of the American Educational Research Association, San Francisco. (ERIC Document Reproduction Service No. ED 270 137)

National Book Award nominee dropped from Norwich faculty. (1991, November 23). *Valley News,* p. 4.

National Center for Education Statistics. (1989). *National higher education statistics: Fall 1989*. Washington, DC: Department of Education.

National Center for Education Statistics. (1990). *Faculty in higher education institutions, 1988* (NCES No. 90-365). Washington, DC: Department of Education.

National Education Association. (1988). *Report and recommendations on part-time, temporary, and nontenure track faculty appointments*. Washington, DC: Author.

National Education Association. (1989). *A survival handbook for part-time and temporary faculty*. Washington, DC: Author.

National Labor Relations Board v. Yeshiva University, 444 U.S. 672 (1980).

Office of the Chancellor, California Community Colleges. (1987). *Study of part-time instruction*. Sacramento: Author. (ERIC Document Reproduction Service No. ED 278 449)

Office of the Chancellor, California State University. (1990, 1991). *Systemwide EEO-6 Report*. Long Beach: Author.

Palmer, J. (1987). *Community, technical and junior colleges: A summary of selected national data*. Washington, DC: American Association of Community and Junior Colleges. (ERIC Document Reproduction Service No. ED 292 507)

Parsons, M. H., ed. (1980). *Using Part-Time Faculty Effectively*. San Francisco: Jossey-Bass.

Pedras, M. J. (1985, July). *A model for the staff development of community college part-time faculty*. Paper presented at the International Seminar on Staff, Program, and Organizational Development, Leysin, Switzerland. (ERIC Document Reproduction Service No. ED 257 514)

Phelan, A. (1986, June). *Boundary-spanning professionals: Value-adding roles for part-time faculty. Pratt Institute's strategy to enhance its curriculum*. Paper presented at a conference sponsored by Empire State College on value-added learning, Saratoga Springs, NY. (ERIC Document Reproduction Service No. ED 279 233)

Rajagopal, I., & Farr, W. D. (n.d.) (a). *Hidden academics: The part-*

time faculty in Canada. Unpublished manuscript, York University, Toronto.

Rajagopal, I., & Farr, W. D. (n.d.) (b). *Mediative roles for management: Collective bargaining with part-time faculty.* Unpublished manuscript, York University, Toronto.

Rajagopal, I., & Farr, W. D. (1989). The political economy of part-time academic work in Canada. *Higher Education, 18,* 267–285.

Rosenberger-Webb, S. (1991). *An examination of the institutionalization of staff and program development in Florida community colleges: Case studies of a changing climate.* Unpublished doctoral dissertation, Florida State University, Tallahassee.

Saint Mary's College. (1989). *Data book: School of Extended Education.* Moraga, CA: Author.

Southern Association of Colleges and Schools. (1991). *Criteria for accreditation: Commission on Colleges.* Decatur, GA: Author.

Study Group on the Conditions of Excellence in American Higher Education. (1984). *Involvement in learning: Realizing the potential of American higher education.* Washington, DC: National Institute of Education.

Tucker, A. (1984). *Chairing the academic department: Leadership among peers* (2nd ed.). New York: American Council on Education/Macmillan.

Tuckman, H. P. (1978, December). Who is part-time in academe? *AAUP Bulletin, 64,* 305–315.

Tuckman, H. P., & Pickerill, K. L. (1988). Part-time faculty and part-time academic careers. In D. W. Breneman and T.I.K. Youn (Eds.), *Academic labor markets and careers.* New York: Falmer Press.

Unit 2 collective agreement between York University and Canadian Union of Educational Workers Local 3, 1989–91 (1989, November). Toronto: York University.

Vermont State Colleges. (1990, January). *Review of the roles of adjunct faculty in the Vermont state colleges.* Waterbury: Author.

Vermont State Colleges Faculty Federation v. Vermont State Colleges. 566 A2d 955 (Vt. S. Ct., 1989).

Williams, J. M. (1985). *A study of professional development practices of part-time instructors at selected League for Innovation community colleges.* Laguna Hills, CA: League for Innovation in the Community Colleges. (ERIC Document Reproduction Service No. ED 269 093)

Working Party on Effective State Action to Improve Undergraduate Education. (1986). *Transforming the state role in undergraduate education: Time for a different view.* Denver: Education Commission of the States.

Index

317